THE *Replica* OF THE ARK OF THE COVENANT IN *Japan*

THE *Replica* OF THE ARK OF THE COVENANT IN *Japan*

The Mystery of *Mi Fune-Shiro*

GENE JINSIONG CHO

iUniverse, Inc.

New York   Lincoln   Shanghai

THE Replica OF THE ARK OF THE COVENANT IN Japan
The Mystery of MiFune-Shiro

Copyright © 2007 by Gene J. Cho

iUniverse books may be ordered through booksellers or by contacting:

iUniverse
2021 Pine Lake Road, Suite 100
Lincoln, NE 68512
www.iuniverse.com
1-800-Authors (1-800-288-4677)

Because of the dynamic nature of the Internet, any Web addresses or links contained in this book may have changed since publication and may no longer be valid.

The views expressed in this work are solely those of the author and do not necessarily reflect the views of the publisher, and the publisher hereby disclaims any responsibility for them.

ISBN: 978-0-595-45404-4 (pbk)
ISBN: 978-0-595-69427-3 (cloth)
ISBN: 978-0-595-89717-9 (ebk)

Printed in the United States of America

Contents

FIGURES

PROLOGUE

In Quest of An Incredible Story

I was in my first year of doctoral study at Northwestern University in 1970 when it opened its new multi-million dollar library. While making my way from the new library to the parking lot one wintry evening, I overheard two female students' conversation while they were walking in front of me. They were referring to piles of old discarded books in the basement of the old library, that were free for anyone who cared enough to rummage and salvage.

The twilight was fast ebbing, but I turned my heels around and hurried to the gray and stately majestic library. I walked down the wide and deserted staircase and, there, saw a huge pile of books about two feet high and at least ten feet in diameter. There were no staff members, no guards, and no posted "DO NOT REMOVE" sign. I stood there for a moment at a loss, wondering how anyone could find anything of value and worth salvaging in this obvious pile of discards. I walked around the pile and, in one area of the heap, I noticed bundles of books with Chinese characters. Perhaps I felt a little sentimental, a bit sad that these *Asian* books were so ignobly discarded by an elite American university. I stooped down, and found that there were Chinese and Japanese books of different disciplines. There were also journals (mostly academic) but also a few magazine types, all from the pre-World War II period. I picked up an old Japanese magazine and spent a few minutes flipping through it, looking at headlines of articles and drawings, reminiscing about the *fuzin zasshi* (lady's journal) my mother had subscribe and I also enjoyed reading occasionally. In those years I was especially fond of reading *jidai-mono,* colorful *tales from the feudal era* before the Meiji Restoration in Japan's history.

Then something caught my eyes: a thick and slightly *deformed* book, caused no doubt by water damage, perhaps a long, long time ago. But what had aroused my curiosity was not the water damage but the fact that the book had the gold-

1

color STAR OF DAVID on the upper right-hand corner of its discolored blue-grey cover, and the title of the book and the name of the author, also in gold lettering, printed on the ridge (*cf. Fig.* 1-3):

NINON OYOBI NIHON KOKUMIN NO KIGEN
[ORIGIN OF JAPAN AND JAPANESE]
[by] JENICHIRO OYABE

I opened the book and saw on the inside cover the title and the author's name printed in both *kanji* (Chinese ideogram) *and* English (as shown above). Then I noticed the inscriptions inside the front cover, not at all carefully written but as if in haste, yet with an unmistakable flair of authority:

DELETE [a seal]; [dated] Sho-wa 14.7.25
[1939 July 25]

on the right-hand page and, on the opposite page:

Sho-wa 15-nen 10-gatsu-12-nichi [1940 October 12]
Annin Zeppan Ho Keikoku [warning of ceased printing
issued by the Bureau of Censor (of the city?)* of Annin]

(*The word *Annin* could be read either as the name of a city
in northeast China, or possibly in reference to the *function*
of that government agency as that of 'peace-keeping,'
somewhat paralleling the 'homeland security' of today.)

The period of these dates suggests that it was right about the time of the beginning of the World War II, when Japan's patriotic zeal and anti-Western sentiments ran high. Obviously, this was one of countless pro-Western or suspected anti-Imperialist publications that were censored, black-listed and banned by the Japanese government inspection agency. The inscription even identified the surname of the inspector: *Iwanaga*, a certain detective of *Keisatsu Tei*—that is, the bureau of investigation.

However, the most immediately puzzling question for me at that moment was: Why was the STAR OF DAVID—the symbol of the Israelites and even with 'The Voice of God' in Hebrew alphabets inscribed in the center of the Star (as

I came to learn later; *cf. **Fig.*** 4)—so prominent on the cover of the book about the origin of Japan and the Japanese people?

I took the book home and could hardly suppress the urge to read just enough to ascertain the reason why the Star of David appeared on the book cover. For I felt—and still possess to this day—a deep sense of affinity with both the Japanese people (my first—and the only—language, until the end of the World War II, was Japanese) and biblical history (my father was a Christian minister). But, after reading a few opening pages, I thought the author's claim was most preposterous, and put the book away. While admittedly still curious, I had other much more urgent matters to occupy my attention, such as my study and research papers.

Three years later (1972) I received a faculty appointment at the College of Music, University of North Texas (then North Texas State University), and that curious book followed me to Denton. Still, I was too preoccupied during my first few years with the duty of the new position to pay much attention to the book which I had 'rescued' from the basement of the old Northwestern Library. I did think of it occasionally, however, and always allotted the book a prominent place on the shelves in my little home office, with a good intention of returning to it later and to give it a duly careful reading. For, somehow, I felt I could not—should not—simply dismiss a book only because its claim appeared a bit bizarre. After all, this seemingly preposterous thesis was put forth by an author who—gleaning from statements contained in the book—was a person of national prominence. He was a recognized intellectual who could list among his credentials M.A. and Ph.D. degrees from an eminent American ivy-league university, and who was an official government envoy—even as an emissary of the imperial office—to the minority tribe of *Ainu* in the northern-most island of Japan's archipelago. He had done extensive anthropological study on the Ainu people and on ethnic and cultural lineage in Japan, and was given an audience with the Emperor. As a matter of fact, this book on its first issuance was honored with an audience with the emperor, the occasion witnessed with the two prestigious red seals of "BESTOWAL OF THE ROYAL READING" printed on the page facing the inside title cover.

For over ten years from about 1980, I had picked up Oyabe's book numerous times. With each successive rereading, I began to realize that, while many 'proofs' Oyabe had cited could be argued and even dismissed as mere curious coincidences between the two cultures, a number of evidences he had stated repeatedly could not be so summarily dismissed but, instead, should be given a more careful assessment. Also, this nagging feeling inside of me was in no small part sustained by a notion—call it a providential selection—that, in that particular and most precarious occurrence so many years ago when I had found and rescued his book from the pile of discarded documents at the foot of the basement staircase of the old Northwestern University Library, there may indeed be a reason—an obligation—that I should more fully pursue *his* line of inquiry. I felt also that I must pursue this research with caution, since Oyabe's voice—now with my own added—would most assuredly invite scrutiny and scoffing from the academic community if the subject was not treated with care, made credible with a measurably persuasive evidence. For I possess no academic credential to claim any degree of expertise in any of the areas of anthropology, archaeology, biblical history, or the history or the language of the Near-East or Far-Eastern countries.

Meanwhile, in the ensuing years, I also read on various related topics, and made copious notes. I even had a couple of articles related to the subject published in a local newspaper in 1994 (*Pipeline*, a weekly in Flower Mound, TX). But this good intention was again interrupted by a professional engagement: a two-year (1994–96) visiting-professor appointment at Hong Kong Baptist University, and completing a musical monograph.

It has been over three and a half decades since the day of my rescuing the book, and about a decade since returning home from a two-year stint in Hong Kong. And I now felt a renewed urge to finish the task, to complete the self-appointed but slow, haltering and at times faltering journey that had begun more than thirty-five years ago. Also, this sense of urgency is prompted by a good number of books I have consulted in recent years, books on coding and decoding, ciphering and deciphering of secret traces of religious relics such as the holy grail and the *lost Ark of the Covenant*, not to mention the other wild chases down the not-wholly-credible alleys of historical maze. Nearly all of these historical detective works focus on the same two most famous sacred relics—the holy grail and the Ark of the Covenant, the subject matters which have even been treated on silver screens as in the adventure saga of an archaeology professor Dr. Indiana Jones (movie series by Stephen Spielberg) more than a decade ago.

Much has been speculated, studied, and pronounced in print on the topic of the Ark of the Covenant, created by Moses over three thousand years ago as commissioned by God on Mount Sinai (also called Mount Horeb). This Ark was (presumed) lost in (one of) the three Babylonian raids on Jerusalem, the last of which was said to have brought a total destruction to the City of *Peace* ('-*salem*'), also called the City of David, and the City of Zion. This was also the site of David's *Tabernacle* for the Ark of the Covenant where, later, King

Solomon would build the *Temple* as the permanent dwelling place of the Lord and for *His* Ark.

Since the destruction of the City of Peace and throughout history, there have been literally hundreds of attempts at tracing and discovering the lost holy relics; from the Crusaders to Freemasons to the Templars, to modern-day scholars of archaeology, religious zealots and serious researchers, many in the fashion of the fabled Dr. Indiana Jones. There are even claims of "actual" discovery or sighting of the lost holy relics, in Ethiopia, in or near Jerusalem, in England, France, or elsewhere in Europe. A few even claim eyewitness accounts for which they alleged to have in their possession photographic evidences of their sighting of the Ark. Yet, curiously, no objective verification has ever been offered by the 'first party' or conducted by an unbiased 'third party' on these evidences of proof, and all the photographic evidences are curiously blurred. This includes highly regarded and meticulously researched works by Graham Hancock and Laurence Gardner. Or, to this list, may we also add the recent "discovery" of the family tomb of Jesus Christ, along with the boxes of remains of mother Mary and father Joseph, so claimed in a book and a movie.

In the present book I intend no such claim of sensationalism of discovery. Indeed, most of this study is done in terms of critical reading and comparative interpretation of primary and relevant secondary source material. For, in my view, "textual archaeology" is the best course I could pursue in re-examining Oyabe's book which bears the Star of David. In resurrecting Oyabe, I had laid aside a number of his claims which I regarded as rather tenuous, and focus only on those that appear to merit further inquiry. And I present them here, along with additional documentary citation from my own study.

In essence, my singular purpose for putting forth this book is to make public, for the first time in the Western world, the documentary evidence on some of the unimaginably incredible parallels between the ritual practices and cultural heritages of the Israelites, the ancient Middle Eastern and Central Asian peoples, and the Japanese. The credence of evidence of the latter rests solely on the citations from various ancient Japanese historical chronicles. For I firmly believe that these documentary evidences constitute a body of knowledge that is worthy of serious future archaeological inquiry, that the inquiry into the *fact concealed between the written pages* may unveil an incredible truth which had been hidden behind the doors of the inner sanctum of the *Grand Ise Shrine* in Japan for some two millennia.

Based on the evidence which will be presented more specifically and in detail in PARTS TWO and THREE, my speculative propositions are as follows:

1) That, deep inside *Ise Dai Jingu* (the Great Shrine of Ise), there is a wooden chest called *MiFune-Shiro*, its literal meaning being the "Replica of the Sacred *Ark*" (or *Boat*), of the size which approximates the size of the Ark of the Covenant as described in the Old Testament;

2) That the legend has it that three treasures are contained in this *MiFune-Shiro*:

 (a) *magatama* (crescent-shaped stones), paralleling the stone tablets in the Israelite's ark of the Covenant, or in the likeness of the *cursive symbols* on the tablets;

 (b) *tsurugi* (sword), paralleling Aaron's rod that also was placed into the Ark;

 (c) *kangami* (mirror), no parallel article in the ark (but see 3 and 7 below);

3) That several passages in a number of ancient and official chronicles of Japan described the mirror *not* like a mirror but more like an urn, a golden vessel which contained an amount of white powder;

4) That the *kangami* (mirror) was, in most likelihood, an erroneous 'reading' during the course of committing oral tradition to writing (seventh to eighth centuries, C.E), that it was in fact a mistaken ideogramming (*i.e.*, *ateji*) for *kan-game* (divine urn) and, if so,

5) This urn may very well be the golden urn which, as commanded by God Yahweh, contained a portion of *manna* and was kept in the Ark, but that the urn (along with Aaron's rod) was found missing when the Ark was opened at the dedication of the Temple of Solomon (*cf.* I Kings 8:9);

6) That many rituals associated with the *Shinto* festivals still practiced today are reminiscent of the Hebraic festival of the Ark, in the movements of the carriers, in the names and even in the season (month and date) of the festival;

7) That ancient Chinese court (*i.e.*, official) chronicles and the recent reports in genetic science provide additional support to the hypothesis that (at least one stock of) the proto-Japanese had migrated from the Near East regions, passed through the Central Asian steppes and the central plain region of China, continued its eastward migration through the Korean peninsula, and finally arrived and settled in (the western and southwestern regions of) the archipelago which is now called Japan; and

8) That, additionally, ancient Japanese legends (*e.g.*, mythological tales) and customs, geographical names and even the (old Japanese) language, would also lend further support to the thesis presented here, that a stock of ancient Japanese did come from the Near East region and carried with them (or created during its migratory journey) a *replica of the Ark* (*of the covenant*) as the emblem of their cultic (and ethnic) lineage.

The very notion that (the ancient or the proto-) Japanese were in their ethnic lineage related to a Near Eastern stock (possibly later mixed with Central-Asian people) and, therefore, there may still be identifiable residues in their customs and language, and that, amid the parallel practices between the Japanese (the *Shintoism* and its supreme goddess *Amaterasu*) and Near Eastern religions (*i.e.*, Judaism but also Persian *Mithraism* and Hittites' *Mezzullashism*), would seem to many as most improbable. But to claim that there is a credible evidence to the possibility that, in Japan, there is still preserved the lost sacred article(s) from the *very* Ark of the Covenant, would assuredly be regarded as incredulous and utterly preposterous. To such understandable skepticism, this author would only wish to submit a body of findings which he believes deserves our objective and unbiased assessment. A certain number of documentary evidences, referring to the passages in the official chronicles of Japan and elsewhere, constitute the core of Dr. Oyabe's claim, and I have found through further reading of nearly three decades many additional and *credible* evidences from more recent works which would further substantiate Oyabe's incredible claim.

In presenting this incomplete study of a potentially incredible story, the author only asks that the readers would keep an open and inquisitive mind. For the truth may indeed yet again be shown to be stranger than fiction.

GJC, Denton, TX March 2007

[Oyabe's book was first published in 1929 by Kosei Kaku Publisher, Tokyo. The copy in my possession is of the eighth printing, dated Fifth of May, 1931. To my knowledge, the book is *permanently* out of print, never reissued even after the World War II when the deity of emperor was no longer in Japan's national psyche.]

THE *Replica* OF THE ARK OF THE COVENANT IN *Japan*

The Mystery of *Mifune-Shiro*

PART ONE

THE ARK OF THE COVENANT

CHAPTER ONE

THE ARK OF THE COVENANT
AND THE MISSING CONTENTS

The Lord *Yahweh* (or, more commonly, *Jehovah*) ordered Moses to construct a receptacle for the *Decalogue*, that is, the Ten Commandments, written on two stone tablets. This receptacle, essentially a rectangular chest, was to become not only the symbol of God's presence amidst the Israelites but, more importantly, as the *testimony* (*i.e.*, covenant, contract, witness) to the "contractual" relationship between God and his chosen people for all future generations. With the help of Bezaleel who was known as a skilled craftsman of wood, metal and precious stones, Moses constructed the Ark according to the specifications given by God. Hence, for the Israelites, the Ark was their most sacred and ever-present companion. It was regarded as the seat of the Lord who had promised to protect, defend and sustain them. Indeed, the Ark brought victory to and in miraculous ways met the needs of the Israelites during their forty years of wandering in the Sinai Desert, and it was revered and honored well into the periods of the judges and the kings in Israelite history.

During the course of this history, however, the Ark was not only moved about but also had fallen into the hands of the enemies of the Israelites. After some unstable periods and curious encounters, the Ark was finally brought back into the Israeli camp. Soon afterward, the Ark was brought to Jerusalem (then the name of the city had been changed to the City of David) amid a jubilant—even wild and frenzied—celebration, and was ceremoniously housed in a *tent* erected by King David. This tent was made specifically as the "*Tabernacle* of the Lord" where the Lord and the symbol of His very presence was to securely repose. Finally, as demanded by the Lord to have His own *permanent house* (as opposed to the *impermanent tent*), King Solomon built the (first) Temple, and the Ark was brought to repose therein. The installment ceremony of the Ark in the Temple took place in the ninth century B.C.E., and the jubilation was arguably the greatest of all the festivities the Israelites had ever witnessed before or since.

As the most sacred article in the monotheistic Judaism, the Ark was held in the greatest of reverence. It was strictly forbidden that human hands would ever defile it by touching, and that even an unwitting gesture would—and did—invite a sudden death for the sin of disrespect. Several references in the Bible indicate that not only enemies of the Israelites but also both King David and Solomon "feared" the Lord and the Ark. It was inconceivable, therefore, that anyone would dare to pry inside this fearsome and awe-inspiring chest of holy regalia.

However, there is a deeply puzzling passage in the Old Testament, clearly implying that the divine Ark was seriously defiled. It was not only intentionally touched by human hands but also the contents were invaded and stolen. In the First Book of Kings, it is told that, when King Solomon and the Levites placed the Ark in the Temple, it was discovered (by opening the lid and looking inside the ark?) that

> "… *there was nothing in the ark except the two tablets of stone*
> which Moses put there at [Mount] Horeb, where the Lord
> made a covenant with the people of Israel when they came out
> of the land of Egypt"
>   (I Kings 8:9, also II Chronicles 5:10; *italics* mine)

This statement must be seen as possessing a considerable historical signification and intrigue. That there was "*nothing else*[?]" in the chest of Promise *except* the two stone slabs bearing the *Decalogue*, the *Ten Words*, also called the Law of Moses, believed to have been written by the very finger of God, clearly implies that something else was or were inside the Ark but, now, were found to be missing. If this were indeed the case, then this discovery of the loss begs the next two questions: (1) *what* were the missing articles; and (2) *where* were they taken and where might they be? This discovery should pose an enormous investigative prospect for all the modern "raiders of the Lost Ark."

It is therefore somewhat curious that none of the books this writer has consulted on the subject of the "lost Ark"—including those published in the most recent years, among them a few on the 'New York Times Best Sellers' listing—has ever considered the ramification of this passage, or even mentioned it in passing. Indeed, there are several Bible passages that clearly identify the *other* sacred items placed inside the Ark during the Israelites sojourning years in the desert. We can state with a measure of certainty that there were *two other arti-*

cles besides the two stone slabs that were placed in the Ark itself, not to mention the various other ritual and precious items of gold that were placed close to the Ark, within the Holy of Holies in both David's Tabernacle and Solomon's Temple.

For this, we need to examine certain passages in the various books of the Old Testament, not only to get the information but also to recount the narratives on how and for what purpose the Ark was created, what else and when were the other sacred articles placed in the Ark, and how were the various encounters on the Ark's journey through the wandering years in the dessert and after the crossing of the Jordan into the land of the Canaanites. Also, there are many aspects of interest: How had the Ark fought for the Israelites? How was it 'housed' by David in the Tabernacle and then by Solomon in the Temple? What was the legend that tells of the removal of the Ark from Jerusalem to Ethiopia by the alleged son of Solomon and Queen Sheba, and how was the Temple, along with all the sacred ritual articles, destroyed and taken away by the ravaging hands of Babylonian armies not only once but thrice, and how the Ark, with all its contents, became lost. We also need to understand the role and function of an ark in the cultural environment of the ancient Near East (including Egypt) and, as importantly, the etymological signification of the word "ark" in referring to an *ordinary* chest and to this specific *holy* chest of the ancient Israelites.

CHAPTER TWO

THE EXODUS AND
THE CREATION OF THE ARK

Moses, after several frustrating attempts and engaging various 'magical' means to persuade the Pharaoh to recognize the legitimacy of his request, was finally able to free the enslaved Israelites from Egyptian bondage and led them out into the desert (Exodus Chapter 12). This massive exodus took place in the night, in late-March (to mid-April). In leaving Egypt, all the Israelites were instructed to observe certain instructions from the Lord: (1) ask for valuables—such as gold and silver jewelry and clothing—from their Egyptian neighbors (Exodus Chapters 35 to 36); (2) splatter animal *blood on their door posts* (so that the Lord will *pass over* their households without any harm on their first-born sons); (3) put on their traveling clothes and eat u*nleavened bread* and *bitter herbs* in haste (*cf.* Exodus 12:8; also Numbers 9:11); and (4) *depart in the darkness of night* as quickly and *quietly* as possible. This was—and is still observed as—the beginning of the annual solemn observation of the seven-day *Feast of* the Lord's *Passover* (also called the Feast of *Unleavened Bread* and, to many Christians, as the *Seder* Feast), to commemorate the night when the LORD YAHWEH delivered his people from bondage.

The exodus encountered more than its share of travel difficulties: pursuit by the vengeful armies of the Pharaoh, shortage of food and lack of water in the vast Sinai Desert, and others such as disease and want of idol of worship. But the Lord wrought wonders, and at each turn provided deliverance: pillars of clouds and light to shield them from the enemies, fresh water from the rock to quench their thirst, and *manna* in the field and flocks of quail to feed their hunger. But above all else, feeding of the hungry multitudes with *manna—the bread from heaven*—was such a memorable experience that the people regarded it as one of the most powerful witnesses to the Lord's promise to His chosen people, that He will forever be their God. It was for this reason that the Lord had commanded that a *testimony* to this event be created, so that later generations would see in *remembrance* what the Lord had done. In Chapter 16 of Exodus are the following narratives:

> "And when the dew had gone up, there was on the face of the
> wilderness a fine, flake-like thing, fine as hoarfrost on the ground.
> When the people of Israel saw it, they said to one another,
> "*What is it?*" For they did not know what it was. And Moses said
> to them, "It is the bread which the Lord has given you to eat." ...
> "Now the house of Israel called its name *manna*; it was
> like coriander seed, white, and the taste of it was like wafers made
> with honey. And Moses said, "This is what the Lord has commanded:
> 'Let an *omer* of it be kept throughout your generations, that they may
> see the bread with which I fed you in the wilderness, when I brought
> you out of the land of Egypt.' And Moses said to Aaron,
> 'Take a jar, and put an omer of *manna* in it, and place it before
> the Lord, to be kept throughout your generations.'
> As the Lord commanded Moses, so Aaron *placed it before the
> Testimony, to be kept.*"
> (verses 14-15, 31-34; *italics* mine)

The word *Testimony* (as well as *Witness*) is in reference to the *Covenant*; in other words, it is the Ark of the Covenant. It should be pointed out that the jar was not placed in *the* ark when the *manna* was put in it, since at that time *the* Ark was not yet created. After it was created, this particular Ark (the chest) became the "sacred place," and it was at this point that the jar—or an urn—was dutifully placed inside the Ark, according to God's instruction.

This also was the case with Aaron's rod which, as we shall note below, was the third article that was placed inside the Ark. It should be mentioned that there are various legends on what other ritual relics were put inside the Ark. Among them is the one which alleges that the remains of Joseph were placed inside the ark when Moses led the Israeli people out of Egypt. Clearly this was *another* ark made long before *the Ark of the Covenant* was created by Bezaleel and Moses. This reference is found in Exodus, Chapter 13:19:

> "... Moses took the bones of Joseph with him, for Joseph had
> solemnly sworn to the people of Israel, saying,
> 'God will visit you; then you must carry my bones with you from here.'"

In the narratives regarding the placing of the urn of *manna* inside the Ark, there is even a mention—in parentheses—of the unit in measuring the amount of *manna*: an *omer*, described in verse 36 as "the tenth part of an *ephah*, or a tenth of a bushel." In terns of present-day measurement, an *omer* is about two quarts (or one-half gallon).

Besides the food and water, healing and safety from enemies' harms ways, the wandering Israelites had one other need: they demanded to have an object for their worship festivities. After more than four hundred years in Egypt where statues of gods—great and small, female and male, animal and human—were in the magnificent temples for all the people, the Israelites had become accustomed to the idols of worship. Therefore, the people, now wandering in the wide-open desert, far from the glorious Egyptian civilization, must have felt somewhat lost in not having any idol of worship. (There is little doubt that some Israelites in Egypt had worshipped Egyptian gods, for the Israelites did not yet have a clearly defined concept of God Yahweh. It was only on Mount Sinai and to Moses that God for the first time revealed himself, with the name "I AM," an awesome and jealous God, almighty yet *invisible*.) Therefore, when they requested to have an idol for worship and it was denied by Moses, they resorted to creating for themselves a golden calf, an Egyptian deity, while Moses was away for forty days and nights up on Mount Sinai, communicating with God. It is well to remember that this golden calf was created with the approval of Aaron, Moses' own brother, the assistant to Moses and himself a priest. But when Moses descended from the mountain, he was so angered by the sight of idolatry that he cast down the stone tablets of holy writ, and smashed them to pieces. Hence the Lord commanded Moses to make the *second* set of tablets to engrave the law, thus to ensure that the people will have written commandments for this otherwise all-but-lawless multitude (Ex. 20-23). And it was for safe keeping of the stone tablets bearing the holy writ that God commanded Moses to build an ark—essentially a wooden container.

This receptacle, the Ark of the *Covenant*, was also called by other names: the Ark of the *Testimony*, the Ark of the *Promise*, or the Ark of *Witness*. Though different, all these words have essentially the same etymological connotation of "pact, contract, or testament." In other words, it was a *legal* term. Hence the Bible may be said to consist of two contractual (legal) papers: one created in the former period (the Old Testament) and the other in the new period (the New Testament).

In fact, the Ark was created not only for safe keeping of the stone tablets as the visible representation of the Lord's Commandments to the Israelites, but also as the *seat and dwelling place for God* himself amidst the people. Hence the

Lord also commanded Moses to erect a tabernacle (a tent) to house the Ark and as His dwelling place. In turn, this tabernacle also was to serve for the people as the sanctified ground of worship and the place to meet with the Lord, to remember and be instructed on the pledge and promise between the Lord and His people.

Therefore, the Law, the Ark, and the Tabernacle were an inseparable and tangible symbol of the bond between God and the Israelites. And the tribe of the Levites—the priestly caste among the Israelites, with Aaron being the first—was assigned the task of ministering to this most important ritualistic representation of God, to guard it and to carry it on their wandering journeys. The degree of importance that the Lord—and the people of Israel—had put on the Ark and the Tabernacle can be easily gauged from the fact that the Lord gave the most elaborate and exact instructions in the making of possibly one of the most luxurious articles—nearly all in solid gold—in the whole history of human culture. From Chapter Twenty-Four to Chapter Forty—the end—of the Book of Exodus, we find one of the most lengthy narratives in the entire Bible devoted to a single subject: the establishment of the Ten Commandments and the creation of the Ark of the Covenant, and all the priestly items, including the specification of clothing for the presiding priests, all associated with the rituals of the Ark.

The specification for constructing the Ark of the Covenant is given in Exodus Chapter Thirty-Seven. (A nearly identical narrative on the construction of the Ark is also recorded earlier in Exodus, in Chapter 25, immediately following the instruction on the construction of the Tabernacle.) The following passages provide sufficiently detailed information on the ark:

> Bezaleel made the ark. This was constructed of acacia wood and was $3^{3/4}$ feet long, $2^{1/4}$ feet wide, and $2^{1/4}$ feet high. It was plated with pure gold inside and out, and had a molding of gold all the way around the sides. There were four gold rings fastened into its four feet, two rings at each end. Then he made poles from acacia wood, and overlaid them with gold, and put the poles into the rings at the sides of the ark, to carry it. Then from pure gold, he made a lid called "the place of mercy"; it was $3^{1/3}$ feet long and $2^{1/4}$ feet wide. He made two statues of Guardian Angels [the cherubims] of beaten gold, and placed them at the two ends of the gold lid. They were molded so that they were actually a part of the gold lid—it was all one piece. The Guardian Angels faced each other, with outstretched wings that overshadowed the place of mercy, looking

down upon it. Then he made a table, using acacia wood ...
It was overlaid with pure gold ... Then he made the lamp stand,
again using pure, beaten gold. Its base, shaft, lamp-holders,
and decorations of almond flowers ... The lamp stand had six
branches, three from each side ... The incense altar was made of
acacia wood ... He overlaid it all with pure gold ...
(Ex. 37: 1-25)

The chest piece was ... nine inches square, doubled over to form a
pouch; there were four rows of stones across it. In the first row were
a sardius, a topaz, and a carbuncle; in the second row were an emerald,
a sapphire, and a diamond. In the third row were a jacinth, an agate,
and an amethyst. In the fourth row, a beryl, an onyx, and a jasper
—all set in gold filigree. The stones were engraved like a seal, with
the names of the twelve tribes of Israel.
(Ex. 39: 8-14)

The Ark which symbolized the presence and the commandments of the
Lord was indeed an awe inspiring vessel and as such was in constant presence
with the Israelis throughout their wandering years in the desert. During the
forty-year sojourn in the wilderness and until the final crossing of the Jordan
and the subsequent conquest of the land of the Canaanites, the Israelites had
witnessed the Ark's awesome demonstration of its power, manifesting God's
wrathful vengeful hand against the enemies of His people. At the same time,
the object of God's wrath was at times directed at His own people (Israelites
and their friends); anyone who showed any manner of disrespect (for example,
in touching the Ark), whether intentionally or unwittingly, was accorded with
immediate and sudden death.

Finally, the Ark led the Israelites to victory over the Canaanites, and the
Israelites overtook the Promised Land, the land which the Lord had promised
to give them and to be their homeland for all future generations. The miraculous power of the Ark was also shown when the Levites carried the Ark *over* the
waters of the Jordan. Such power was believed, more than any other articles
that were inside the Ark, to be from the stone tablets with the writings of God.
For, repeatedly, the Bible makes reference to the two tablets of stone on which
the Lord had written the ten commandments—the *Decalogue*—as *the* contents
in the Ark, referring to them as if they were the living thing.

It may be of interest to note that, actually, this set of stone tablets was the
third set of stone tablets. As mentioned, Moses had broken the first set into

pieces in rage. Hence, the Lord commanded *Moses to write* another set—the *second* set—of tablets. Then, in Chapter 8 of the Book of Joshua, we read the following passage:

> "… And there, in the presence of the people of Israel, [*Joshua*] *wrote upon the stones a copy of the law* of Moses, which he had written. And all Israel, sojourner as well as home-born, with their elders and officers and their judges, stood on opposite sides of the ark before the Levitical priests who carried the ark of the Covenant of the Lord, …"
>
> (vs. 32-33a; italics mine)

It is not difficult to see how a great emphasis was placed on the importance of the Ten Commandments and the stone tablets which bore the writings of the Lord (and of Moses and, perhaps, of Joshua). But it is this manner of emphasis of the Law of God (and Moses as the law-giver of Israel) that perhaps eclipsed the importance of the other articles that also were regarded by the Israelites as sacred ritual articles, sacred enough to warrant a space alongside the *Decalogue*. These *other* articles, though not as important as the Law and certainly not as awe-inspiring as the mercy seat that symbolized the very presence of the Lord, were still regarded by the Israeli people of both the Old Testament and the New Testament times as co-members residing within the Ark. The other sacred articles that are mentioned in the Old Testament are the following two:

> The *rod of Aaron* which also had miraculously budded, symbolizing the living [and resurrecting] power of God (*cf*. Numbers 17:8-10); and
>
> The *urn of Manna*; a container in which a quantity of *manna* was deposited for safe-keeping and for remembrance of and by later generations
>
> (cf. Exodus 16:33-36)

These same *three sacred articles* are again mentioned in the New Testament. In Chapter 9 of the Book of Hebrews, we find the passage—in a mater-of-fact "inventory" manner—on the three sacred articles, as well as other items behind the curtain in the Holy of Holies:

> Now in that first agreement (*i.e.*, covenant) between God and his people there were rules for worship and there was a sacred tent

down here on earth. Inside this place of worship there were two rooms. The first one contained the golden candle-stick and a table with special loaves of holy bread upon it; this part was called the Holy Place. Then there was a curtain and behind the curtain was a room called the Holy of Holies.

In that room there were a golden incense-altar and the golden chest, called the ark of the covenant, completely covered on all sides with pure gold. Inside the ark were the tablets of stone with the Ten Commandments written on them, and a golden jar with some manna in it, and Aaron's wooden cane that budded.

Above the golden chest were statues of angels called the cherubim —the guardians of God's glory—with their wings stretched out over the ark's golden cover, called the mercy seat ...

(vs. 1-5; italics in bold face mine)

CHAPTER THREE

ARK IN THE ANCIENT NEAR-EASTERN CULTURE

The Bible tells how the Lord gave a very specific instruction on the construction of the Ark, the Tabernacle, and all the ritual articles of worship to be used in the Tabernacle. The description in the divine instruction was most precise, down to the details of the garments that were to be worn by the priests, and that Moses and Bezaleel—Moses's skilled assistant—made them in strict adherence to the specification given by the Lord.

Contrary to the general belief (*i.e.*, held by both the Christian and Judaic faithful) that the Ark of the Covenant was a unique religious article of the ancient Israelites, archaeological studies suggest that the ark (notice the word is not capitalized) was not at all singularly unique. In fact, the ark most likely resembled any other chest or receptacle of the time for transporting religious articles, and that there are also evidences to support the view that Israel's ark in so many respects was created after the tradition and in the *fashion* of Egyptian royal-ritual chests, even the *sarcophagus*. In fact, the Israeli culture and civic codes owed much to the religious polity of Egypt and other neighboring peoples.

We know, for example, that the name Moses (or *Moshe* in Hebrew) is in fact of Egyptian origin: '*mou*' was an Egyptian word for water, and those who were saved were called '*eses.*' Hence the name *Mo(u)ses* connoted 'the one who was saved from water.' Additionally, the Bible clearly states that all of Moses' knowledge and wisdom was of the 'learned' heritage of the elite institutions of Egypt, created to nurture the distinguishing qualities of members of the house of Pharaohs from commoners (*cf.* Acts 7:22). The famous ancient Jewish philosopher-historian Josephus provides an account of the subjects in which Moses more than likely received his instruction: the 'lower-division' subjects such as logic, grammar, rhetoric, and rhythm (poetry), as well as the 'upper-division' subjects of arithmetic, geometry, astronomy (or, more properly, astrology), and harmony (the study of ratios as related to musical intervals). We may take note of the fact that these were the same subject group known as *trivium* and *quadrivium* (the terms coined by Boethius, the last in the lineage of Greek philosophers) in the Medieval monastic curriculum and, as such, were the main curricular requisites well into the Renaissance era, regarded as the intellectual underpinning for societal (male) elites. In addition and particularly as a member of the royal family, Moses also received instruction in the *priestly wisdom* of the *star-knowledge* (or *astrology*), *necromancy*, *occult lore*, and *divination*.

(It is of considerable interest to note that Isaac Newton, the most illustrious of Renaissance scientists and one of the greatest intellectuals in the entire human history as well as an alleged member of the Brotherhood of *Freemasons*, had noted in his writing that he had owed much to Moses—or, rather, the intellectual lineage associated with the Egyptian priests and royal family members—for the "secret of deep wisdom," perhaps in reference to the science of alchemy. In turn, Pythagoras also, who was among the most famous of the early Greek philosophers, was said to have obtained all his knowledge and wisdom from Egypt. This particular subject and historical perspective, however, is outside the bounds of this study and, therefore, would let suffice with this brief mention without further pursuit.)

It is not surprising, therefore, that the ark would have been conceived and constructed in the tradition of the Egyptian ritual chest. Such a ritual chest was also found to be in common usage in religious practices in the ancient world, not only in northern Africa—including Egypt and Ethiopia—but also in the Near and Middle East. It may be said that most of these ritual items were most likely a testimony to a wide influence of the Egyptian tradition, the country which possessed the earliest, the most advanced and systematized civilization in that part of the ancient world. Graham Hancock, the author of *The Sign and the Seal* (a national best seller) alludes to the fact that the caskets from Tutankhamen's tomb, with the wooden box covered with gold inside and out, could be correctly regarded as a prototype for the Israelites Ark of the Covenant, and that it was with Moses' own familiarity with such a Egyptian ritual chest that he was able to construct the Ark of the Covenant.[1] (Hereafter, the word ark, whether in referring to the Ark of the Covenant, or a ritual chest, will not be capitalized.)

Christopher Knight and Robert Lomas, the authors of *The Hiram Key* which was lauded by Graham Hancock as a "breakthrough book," also state that even the two golden cherubims on the ark's lid—the mercy seat—"have been Egyptian in style, looking exactly like the figures depicted on the walls and sarcophagi of the pyramids."[2] This is also supported by the late Dr. G. Ernest Wright, one of the most respected biblical archaeologists of the mid-Twentieth Century (*e.g.*, as the Parkman Professor of Harvard Divinity School). Wright writes (p. 124, *The Book of the Acts of God*) that the cherubims in the holy of holies in Solomon's Temple were, borrowing from a Phoenician art motif, in the form of [crouched] "lions with human heads and with wings stretched out ..." This, it is to be noted, is also the exact same image on an Egyptian sacred sarcophagus.

In fact, various writers on the subject further propose that the *Decalogue* was [more than likely] written in *hieroglyphics*, the only script that Moses was familiar with (but the commoners, especially the illiterate Israelites, were not). We must take note also of the fact that the Bible not only makes reference to Moses writing down the commandments of God but actually doing so again, on the *second* set of stone tablets. In Exodus Chapter 34 is the following narrative:

"... And *the Lord said to Moses*,
'*Write these words*; in accordance with these words I have made
a covenant with you and with Israel. And [Moses] was there with
the Lord forty days and forty nights; he neither ate bread nor drank
water. And *he wrote upon the tablets the words of the covenant*, the
ten commandments.
(Ex. 34:27-28; also Ex. 17:14; *italics* mine)

In this regard, it should be of special interest that hieroglyphics were called 'the Word of God' by the Egyptians—the term repeated throughout the Bible.[3]

Archaeologists make further inference to the fact that it was common practice in the Near Eastern cultures to make a *replica of ritual articles*. This practice was out of necessity, believed by many ancient people, that the extent of the power and the magical potency of a deity had a localized boundary. In other words, a deity and the range of his power was a *territorial* one, much like the range of juridical authority, be it a country, a county, a city, an office or institution. This concept of *territorial god* was clearly implied in the story of prophet Jonah, for example, in how he had attempted to escape from the range of God's command for him to go to Nineveh, by

"... *flee*[-ing] ... *from the presence of the Lord* [and] went down to Joppa."

Jonah was trying to evade his duty by literally trying to sneak out of the boundary of the Lord's authority by getting on a boat to Tarshish, going in the *opposite direction* of Nineveh (Jonah 1: 1-3).

In religious worship, the people had the need for a visible presence of (a representation of) god. Hence, it was necessary to make the statue of a deity available to the faithful in different locations by making the idol of god mobile from one location to another. This would indeed make possible for the people to have their gods wherever and whatever the rituals were in need, for bestowal of blessing and offering supplication or for praying for victory over enemies when going into battle. From this, then, as many *replicas* were created (at least the most prominent ritual articles), even the ark and the stone tablets of the *Decalogue*, to meet the religious need of the people in different locations and on various occasions. The fact that, today, many people and various researchers claim the existence of the supposedly *lost* ark of the Covenant—the very ark which Moses and Bezaleel constructed—in various locations, could only be regarded as the contemporary testimony to the survival and preservation of not only the belief and practice but also the possible artifacts of the *replicas* of the sacred articles.

The Church of Saint Mary of Zion, in the city of Axum (variously spelled such as Aksum) in Ethiopia, has been widely claimed to be the last resting place of the one and the *true* ark of the Covenant. Perhaps it is not altogether difficult to understand, therefore, that every Orthodox (Christian) church in not only the city of Axum but also throughout entire Ethiopia would and does claim to house the "true" ark of the Covenant in the holy of holies of their local and not-as-well-celebrated church.

One of the most vivid and credibly detailed accounts on the existence of literally countless replicas of the sacred articles of worship—even the ark itself—in many places in the Near East and Ethiopia in particular is given by Hancock. In his fascinating, most thoroughly researched and extraordinarily informative book titled *The Sign and the Seal: ... The Quest for the Lost Ark of the Covenant*, Hancock states that, based on his own research, interviews and personal eye-witness,

> "Every Orthodox church in Ethiopia, it seems, had its own Holy
> of Holies, and in every Holy of Holies was a *tabot* [Ethiopian name
> for ark]. No claim was made that any of these objects were actually
> *the* ark of the Covenant. There was only one true ark and that,
> properly known as *Tabot Zion*, had indeed been brought by Menelik
> [the alleged son between Solomon and the Queen of Sheba] to Ethiopia

in the time of Solomon and now stood in the sanctuary chapel in Axum. All the others throughout the length and breadth of the land [are] merely replicas of that sacred and inviolable original."
"These replicas (or *tabotat*), however, were important. Indeed they were supremely important. Symbolic on several levels, it appeared … that they fully embodied the intangible notion of sanctity … [4]
"These objects, which were often spoken of as replicas of the original in Axum, were not boxes or chests but took the form of flat slabs. The ones I had seen had all been made of wood. Researching the matter further, however, I discovered that *many were indeed made of stone.*"[5]

We know from the Bible that the ark was specifically made to house the two stone tablets bearing the *Decalogue*, the Ten Commandments of the Lord. Regarding the question of stone tablets, Hancock as well as a number of scholars writing on the subject assert that these were not mere ordinary and commonly found rocks but, rather, meteorites. Indeed, the Islamic Holy of Holies, the Temple of the Dome in Mecca, houses a giant Black Stone which is also believed to be a meteorite, the stone which had fallen from the sky that also has markings on its surface. On this, Hancock states that,

"… Since ancient times, Semitic tribes such as the children of
Israel had been known to venerate stones that 'fell from heaven'.
"Geologists … unhesitatingly attributed a meteoric origin to the
Black Stone. Likewise the pairs of sacred stones, known as *betyls*,
that some pre-Islamic Arab tribes carried on their desert wanderings
were believed to have been aerolites—and it was recognized that
a direct line of cultural transmission linked these *betyls* (which were
often placed in portable shrines) with the Black Stone of the *Ka'aba*
and with the stone Tablets of the Law [placed inside] the ark.
And that *betyls* had been known in medieval Europe as *lapis betilis*
[the name] stemming from Semitic origins … [which in turn was a
derivative] from *lapis ex caelis* ('stones from heaven') *lapsit ex caelis*
('it fell from heaven'), or even *lapis, lapsus ex caelis*, 'stone fallen
from heaven.'"[6]

On the other hand, there are *tabotat* that are in fact made as a box "about the size of a tea chest." It is worth noting, therefore, that, in a highly ritualistic and secretive society and in regard to sacred objects, a replica of one or even a small part of the "original" sacred articles was often regarded as a sufficient representation of the whole. Such appears to be the case also when the ark of the Covenant was addressed numerous times in the Old Testament as if the box—elaborate and made of pure gold but essentially still a mere container for carrying the stone tablet—was God Himself (*cf.* above quote in *Note 4*). It may be said, therefore, that the power and the worthiness of the ark was not in the ark itself but, rather, its contents, especially the tablets that bore the handwriting of God.

From this, we also read that stone—rather than wood—was often used as a representation of God or a memorial for the manifested act of God. The stone may be a smaller slab or a sizeable column such as a pillar, but they were equally used and erected to symbolize the place where God visited, or even the place where a covenant was established between the two parties with God as witness. In fact, archaeological scholars inform us that "in the Canaanite religion the pillar had so far become identified with deity (particularly a male deity) as to be an object of veneration,"[7] as opposed to mere commemoration. And it was with this theological precept that the Israelites went forth to destroy all the stone pillars they found in every conquered land of their enemies (*cf.* Exodus 23:24, Deuteronomy. 16:22).

The Old Testament tells many episodes that give accounts of the practice of erecting stone pillars as a representation of God or the place of His visit. Perhaps the most famous and familiar to many is the story of 'Jacob's ladder' told in Genesis Chapter 28: 12-22:

> "And he dreamed that there was a ladder set up on the earth, and
> the top of it reached to heaven; and behold, the angels of God
> were ascending and descending on it! And, behold, the Lord stood
> above it and said,
> 'Behold, I am with you, and will keep you …'
> Then Jacob awoke from his sleep and said,
> 'Surely the Lord is in this place …'
> So Jacob rose early in the morning, and he took the stone which
> he had put under his head and set it up for a pillar and poured oil
> on the top of it [and said] … 'And this stone, which I have set
> for a pillar, shall be God's house.'"

And it is in the course of Jacob's colorful life that we also read several other instances of his erecting stone pillars and monuments (such as piles of stone or an altar of stone), to either commemorate his encounter with God (*e.g.*, Gen. 35: 6-7; 13-15) or as a sign of contractual pledge—that is, a covenant—with other people, such as Laban, his father-in-law (*cf.* Gen. 31: 51-52). This also was the case when Joshua, who became the leader of the Israelites after Moses' death, took

> "… a great stone, and set it up under an oak, that was by
> the sanctuary of the Lord. And Joshua said unto all the people,
> 'Behold, this stone shall be a witness unto us; for [the stone] hath
> heard all the words of the Lord which he spake unto us; it shall be
> therefore a witness unto you, lest ye deny your God.'"
> (Joshua 24: 26-27)

From the above, it is clear that, for Joshua and the Israeli people, the stone was capable of "hearing" and understanding and remembering their oath. In other words, they regarded the *stone to be a living thing*, even the living representative of their God and, hence, far more trustworthy than mere mortals. In fact, stone pillars as a representation of deity and a symbol of covenant was a common feature in the cultic practices of not only the Israelites—God's chosen people—but also of the 'enemy of the Lord.' There is a clear reference to this common religious practice, in Egypt also, as was pronounced in one of Isaiah's prophesy (Is. 19:19-20). This also has its New Testament reference; perhaps the most famous mention of stone as representation of deity or, here, the signification of the divine *persona* of Christ, is when Jesus likened himself to the 'cornerstone,' one which was once despised and rejected by the builders (*cf.* Matthew 21:42; Mark 12:10; Luke 20:17; also see Psalms 118:22).

And, as we shall see, this regard of stone as a living thing and as a representation of deity was also held by the early people of the *shinto* cult in Japan. (In China, in contrast, stone pillars were used as grave headstones, but seldom as the representation of a deity. Images of deities, such as Buddha and Bodhisattva, may be carved out of stones, but natural stones were seldom used as the image of God.) In Japan, the word *hashira* (meaning column or pillar, of stone or wood) was used especially in the *shinto* narratives in reference to and to enumerate their deities, the *kami*.

CHAPTER FOUR

ON THE MYSTERIOUS POWER OF THE ARK

In a most fundamental sense, the ark was a visible representation of the solemn vow between God and His people Israel, that God will be the only God (for He is a *jealous* God) for them. But this relationship was founded on one condition (the *covenant*): that they would walk in the way God had prescribed for them. In other words, if the people observe and keep His conditions (the Laws), He will promise to protect them and make them prosper. Hence, it is told in many passages that the ark of the Lord led the Israelites into battle and had won them victory over their enemies. However, when the Israelites went into battle without the presence of the ark, the defeat was inevitable (*cf.* Numbers. 14:44 *ff.*).

The ark was not only the tangible presence of the Lord of Hosts (*i.e.*, the Lord of the heavenly armies), it was also described in many instances as a vehicle which possessed inexplicably awful power. Testimonials of such a power are told in many biblical passages. In crossing the River Jordan under the leadership of Joshua, for example, we read the following story in Chapters 3 and 4 of the Book of Joshua:

> "At the end of three days the officers went through the camp
> and commanded the people, "When you see the ark of the Covenant
> of the Lord your God being carried by the Levitical priests, then
> you shall ... follow it ... there shall be a space between you and it,
> a distance of about two thousand cubits; do not come near it ...
> And when the soles of the feet of the priests who bear the ark of
> the Lord ... shall rest in the waters of the Jordan, the waters of
> the Jordan shall be stopped from flowing, and the waters coming
> down from above shall stand in one heap ... and the people passed
> over opposite Jericho.

And while all Israelites were passing over on dry ground, the priests who bore the ark of the Covenant of the Lord stood on dry ground in the midst of the Jordan, until all the nations finished passing over the Jordan." (Ch. 3, vs. 1-17)

"And the Lord said to Joshua, 'Command the priests who bear the ark of the Testimony to come up out of the Jordan.' Joshua therefore commanded the priests, 'Come up out of the Jordan.'

And when the priests bearing the ark of the Covenant of the Lord came up from the Jordan, and the soles of the priests' feet were lifted up on dry ground, the waters of the Jordan returned to their place and overflowed all its banks, as before." (Ch. 4: vs. 15-18)

The famous tale of the conquest of Jericho described how the walls came tumbling down at the sound of the trumpet blasts and the shouts of the people. During the siege, the ark of the Covenant occupied a position of importance. The story is narrated in Joshua, Chapter 6:

"Now Jericho was shut up from within and from without because of the people of Israel ... and as Joshua had commanded the people, the seven priests bearing the seven trumpets of rams' horns before the Lord went forward, blowing the trumpets, with the ark of the Covenant of the Lord following them ...

"... and the armed men went before them, and the rear guard came after the ark of the Lord, while the trumpets blew continually ... So they did for six days.

"On the seventh day they rose early at dawn, and marched around the city in the same manner seven times: it was only on that day that they marched around the city seven times. And at the seventh time, when the priests had blown the trumpets, Joshua said to the people,

"Shout; for the Lord has given you the city" ...

So the people shouted, and the trumpets were blown ... And the wall fell down flat ... [and] the [Israelites] took the city.

Then they utterly destroyed all in the city, both men and women, young and old, oxen, sheep, and asses, with the edge of the sword [*except the silver and gold, and vessels of bronze and iron, which are sacred to the Lord ... these shall go into the treasury of the Lord*]."

(vs. 1-21)

It must be noted, however, that now the ark of the Covenant *did not lead* in the march around with the Israelite armies in the seize of Jericho but, rather, was positioned as a *rear guard*. And we may further note that, after the conquest of Jericho and in the ensuing battles against the numerous tribal citadels of the Canaanite people, during which the Israelite armies under the leadership of Joshua had committed countless atrocities of genocidal massacre, the ark was never again figured prominently. Instead, it was mentioned only occasionally.

It is in this larger context of the history of the ark of the Covenant that we detect the declining importance of the ark in the life of the Israelites, that its mysterious power began to diminish gradually, from one scene to the next, in a detectibly "reduced" level of potency. Its power declined visibly and continually, from the awesome power at the head of the victorious army to a position which was passive and defensive rather than active and offensive. And the final blow to the pride of Israel came when, as Samuel's daughter in-law had lamented on her deathbed, "*the glory [of the Lord] has departed from Israel, for the ark of the Lord has been captured*" by the enemy (*cf.* I Samuel 4:21-22; also see below).

It would seem somewhat curious, in the context of the history of the ark, that after the days of Moses and Joshua, the ark was not mentioned in several events of national importance in the history of Israel. For example, the ark did not figure in the "coronation" of Saul as the first King of Israel, and it also was not mentioned when David was crowned King at Hebron and later in Jerusalem. In short, the ark appeared even to have lost its ritual importance since the days of Moses and Joshua.

The beginning of the decline of the importance of the ark may be traced back to the seize of Jericho. That is, after Joshua and the battle of Jericho, the ark of the Covenant no longer led the Israeli army into battle to secure the victory for the people. On the contrary, the presence of the ark may even have proven to be *no guarantee* for military victory. The defeat of Israel and the capture of the ark by the Philistines is described in vivid terms in First Samuel, Chapter 4:

"Now Israel went out to battle against the Philistines; ... and
when the battle spread, Israel was defeated by the Philistines ...
And when the troops came to the camp, the elder of Israel said,
'Why has the Lord put us to rout today before the Philistines?
Let us bring the ark of the Covenant of the Lord here from Shiloh,
that [the Lord] may come among us and save us from the power of
our enemies.' So the people sent to Shiloh, and brought from there
the ark of the Covenant of the Lord of hosts, who is enthroned
on the cherubim;

... When the ark of the Covenant of the Lord came into the [Israeli]
camp, all Israel gave a mighty shout, so that the earth resounded ...
[But] the Philistines fought, and Israel was defeated, and they fled,
every man to his home; and there was a very great slaughter, for there
fell of Israel thirty thousand foot soldiers.
And the ark of God was captured; and the two sons of Eli [the
mentor-judge of Samuel] were slain.
... [Then] a man of Benjamin ran ... and came [to Shiloh] and
told Eli ... and said,
'Israel has fled before the Philistines, and there has also been
a great slaughter among the people; your two sons also ... are dead,
and the ark of God has been captured.'
When he mentioned the ark of God, Eli fell over backward from
his seat ... and his neck was broken, and he died ...

(vs. 1-18)

The victorious Philistines brought the Israeli ark to their camp and set it up beside Dagon, the god of the Philistines. There, the ark was said to have caused the statue of Dagon to fall and to break its head and arms. Thereby the Philistines moved the ark to another city where, again, it had caused tumors among men of all ages, creating a citywide panic. The ark was then moved to another place, but no city would dare accommodate it for fear of any inexplicable harm such as tumors and death to those who had dared touch or look into the ark. Finally, the Philistines, finding themselves at wits end, decided to return the ark to the Israeli camp. Their efforts did not bring much success but, instead, caused sickness and death along the way (*cf.* I Samuel Chapters. 5-6).

One of the last manifestations of the mysterious power of the ark of the Covenant was in the leading of the cows and the cart to go straight away from the camp of the Philistines to a specific destination. Without any guiding hands of men (*cf.* I Sam. 6:1-15), the cows and the cart brought the ark away from the Philistine camp, along with a rich coffer of gold and jewelry that was returned by the enemy. However, arriving there, the ark

"slew some of the men of Bethshemesh, because they looked
into the ark of the Lord; he slew seventy men of them, and the
people mourned because the Lord had made a great slaughter
among the people ..."

(I Sam. 6:19)

From there, the ark was again moved, now to Kiriathjearim, to the house of Abinadab, who consecrated his son for the service of the ark. And it is recorded that

"From the day that the ark was lodged at Kiriathjearim, a long
time passed, some twenty years, and all the house of Israel
lamented after the Lord"
(I Sam. 7:2)

However, Samuel, then the judge over Israel, seemed not overly concerned with the fact that the ark was in the hands of other people. Instead, this last judge of the Israelites used the occasion to admonish the people of the error of their ways. Eventually Samuel installed Saul as the (first) king of Israel and, later, David as the king when Saul failed in his duty as a king and had sinned in the sight of God. On both of these occasions of national importance (coronation of a king), the ark was not featured or even mentioned. During the post-Exile period and especially after the days of Joshua until the days of King David, the ark was still shown to possess mysterious power but only in terms of a non-military nature.

Finally, the ark was on its way back to the Israeli camp, and King David and all Israelites came out to welcome back the ark, with jubilant procession. However, on its way, a man by the name of Uzzah stretched his hand in an attempt to steady the ark when the cows leading the cart stumbled, and the Lord struck him dead on the spot. Fearful of the power of the ark and angry, David sent the ark elsewhere, this time to another Philistine camp, to the house of Obededom of Gittite (*i.e.*, of Gath). The ark stayed with Obededom for three months, and the Lord greatly blessed the Philistine's household. When King David heard about how the Lord had blessed Obededom and his household, he again changed his mind and asked for the return of the ark. Eventually the ark was brought back into the camp of David, and reposed in the tabernacle which David had erected.

At the same time, we may wonder why there were never any recorded accounts or oral legends on the death or other calamities that had befallen the Babylonians, when their armies raided the Temple time and again and, sometime during the course of the battle, carried away the sacred treasures, including the golden ark of the Covenant, from the Holy of Holies of Solomon's Temple. If God Yahweh was indeed a jealous God of *Hosts* (heavenly armies) who, without any human hands, could not only performed the most incredible miracles, from letting the water gushing out from the rock in the dry desert, raining *manna* from heaven, shielding and guiding the Israelites with clouds and fire, massacring enemies by the thousands, and levitating the train of priests across the River Jordan and into Canaan, or even striking dead a hapless man who was only trying to steady the ark by unwittingly upholding its side, would it not be expected that this same God would never allow the enemy of His chosen people to go unpunished especially when they so violently transgressed His own dwelling place, the Mercy Seat?

Perhaps the glory of the Lord had indeed departed from the ark, as the prophets lamented. Or was it because the people, including their kings and judges and even prophets, had ceased to believe in the miraculous power of the ark, regarding it as nothing more than an emblem, rather than the very presence of their God? Could this not be the reason why the people had let the tabernacle fall into a state of disrepair? Why were there no more feasts of sacrifices, no more glorious festivities of the ark? Even if God did not desire fat burning offerings and elaborate sacrificial festivals, he surely would still desire some gestures of a repentant and contrite heart, indicating thereby that the people still believed in and depended on their God.

But the people had become content and complacent, and their Kings who were the mightiest, wisest and wealthiest, with several hundred wives, princesses and concubines, sat on the lion's throne made of gold and ivory. And God's favored King Solomon not only built the Temple for Him but also many temples for other gods, gods who came into Jerusalem with Solomon's exotic wives. God Yahweh was no longer a jealous god. The people's faith and belief was no longer unfailing.

When the people's faith and belief in their deity declined, the potency of the sacred relics also diminished. When Moses and Joshua made people believe in the awesome power of the ark, it performed miraculous deeds. But when David and Solomon ceremoniously 'housed'—or moth-balled, as it were—the ark, and then kept a respectable *distance from it*, the ark "proportionally" ceased to exert observable power. The once-awesome ark had now become an ordinary chest, a common receptacle, to keep human remains (*cf.* Joshua 23:32) along with a few curious cultic artifacts, remnants from the legendary bygone days. After all,

"There was *nothing* [*else*] *in the ark except* the two stone tablets."

CHAPTER FIVE

KING DAVID'S CONQUEST
OF JERUSALEM AND THE RETURN OF THE ARK

King David proved himself over and over again a masterful warfare strategist and an indomitable warrior. In a relatively short period, he had subjugated nearly all the neighboring Semitic tribes. A partial list of David's conquests and the war booties he had taken for himself and as offering to the Lord in thanksgiving to the Lord for all his victories can be found in Chapter Eight of II Samuel:

> "After David defeated the Philistines and subdued them,
> David took Metheghammah out of the hand of the Philistines.
> And he defeated Moab ... David also defeated Hadadezer ...
> David slew twenty-two thousand men of the Syrians.
> ... And Joram brought with him articles of silver, of gold, and
> of bronze; these also King David dedicated to the Lord, together
> with the silver and gold which he dedicated from all the nations
> he subdued, from Edom, Moab, the Ammonites, the Philistines,
> Amalek, and from the spoils of Hadadezer ... And David won a
> name for himself. When he returned, he slew eighteen thousand
> Edomites in the Valley of Salt. And he put garrisons in Edom;
> throughout all Edom he put garrisons, and all the Edomites
> became David's servants."
>
> (vs. 1-14)

Indeed, the litany of David's military conquests is long, and the tribes he had subjugated were not limited to those listed above. For the purpose of the present study, two conquests will be mentioned: the battles against the Edomites and against the Jebusites.

One of the most famous tales on David's strategic successes is his taking of Jerusalem, a fortified city with a long history. Chapter Five of II Samuel tells how David, now the king over the tribes of Israel who had reigned from Hebron for seven and a half years, had decided to take on the Jebusites, living in the ancient but fortified and strategically situated city of Jerusalem. (The name *Jebusite* was in fact derived from *Jeru*salem, the city in and around which the *Jebu*sites lived.) In penetrating the heavily fortified city, David devised a clever strategy: to use the underground water passages into the city to infiltrate the impregnable Jerusalem. Once inside Jerusalem, David and his army committed horrendous atrocities against the people of the City of *Peace* (-*Salem*). And, having conquered the city, King David renamed it after his own vainglory: the *City of David*.

But perhaps the most horrific battles were fought against the Edomites, the descendants of Esau (*cf.* Gen. 25:30), the hapless elder brother who lost his birthright to his more cunning younger brother Jacob whose name was to become Israel. The battles of the Israelites against the Edomites are recorded in Chapter 11 of I Kings, as well Chapter 14 of II Kings and Chapter 25 of II Chronicles. However, one should take note of the fact that the tenor in these different narratives is markedly different. In II Samuel, the victory was seen as a gift from the Lord (*cf.* verse 14b), while it was cast in a much less favorable light elsewhere. In reading these several passages in different books of the Old Testament, it is apparent that the conquest of the Edomites—the original inhabitants of the ancient fortified city of *Jerusalem*—was nothing short of savage atrocities, of the category of genocide: merciless and thorough carnage of all the male inhabitants, and enslaving of all others—female and children. Such atrocities, whether they were committed by David, his army commanders, or other later Israeli kings such as Joash, against the Edomites were apparently regarded by the authors of these other (later) chronicle passages as among the sins of David as well as the bitter seeds for Solomon. Indeed, the annihilation of the Jebusites and Edomites, who were the Israelites' own Semitic kin, was regarded by the later prophets as of the same gravity with the other great sins of both David and Solomon, such as taking foreign wives and worshipping their alien gods in the land of Israel.

> "And the *Lord raised up an adversary against Solomon*, Hadad the Edomite; he was of the royal house of Edom. For when David was in Edom, and Joab (the commander of the army) went up to bury the slain, he slew every male in Edom. (Joab and all Israel remained there six months, until he had cut off every male in Edom;

but Hadad fled to Egypt, together with certain Edomites of his
father's servants, Hadad being yet a little child...."
(I Kings 11:14-17; RSV).

"[Joash] killed ten thousand Edomites in the Valley of Salt and
took Sela by storm, and called it Joktheel ..."
(II Kings 14:7; RSV)

"But Amaziah took courage, and let out his people, and went
to the Valley of Salt and smote ten thousand men of Seir.
The men of Judah captured another ten thousand alive, and took
them to the top of a rock and threw them down from the top of
the rock; and they were all dashed to pieces. But the men of the
army whom Amaziah sent back ... fell upon the cities of Judah,
from Samaria to Beth-horon, and killed three thousand people
in them, and took much spoils. After Amaziah came from the
slaughter of the Edomites, he brought the gods of the men of Seir,
and set them up as his gods, and worshipped them, making
offering to them. *Therefore the Lord was angry* with Amaziah ...
(II Chronicles. 25:11-15a; *italics* mine)

(Here, it may be of interest to take note of the name *Amaziah*, appearing in
the above citation as an unrighteous man, even if the name itself meant "*Yahweh
is Mighty*." In terms of change in word signification, the name Amaziah may
have come to mean, instead of "*Yahweh is mighty*," a "*bad person*," particularly
for the Edomites who had suffered horrendously at the hands of Amaziah who
was a general in David's army. This possible change in the name signification
may be related to a peculiar etymological similarity: a particular Japanese slang
word which had originated in the district of Izumo—the site of Izumo Shrine,
perhaps the oldest *shinto* shrine in Japan, in the area where the descendants of
Esau of the Old Testament and the people who were later called the Edomites
might have come to settle. The word is pronounced variously as *aman-jaku*
or *ama-no-shaku*, and this word is used not only in Izumo but also in nearby
districts such as Akita. An adjective, the word is used to describe a "man of ill
intent" or "man of wanton nature." One can only wonder if there is any connection between *Amaziah* who had massacred the *Edomites*, and the *Izumo* word
amanjaku to mean a person with harmful intent.)

Having conquered both the southern and northern regions of the kingdom,
and having taken the strategically located city of Jerusalem, King David now
reigned over the entire Israel from his palace in the newly renamed City of

David. And it is there, in the City of David, that we witness the sudden resurface of the ark of the Covenant, and read how the ark was received by King David and all the people, amidst a wild and frenzied jubilation.

First, we read the story about the return of the ark of the Covenant, essentially from the hands of the enemy Philistines to the camp of King David. In Chapter Six of II Samuel, the following narrative is given:

"David again gathered all the chosen men of Israel, thirty thousand.
And David arose and went with all the people who were with him
to Baale-judah, to bring up from there the ark of God, which is called
by the name of the Lord of hosts who sits enthroned on the cherubim.
And they carried the ark of God upon a new cart, and brought it out
of the house of Abinadad ... And David and all the house of Israel
were making merry before the Lord with all their might, with songs
and lyres and harps and tambourines and castanets and cymbals.
And when they came to the threshing floor of Nacon, Uzzah put
out his hand to the ark of God and took hold of it, for the oxen
stumbled. And the anger of the Lord was kindled against Uzzah;
and God smote him ... and he died there beside the ark of God.
And David was angry ... and David was afraid of the Lord that day ...
So David was not willing to take the ark of the Lord into the city
of David; but David took it aside to the house of Obededom the Gittite.
And the ark of the Lord remained in the house of Obededom the Gittite
for three months, and the Lord blessed Obededom and his household.
And it was told King David, 'The Lord has blessed the household of
Obededom and all that belongs to him, because of the ark of God.'
So David went and brought up the ark of God from the house of
Obededom to the city of David with rejoicing [and, at every six paces
he offered sacrifice of an ox and a fatling]
And David danced before the Lord with all his might; and David was
girded with a linen ephod. So David and all the house of Israel brought
up the ark of the Lord with shouting, and with the sound of the horn.
As the ark of the Lord came into the city of David, Michal the daughter
of Saul looked out of the window, and saw King David leaping and
dancing before the Lord, and she despised him in her heart.
And they brought in the ark of the Lord, and set it in its place, inside
the tent which David had pitched for it; and David offered burnt
offerings and peace offerings before the Lord ..."

(vs. 1-19)

Here, we should take note of the reaction of Michal, David's wife and the daughter of King Saul, and ask why she "despised him in her heart" (vs. 16). Was it because she saw how her own husband had disgraced himself before all of his servants and maids, acting "as one of the vulgar fellows shamelessly uncover[ing] himself!"? (vs. 20). Surely, as the daughter of King Saul, she should have been familiar with the ritual celebration before the ark, and would have regarded David's behavior normal and acceptable on such a festive occasion. But the fact that Michal despised David of his behavior before the ark would strongly suggest that the ark was not a part of any religious rituals during the reign of King Saul. In fact, the ark was not in the Israeli camp. Thus the jubilant and frenzied celebration with dance and music before the ark was totally alien to Michal. The response of David to the spiteful accusation of Michal (*cf.* v. 21-23) should also be of considerable interest in the history and the ceremony of the ark.

Then we read a most interesting passage regarding the ark of the Lord. The Lord desired a place of rest, and He gave Nathan the prophet a message that He wanted conveyed to David. First the Lord pointed out that David has now built himself a nice house or a palace, then He literally begged David to *also* build Him a dwelling place, even just a tabernacle—essentially a tent—by recounting how He had blessed David and made him victorious and, *therefore*, David should now repay the goodness of his Lord (*cf.* II Samuel Chapter 7):

> "Go and tell my servant David, 'Thus says the Lord: Would you
> build me a house to dwell in? [For] *I have not dwelt in a house since
> the day I brought up the people of Israel from Egypt to this day, but
> I have been moving about in a tent for my dwelling. In all places
> where I have moved [to], did I speak a word with any of the judges
> of Israel ... saying, 'Why have you not built me a house of cedar?'*
> Now therefore thus you shall say to my servant David ...
>   (vs. 5-8a; *italics mine*)

The passage that follows can only be seen as David's wheeling and dealing with God. While not ever directly answering to commit himself to build a dwelling place for (the ark of) the Lord, David responded by begging how the Lord must continue to bless him and his household, and to be victorious over his enemies. That David certainly continued to receive God's blessing on his military campaigns of near total annihilation of all the neighboring tribes around Jerusalem and beyond is recorded in Chapters Eight through Ten of the Second Book of Samuel. And it was only after all the slaughters that David eventually erected a tabernacle for the ark. To be sure, this effort in erecting the Tabernacle of the Lord was rather minuscule when compared to his warring efforts and satisfying the needs of his hundreds of wives and concubines (*e.g., cf.* Chapter. 5:13). And we are all familiar with the extent of David's carnal desires which had extended to usurping the wife of his general by devising the death of this hapless husband (Chapter 11).

One thing is clear. After the ark was installed in the Tabernacle, and after David blessed the people and divided the sacrificial offerings among the people and the servants in his own household, the ark, for all practical purposes, was left in repose, and forgotten. Subsequently, the Tabernacle was let to fall into a state of disrepair. The implication here is that, as the result of David's neglect of the ark, the blessing of the Lord did not stay with the household of David. Internal strifes and external battles great and small with new as well as old enemies (*e.g.,* the Philistines) ensued, not the least of which was the struggle among David's own sons on the succession right to his throne (*e.g., cf.* I Kings, Chapters 1-2). And, so, we read about the last days of David's life filled with remorse and repentance, chiefly over his life of great bloodshedding which had created so much hatred which, in turn, had brought on so many tragedies to the people (*cf.* II Samuel, Chapter 24).

CHAPTER SIX

THE ARK SINCE THE DAYS OF SOLOMON AND AFTER THE DESTRUCTION OF THE TEMPLE

After a considerable family feud, Solomon ascended the throne of David. Solomon was the son of King David and Bathsheba who, earlier, was the wife of Uriah the Hittite and a general in King David's army. But King David desired Bathsheba, and sent Uriah to the ill-fated battle to die (*cf.* II Samuel 11:2 *ff*). It was for this and other sins of David that, although David was commanded by the Lord to erect a *temporary* tabernacle for the ark of the Lord, it was to Solomon that the Lord gave the specific command to build the Temple, the *permanent* house of God. For the hands of David were too tainted with the blood of the slain thousands (*cf.* I Kings 5:3). Indeed, the Lord condemned these mighty kings of Israel for their indulgence in luxury and their indifference to the suffering of the people. Therefore, the Lord would regard even the sweet music (of the psalms) of David as abomination (*cf.* Amos 5:21-23; 6:1-6).

Finally, four hundred and eighty years since the day the Lord led the Israelites out of Egypt, the work on building the first Temple of the Lord was begun by King Solomon. The Temple was to be a truly impressive architectural structure, but was far less grand when compared to the palaces which Solomon built for himself and for his thousand wives (many of them political marriages) (*cf.* I Kings 3:1-2). Still, it was an expensive enough undertaking for King Solomon to inquire about; he obtained both the skills and materials from neighboring countries, especially from the kings of Tyre (southern Lebanon) and Egypt.

It is in the narratives delineating the course of plans for and the work on constructing the Temple that we encounter the name Hiram, king of Tyre (I Kings, Chapter 5). Hiram was the king whose life and impact was to figure so prominently in the cultural history and the 'secret' tradition of the *Freemasons*, much more prominently than the brief reference in the Bible would suggest (as more or less a neighboring king who was glad to supply Solomon with building material and manpower). It was clear that the tradeoff was for exchange of other commodities such as wheat and oil, and Solomon's promise to make yearly and partial 'mortgaging' payments for Hiram's help in building the Temple. All in all, it was also a political deal to maintain peace between the two neighboring kingdoms. We should note that Hiram not only supplied building materials for the Temple, but also was the architect of the whole project, for "[Hiram] came to King Solomon, and did all his work" (*cf.* I Kings 7:14; also 15–50).

It took seven years to complete the building of the Temple, and there is a detailed description of the architectural features of the Temple in Chapter Six of the First Book of Kings. In comparison, it took thirteen years—nearly twice the length of time to build the Temple—to complete Solomon's own private residence palace (*cf.* Chapter 7). And in undertaking such massive construction projects, Solomon had to "raise a [very heavy] levy of *forced* labor of nearly two hundred thousand men. At last the temple was completed:

> "Thus all the work that King Solomon did on the house of the Lord was finished. And Solomon brought in the things which David his father had dedicated, the silver, the gold, and the vessels, and stored them in the treasuries of the house of the Lord.
> "Then Solomon assembled the elders of Israel and all the heads of the tribes, the leaders of the fathers's houses of the people of Israel, before King Solomon in Jerusalem, to bring up the ark of the Covenant of the Lord out of the city of David, which is Zion …
> And all the elders of Israel came, and the priests took up the ark. And they brought up the ark of the Lord, the tent of meeting, and all the holy vessels that were in the tent; the priests and the Levites brought them up. And King Solomon and all the congregation of Israel, who had assembled before him, were with him before the ark, sacrificing so many sheep and oxen that they could not be counted or numbered.
> Then the priests brought the ark of the Covenant of the Lord to its place, in the inner sanctuary of the house, in the most holy place, underneath the wings of the cherubim. For the cherubim spread out their wings over the place of the ark, so that the cherubim made a covering above the ark and its poles. And the poles were so long that the ends of the poles were seen from the holy place before the inner sanctuary; but they could not be seen from outside …
> **There was nothing in the ark except the two tablets of stone which Moses put there at Horeb, where the Lord made a covenant with**

the people of Israel, when they came out of the land of Egypt ...
Then the king, and all Israel with him, offered sacrifices before the Lord.
Solomon offered as peace offerings to the Lord twenty-two thousand
oxen and a hundred and twenty thousand sheep ...
So Solomon held the feast at that time, and all Israel with him, a great
assembly, from the entrance of Hamath to the Brook of Egypt, before
the Lord our God, seven days ...

It should be pointed out that the heavy levy and forced labor (described in
I Kings 9:15 *ff*) or the greater use of materials, manpower and armies of forced
labor, did not end with completion of the Temple project. In fact, for thirteen
years following the completion of the Temple building, a much heavier levy was
forced upon the *non*-Israelis in building lavish palaces for the many hundreds
of Solomon's exotic wives and temples for foreign gods of his exotic wives.
Indeed, the listing of the construction expense is nothing short of staggering
(*cf.* I Kings 9:10-28). The passages in Chapter 9 of I Kings allude to aspects relative to this construction project:

"At the end of twenty years, in which Solomon had built the two
houses, the house of the Lord and the king's house, and Hiram king of
Tyre had supplied Solomon with cedar and cypress timber and gold,
as much as [Solomon] desired, [and in exchange for Hiram's work]
King Solomon gave to Hiram twenty cities in the land of Galilee ...
[but Hiram was not pleased with what he saw] ... So [the place of
these cities was] called the land of Cabul to this day, for] Hiram had
sent to [Solomon] one hundred and twenty talents of gold.
And this is the account of the forced labor which King Solomon levied
to build the house of the Lord and his own house and the Millo and
the wall[s] of Jerusalem and Hazor and Megiddo and Gezer.
(Pharaoh king of Egypt had gone up and captured Gezer and burnt it
with fire, and had slain the Canaanites who dwelt in the city, and had
given it as dowry to his daughter, Solomon's wife; so Solomon rebuilt
Gezer) and Beth-horon the lower and Baalath and Tamar in the
wilderness, in the land of Judah, and all the store-cities that Solomon
had, and the cities for his chariots, and the cities for his horsemen,
and whatsoever Solomon desired to build in Jerusalem, in Lebanon,
and in all the land of his dominion. And all the people who were left
of the Amorites, the Hittites, the Perizzites, the Hivites, and the
Jebusites, who were not of the people of Israel—their descendants

who were left after them in the land, whom the people of Israel were unable to destroy utterly—these Solomon made a forced levy of slaves ... But of the people of Israel Solomon made no slaves; they were the soldiers, they were his officials, his commanders, his captains, his chariot commanders and his horsemen ...

(vs. 10-22; RSV)

It is important for us to realize that many of Solomon's wives were from a *political marriage* and, as such, they were not Solomon's 'handmaids' but nearly equal in terms of the degree of political status. Hence, they would demand the right to continue to worship their gods, and Solomon had apparently yielded to their demands. In fact, from all indications, Solomon did so rather *willingly*. The following brief passages should be read and understood in this context:

"*But* Pharaoh's daughter *went up from the city of David to her own house* which Solomon had built for her.

(I Kings 9:24; *italics* mine)

"Now King Solomon loved many foreign women: the daughter of Pharaoh, and Moabite, Ammonite, Edomite, Sidonian, and Hittite women, from the nations concerning which the Lord had said ... 'You shall not enter into marriage with them, neither shall they with you, for surely they will turn away your heart after their gods. [But] Solomon clung to these in love. [Solomon] had seven hundred wives, princesses, and three hundred concubines; and his wives turned away his heart. For when Solomon was old his wives turned away his heart after other gods; and his heart was not wholly true to the Lord his God ... For Solomon went after Ashtoreth the goddess of the Sidonians, and after Milcom the abomination of the Ammonites. So Solomon did what was evil in the sight of the Lord, and did not wholly follow the Lord. Then Solomon built a high place for Chemosh the abomination of Moab, and for Molech the abomination of the Ammonites, on the mountain east of Jerusalem. And so he did for all his foreign wives, who burned incense and sacrificed to their gods. And the Lord was angry with Solomon ... [and said to Solomon] since ... you have not kept my covenant and my statutes ... I will surely tear the kingdom from you ...

(I Kings 11:1-11)

All this while, the ark of the Lord was left reposed in the Temple, not to be figured prominently again in all the affairs of Solomon, whether they were political, ritual, or domestic. In short, the ark was virtually forgotten since the day of the sumptuous dedication festivity.

Why had the once mighty, invincible and fearsome ark of the Lord become minimized in the otherwise ever ascending and increasingly glorious court of Solomon's empire? Why, indeed, when the fame of Solomon the Wise had attracted admirers from every region of the then known world, and the glory of Solomon even "took away the breath" of the Queen of Sheba (*cf.* I Kings 9)?

We could only surmise whether the loss of the two other sacred articles stolen from the ark had any psychological impact on the Levites, on King Solomon himself, or on the collective psyche of the people of Israel. After all, the ark had been invaded and taken by the enemies, and now was found to have been *violated* by persons unknown, the *sacred contents stolen*, and there was no knowledge of the whereabouts of the missing articles. We know, from the vantage of historical hindsight, that the kingdom of Solomon and the dynastic period of Israel was coming to a close. We may surmise that the most luxurious life of Solomon's many exotic wives and the unbridled expenditure in the worship of their exotic gods around the Temple and *within the "sight" of* (the ark of) *the Lord*, had collateral effect of sapping not only the coffer but also the spirit of the people of Israel. As David had done to grieve the Lord with his bloodsheding, so did Solomon anger the Resident of the ark with his arrogance and idolatry.

Immediately after Solomon's death, there followed a period of turmoil, of power struggle among the leaders of the Israelites including Solomon's sons. For example, Jeroboam, once a confidant of King Solomon, eventually left Jerusalem for Egypt, disenchanted with Solomon. His departure and alliance with Egypt also spelled disaster for the kingdom of Judah. For the following event is recorded in I Kings, Chapter 14:

> "In the fifth year of King Rehoboam [a son of Solomon], Shishak king of Egypt came up against Jerusalem; he took away the treasures of the house of the Lord and the treasures of the king's house he took away everything. He also took away all the shields of gold which Solomon had made; and King Rehoboam made in their stead shields of bronze, and committed them to the hands of the officers of the guard, who kept the door of the king's house. And as often as the king went into the house of the Lord, the guard bore them [*i.e.*, the bronze replica, the substitute] and brought them back to the guardroom."
>
> (v. 25-28)

This then was the period of the prophets of doom—the era of Elijah, Elisha and Amos—whose ministry was, for all practical purposes, a failure, forcing Prophet Elijah to escape to the land of Tishbet (the modern Tibet?), and later, Elisha too to ride off to a region beyond the clouds (implying perhaps to high mountain regions above the cloud level?). Israel was invaded repeatedly, by such mighty foreign powers as Assyria and Babylonia (and, finally Rome), in whose hands Jerusalem was utterly destroyed, and the ark—with all its contents and the companion vessels in the Holy of Holies—was carried away by the raiders.

The historians and archaeologists tell us that the City of David was attacked by King Nebucadnezzer, not only once but three times. The Babylonian armies utterly devastated Jerusalem, and the Temple crumbled to its foundation. Today, with only the section of the outer walls known as the "wailing wall" left standing, we gaze on a sorry reminder of the glory that once was the emblem of pride but now the symbol of shame for Israel. It was the shame the Lord had allowed to happen, for both King David the Warrior and King Solomon the Wise had turned their hearts away from the Lord, and had given them to satisfying their carnal desires, vain glory, with a palace-full of foreign wives and their alien gods. It is no wonder that the "glory of the Lord" had departed from amidst His chosen people. And the ark with all its contents and all the other holy vessels in the Holy of holies disappeared, was taken, destroyed, recast, hidden, no one seemed to know with any degree of certainty.

In hindsight, the Lord had forewarned this national disaster right after the dedication of the Temple. For the Lord appeared *for the second time* to Solomon, and delivered him the following warning:

> "But if you turn aside from following me, you or your children,
> and do not keep my commandments and my statutes which I have
> set before you, but go and serve other gods and worship them, then
> I will cut off Israel from the land which I have given them; and the
> house which I have consecrated for my name I will cast out of my
> sight; and Israel will become a proverb and a byword among all peoples.
> *And this house will become a heap of ruins*; everyone passing by it
> will be astonished, and will hiss; and they will say,
> 'why has the Lord done thus to this land and to this house?'
> then they will say,
> 'because they forsook the Lord their God who brought
> their fathers out of the land of Egypt, and laid hold on
> other gods, and worshiped them and served them;
> therefore the Lord has brought all this evil upon them.
> (I King 9: 6-9)

Both the gradual shift in the emphasis on the ritual importance and the eventual "demise" of the inviolable holiness of the ark were evident in the writings of the later prophets who had ceased to mention the ark. It is clearly implied that the ark simply had faded from the collective memory of the Israelites. One passage would even go so far as to unceremoniously imply that the ark not only had no longer existed among the Israelites at that time (of prophet Jeremiah) but *would never again be remembered* even when Israel was restored in the latter days to its former glory once again:

> "And when you have multiplied and increased in the land, in those days, says the Lord, they shall no more say, "the ark of the Covenant of the Lord." It shall not come to mind, or be remembered, or missed; it shall not be made again."
>   (Jeremiah 3:16)

However, the story of the ark would not end with the destruction of the Temple. It might be said that the ark—or the trace and retracing of it—went underground. The story certainly took a fascinating turn, with its track blurred and itinerary lost in mazes; the story was told, retold, followed, and lingered on in various legends. For we have the stories of the Templars and the Freemasons—the followers and pursuers of the mysterious *Hiram Key*, and the story of an Egyptian emperor Menelik, the alleged son of King Solomon and the Queen of Sheba, who is alleged to have taken possession of the ark after visiting Solomon's court. The story of Menelik obviously had existed in several oral traditions, and also was committed to a writing in a much later but still sufficiently ancient time (in the thirteenth century, C. E., and hence believed to be credible), in the book known as *Kebra Nagast* (the title means *The Glory of Kings*). Surviving legends and *Kebra Nagast* together have kept alive the belief that Menelik in fact had 'inherited' the ark, and that the ark is now kept in the city of Axum in Ethiopia, in the holy of holies of the Mary of Zion Church. Meanwhile, other claims of the existence and location of the ark, or the Holy Grail, and even eyewitness (but unvalidated) testimonials, abound. For none of these has received an objective verification by an objective third party.

In this sense, therefore, it may be said that Prophet Jeremiah was not entirely correct when he said that the ark "shall not be remembered" or that "it shall not be made again." For the ark, or its *replica*, was to be made in various places and in various ways, and the memory of and the faith in the ark linger still, to this day, even in the *farthest eastern shores* of the world.

PART TWO

MiFune-Shiro
—*a.k.a.* *Replica* of the *Ark*—
and *Shintoism*

CHAPTER SEVEN

THE ETYMOLOGY OF "ARK" AND *MIFUNE-SHIRO*

The word "ark" is familiar to the people of Christian, Judaic and Muslim faiths, famously associated with Noah's *ark*, as well as the *ark* in which infant Moses was hidden and let afloat on the Nile River to escape the Pharaoh's soldiers on forced-reduction of the Israeli population in Egypt. The word is equally familiar to many as the *ark* of the Covenant, perhaps made a bit more famous by the Spielberg movie "The Raiders of the Lost *Ark*." However, an obvious question that begs to be answered is: "Why was the same word *ark* used to refer both to a square *chest* of a container and a *boat*?" The English word *ark* means a boat and, hence, the large boat or ship which Noah was commanded to build to save his family and a pair of every living creature was rightfully called 'Noah's *ark*.' This same English word (and the same Hebrew word) were also used in reference to 'Moses' *ark*'—the small basket that functioned as a flotation device that Moses' mother had made to save her infant son.

It would appear peculiar, then, that the *ark* of the Covenant was called an ark (at least in the English Bible), when it is obvious that it was never used as a flotation vehicle, as was the case with Noah's ark and Moses' ark. It is therefore necessary in the context of this study to inquire into the etymology of the word *ark*, in providing an important understanding of the historical and cultural lineage of the *ark* of the Covenant.

First, two different Hebrew words were used in the Bible for "ark": one is *tebah* (pronounced with an accented and elongated '*e*'); and the other is '*aron* (with a glottal '*a*' and a similarly accented and elongated '*o*'). *Tebah* is believed to be a 'loan word' from Egypt (also see below, in the Hancock quotation), which means a box or even a coffin (see below), while '*aron* (not a loan word but a Hebrew word proper) also means a box, even an ordinary chest. '*Aron* is an older word in Hebrew history (*i.e.*, used earlier than *tebah* in the *Pentateuch*, the first *five books* of the Old Testament traditionally believed to have been written by Moses); it first appearing in Genesis 50:26, where it is stated that, when

Joseph died in Egypt at an old age of one hundred and ten, "they embalmed him, and he was put in a 'coffin' ('*aron*) in Egypt." However, a different word *tebah* is used for both Noah's ark and Moses' ark .

From this use of the two different words for outwardly two different shaped articles of dissimilar functions, it is not difficult to conclude that '*aron* is meant to refer to a chest, a receptacle, while *tebah* is for a container that is used as a flotation device. Thus we understand why '*aron*, instead of *tebah, was* used for the ark (the chest) of the Covenant. This use of interchanged (or interchanging) meaning of the two words is further confirmed in II Kings, 12:9-10 and 16, where it is stated that a 'chest' (*tebah*, instead of '*aron*) was placed on the right-hand side of the altar at the Temple entrance, for the purpose of collecting the contributions toward the restoration of the Temple (which had, somehow, fallen into a state of disrepair).

It may be added also that, as compared to *tebah* which referred to an ordinary receptacle, '*aron* was used for a receptacle of articles of religious or ritual significance, such as the remains of Joseph, the stone tablets with the Ten Commandments written on them and, still later, the urn containing a portion of *manna*, and Aaron's rod. Hence, the ark of the Covenant was not a mere chest or receptacle; it was in fact the receptacle of a considerable divine dignity as well as the throne *par excellence* of the Lord. In short, this *ark* was a holy and living article, virtual God in bodily form. To wit: when the ark was lifted to begin a journey, the people would cry out: "Arise, Yahweh, let thine enemies be scattered, let them that hate thee flee from before thee!" Similarly, when the ark was to come to rest, the people would cry out: "Return, O Yahweh, to the myriads of families of Israel" (*cf.* Number 10:33-36).

Indeed, the ark of the Covenant frequently displayed unspeakably awesome power. This is most vividly demonstrated by destroying the enemies of the Israelites, or anyone showing the slightest degree of disrespect, intentionally or otherwise. A vivid example of the latter is told about Uzzah, one of Abinadab's sons who was serving as the escort and guard of the ark when it was transported from their hillside homestead to Jerusalem. Uzzah extended his hands to steady the ark when he saw that it was faltering (due to the cart faltering caused by a stumbling of the oxen pulling the cart). The poor soul was immediately struck dead, because his action was impious (*e.g.*, touching the ark), even if his intention was admirable (*cf.* II Samuel 6:68).

But, then, why was the ark of the Covenant—essentially a chest or a box with no expressed purpose or likeness of a ship—called an ark? Here, we must again turn to one of the most fascinating insights offered by Graham Hancock, that there was a cultural and etymological link between '*aron* the chest (the ark) and *tebah* the boat (also ark) (*cf.* **Fig.** 5). In other words, the same translated word "ark" to mean both a chest and boat is not an inappropriate or mistaken use but, indeed, has its unique etymological basis. In order to show this etymological connection, it is necessary to cite a rather lengthy passage from Hancock's work, in order to clarify the double meaning of the word *ark* as used in the Bible.

"Studying first the western wall of the colonnade on which the Tutankhamen reliefs were displayed, my eye was caught by what appeared to be an ark, lifted shoulder high on its carrying poles by a group of priests ...
... With the sole proviso that the object being transported took the form of a miniature boat rather than a casket, the scene ... looked like ... a faithful illustration of the passage in the first book of Chronicles [describing the Levites' carrying of] the ark of God with the shafts on their shoulders ...
[In *Timkat*—the Ethiopian festival of the ark of the Covenant, or festival of ark worship which Hancock had witnessed,] the details of the ceremonies [with] religious frenzy [which was identical to] the ecstatic procession portrayed on the time-worn stones of this Egyptian temple [of Tutankhamen] ... *Timkat* had been characterized by the performance of wild dances and the playing of musical instruments before the arks ...
"... According to established etymologies the original meaning of *tabot* [the ark] had been 'ship-like container.' Indeed ... the archaic Hebrew word *tebah* (from which the Ethiopian term had been derived) had been used in the Bible to refer specially to ship-like arks, namely the ark of Noah and the ark of bulrushes in which the infant Moses had been cast adrift on the Nile. [And it is of significance] that the *Kebra Nagast* [an ancient Ethiopian text of history] had at one point described the *ark of the Covenant* as 'the belly of a ship' containing 'the Two Tablets which were written by the finger of God.' [In an 1884 book by A. H. Sayce, then a Deputy Professor of Philology at Oxford University, titled *Fresh Light from the Ancient Monuments*, it is stated that] the law and ritual of the Israelites had been derived from many sources. Amongst these were 'various festivals and feasts' in which "The gods were carried in procession in 'ships' which, as we learn from the sculptures, resembled in form the Hebrew ark, and were borne on men's shoulders by means of staves.'"

Hancock then continues, that

"… Those ceremonies … had taken place in the Upper Egyptian town now known as *Luxor*, a relatively recent name derived from the Arabic *L'Ouqsor* (meaning 'the palaces'). Much earlier, during the period of Greek influence in Egypt (from about the fifth century, BC) the whole area including the nearby temple at Karnak had been known as Thebai. Modern Europeans had subsequently corrupted this name to the more familiar 'Thebes.' In the process, however, they had obscured an intriguing etymology: the Thebai had in fact been derived from *Tapet*, the name by which the Luxor/ Karnak religious complex had been known in the era of Tutankhamen and Moses. And *Tapet* in its turn was merely the feminine form of *Apet* the great festival for which they had been famous, a festival that had centered upon the procession in which arks had been carried between the two temples. What intrigued me about this … was the phonetic similarity of the words *Tapet* and *Tabot* [which was due to the fact that] the shape of the *Tapet* arks had evolved over the passing centuries, gradually ceasing to resemble ships so closely and becoming instead 'more and more like a chest.'

"I had … established that the Ethiopian term *Tabot* had been derived from the Hebrew *tebah*, meaning 'ship-like container,' [which, in turn, points to the possibility that] the word *tebah* had itself originally been derived from the ancient Egyptian *Tabet* … because the ceremonies derived for the ark of the Covenant had been modelled upon those of the Aper festival.[8]

To the above, the following perspectives may also be added:

The first is that some *liberal* scholars (term used by the fundamental theologians to refer to their more academically *objective* counterpart) are of the opinion that the theological concept associated with the ark was an invention of the "Elohist." (The *original* writers or the source of the material of the Bible have God being referred to as *Elohim*. This is considered to be the more orthodox school of the ancient Hebrew ritualists.) These scholars believe that the Elohist came into being sometime in the mid-9th century B.C.E. and that the ark was used principally as the divination box of the priestly caste, *i.e.*, the Levites. It is their opinion also that, when this older Elohist's view "fell into disrepute under the rise of the [newer] Hebrew legalism [referred to as 'Yahwist' in whose writings God was referred to as *Yahweh, the personal name of God*], the ark was associated with the Covenant and the *Decalogue* in a very close way" (*cf. Encyclopedia Britannica*, under "*ark* ").

The above perspective would at least explain the reason why there are conflicting descriptions of the ark. That is, there was the ark (made by Bezaleel, a Calebite, of a priestly caste) to keep the *second* set of the stone tablets with the additional weight of two solid-golden cherubims with their wings outstretched, mounted on a thick solid lid of gold and, together, were called the Mercy Seat (*cf.* Exodus 25 and 37). This newly designed ark with more sophisticated features would require four men to carry, as opposed to the (earlier?) ark without the cherubim statues and, hence lighter. This ark (which Moses himself had made for the *first* set of stone tablets), the one which appeared to have no lid (*cf.* Deuteronomy 10:1-5), would only require two men to shoulder (*cf.* II Samuel 15:29). From this and other references mentioned earlier, ark was neither a unique religious vessel, nor was it a particularly Israelite ritual item. Instead, there is every reason to believe that ark was a rather common item in the Near East, including Egypt, for both religious purposes and ordinary, every-day life usage. (Perhaps for this reason, too, the word "ark" for the *ark of the Covenant* is never capitalized in all the English Bible. Simillarly, an ordinary word for "chest" is used to refer to the *ark* of the Covenant in all the Bibles in the Asian language: *e.g., xiang* in the Chinese bible, and *hako* in the Japanese bible.)

The second is that, while '*aron* connoted a receptacle for ritualistically or religiously important articles (be it the remains of a revered ancestor such as Joseph, or the stone tablets bearing the written words of God), *tebah*, though used as a common word for an ordinary chest, large or small, was *also intimately associated with the more ancient* (than Israelite's adaptation) *ritual use* of a receptacle, as a vehicle for transporting sacred articles (such as the soul of a dead Pharaoh to the realm of gods). This connotation apparently had come to possess a particular signification in the post-exile period. It is for this reason that the ark was called or translated to mean a *vessel with which to transport sacred articles*, and a vehicle in transmitting messages between terrestrial man and celestial God.

Therefore, the use of the English word *ark* for the ark of the Covenant in the *King James* bible and in all subsequent English bible editions "corrected" by the more recent biblical and archaeological scholars is justified in referring not only to the function of a receptacle but also, and perhaps more importantly, to the *symbolical* ship-shape vessel for transporting the sacred relics. This indeed has been observed to be true in all the traditions of worship and celebration of *aper, tebah, tabot,* or *tabotat* associated with the ark of the Covenant.

And, as it shall be shown, this is also true with the *shinto* festivals and rituals, particularly with regard to *MiFune-Shiro.* This *MiFune-Shiro* is essentially a rectangular wooden chest, a receptacle, which has been kept for countless generations by the Japanese imperial household, as long as two millennia, reposited deep inside the *Nai-gu*—the inner *sanctum,* or the Holy of Holies—of the most revered Grand *Ise* Shrine (*Ise Dai-Jingu*) of Japan (*cf. Fig. 6-8*).

It is here also that students of ancient Japanese history and of *shinto* heritage would find the etymology of *MiFune-Shiro* puzzling and mystifying. For the word *Mi* is a prefix signifying thing of divine or imperial nature, while *Fune* means "a boat," and *Shiro* refers to "an article that it is not the genuine but a mere representation," or a *replica* of the original. Hence, together, the literal meaning of the Japanese name for this sacred imperial regalia is:

"The *Replica* of the *Sacred Boat* (*i.e., the Ark*)"
[*Shiro*]   [*Mi-*] [*Fune*]

CHAPTER EIGHT

MiFune-Shiro and The Grand *Ise* Shrine, the Rituals of *Shingu Shiki-nen Sen-Gu*, and the *Sanpo*—The *Three Treasures*

Ise Shrine is more often referred to as the *Grand Ise* Shrine (*Ise Dai-Jingu*), not only because of its size but, more importantly, because of its hierarchical status in Japan's *Shinto* heritage. It is without doubt the most revered of all *Shinto* shrines in Japan, for the shrine is dedicated exclusively to the worship of *Amaterasu O-Mikami*, the "Great Goddess of Heavenly Illumination." Until the end of World War II, this deity was believed (under national edict) by all Japanese to be the ancestor of the *bansei-ikkei* (one continuous lineage of ten-thousand generations), signifying the *unbroken* imperial bloodline from the sun-goddess *Amaterasu* of the antiquity legend to the present.

The Shrine is built on a secluded gentle hilly ground, nestled amidst tall ancient trees, in the city of Ise on the southwestern shore (near the mouth) of Ise Peninsula. It is some seventy miles southeast of the modern metropolis of Kyoto. Kyoto boasts its rich historical heritage and priceless cultural treasures dating back to the fifth century, with hundreds of historical architectures, from *shinto* shrines to Buddhist temples numbering in the hundreds. As the second oldest capital of Japan (the oldest being Nara), Kyoto also is the site of count-less national historical treasures, the magnificent palaces and opulent pavilions from the early feudal eras. Strangely, the Grand *Ise* Shrine is a good distance and apart from all the ancient cities of Japan's greatest cultural and religious heritage.

Ise Shrine is not a single architectural entity; it consists of two *main* build-ings, and the *Naigu* (inner shrine)—the shrine *proper*—is off limits to all tour-ists, foreign or domestic. Visit to the inner Shrine itself is strictly limited and, unless for a very special reason, is opened only to the immediate members of the imperial household and a few very high-ranking government officials. Still, the Grand *Ise* Shrine remains the most sacred of all *Shinto* shrines and commands the most awe-inspiring reverence of the Japanese people. Thousands of visitors come expectantly, but from a respectable distance all walk in hushed reverence on this sacred ground. Western visitors may observe in amazement how many elder—and even younger—Japanese visitors fall on their knees in a worshipful prostration toward the direction of the *Naigu*.

The *history* of the Grand *Ise* Shrine is said to be about two thousand years. Curiously, however, the shrine building in all its appearance seems fresh and rather recent. This impression is not inaccurate. For the Shrine is *completely rebuilt* every twenty years (with enormous expense, approximately one quarter to one-third of a billion US dollars), and this task of rebuilding the entire shrine structure to be identical in very detail to the earlier—indeed the original—one has been repeated sixty-one times (the most recent undertaking in 1990), beginning in 690 C.E., by the edict of Emperor Temmu who reigned over thirteen centuries ago.

This event is called *sengu*, which literally means "moving of a shrine." (*Sen* means to move; *gu*—pronounced with an elongated U, as in the English word "do" or "two"—can mean a shrine, a temple, a palace, or a residential dwelling of members of the royal family.) As is the Shrine itself, the occasion of *Sengu* is witnessed only by the imperial household and invited guests (mostly high ranking officers in the government). During its thirteen-hundred year history, this enormously expensive tradition of great ritual importance was interrupted only a few times, during the warring periods (*e.g.*, the feudal era of Japan). While the "official" historians summarily attribute this unique ritual to the "need for rejuvenation of the spirit," no other *shinto* shrines—including the ones which also are dedicated to other "equally great" *shinto* deities, such as the parent *kami*, sibling *kami*, the children *kami*, or grandchildren *kami* of *Amaterasu*—observe this most curious (and, to many modern Japanese, unnecessary and wholly wasteful) rite of *sengu*.

The entire *Ise* Shrine as well as all other *shinto* shrines are built with *hinoki* wood. *Hinoki* wood is a unique Japanese timber of cypress species, and hence called by a distinctive name of *Japanese cypress*. However, it is worth noting that this *hinoki* wood is a type of *sugi* or cypress which, in turn, is called by Japanese botanists as *ito-sugi*, as opposed to *hinoki*. This name, therefore, is meant to be a distinct name for a particular cypress wood found only in Japan (and Taiwan). However, *sugi* is also the name of the same or similar cedar which is differentiated by another name (called by the Japanese as) *seiyo-sugi* (*i.e.*, "western" *sugi*, in other words, 'western cedar' or 'western cypress'). Therefore, *hinoki* is to be understood as a particular *Japanese* cedar/cypress wood. And it has been estimated that about 13,000 pieces of cypress/cedar (*hinoki*) lumber, ranging in size and shape from round lumber more than two feet in diameter and over twenty feet in length to rectangular pieces of several inches in thickness and several feet in length, are required to complete the shrine reconstruction project every twenty years.

Each of the two buildings of *Ise* Shrine is in a separate compound within walking distance from each other: one is called *Gaigu* (or *Gaiku*, the *Outer* Shrine), and the other, *Naigu* (or *Naiku*, the *Inner* Shrine). The proper name for the outer shrine is *Toyo-uke Daijingu* (its literal meaning is "the great shrine of bestowal of rich blessing," where 'rich blessing' is in reference to "rich harvest" of rice), and it is at this shrine that the annual rite of "the blessing of rice" is observed, with the *ritual gesture of scattering the rice over the people*. The Inner Shrine, on the other hand, has the near-exact function as the "holy of holies" of the Jewish synagogue, or the Tabernacle and Temple of ancient Israel. Specifically, as the ark of the Covenant was reposed in the holy of holies of the Tabernacle, so the *MiFune-Shiro*—a.k.a. the *Replica* of the *Divine Boat*—the *Ark*—is reposed in the *Naiku* of *Ise* Shrine.

The *shinto* ritual of the blessing of rice and the rebuilding of the entire sacred shrine with the cedar/cypress wood (*hinoki*) may remind us of certain aspects associated with the Israelites' wilderness wandering. One is the Feast of *Manna* which subsequently has become one of the most important religious festivals in Judaism. In fact this *Feast of Manna* (also called the *Feast of Weeks*) is one of the three most important festivals in the Judaic calendar and in the life of the Judaic faithful. The other two are the *Feast of the Passover* (in March to early April, during the *civic* new year season of the Jewish calendar, in contrast to the *ritual* new year which falls in late September), and the *Feast of the Tabernacle* (*cf.* Deuteronomy 16:1-15). One aspect which also bears a peculiar parallel between the *shinto* and Judaic ritual—in this case the building material for sacred buildings—is the exclusive use of *hinoki* in building all the *shinto* shrines (see above), on the one hand and, on the other, the extensive and nearly exclusive use of *cedar* and *cypress* wood in building the Tabernacle and the Temple, as commanded by God (*cf.* I Kings 5:6, 8-10, 15; 6:15-16, 18, 20; 6:36, etc.).

This ritual of rebuilding the entire two-building *Ise* Shrine every twenty years has no plausible explanation except the one offered by *shinto* officials, to the effect that it is for "rejuvenation" of the spirit of the Shrine as well as to maintain the shrine's structural integrity. Considering the material integrity of *hinoki*, however, the second reason would seem rather groundless. There are Buddhist temples and *shinto* shrines in Japan that also were built with *hinoki* over a thousand years ago, and yet they still stand, in remarkably excellent condition.

Perhaps there might be other, deeper historical and ritual signification behind this curious ritual custom of completely *dismantling* the old shrine and *rebuilding* anew the entire structure, and *removing* its sacred contents to the new shrine only a short distance away *every twenty years*. We may cite, for example, that Israel's ark of the Covenant was moved a number of times after it had fallen into Philistine hands, each time several years and as much as *twenty years*. Two references to this may be cited below: one is in I Samuel 7:2:

"… From the day that the ark was lodged at Kiriathjearim, a long time passed; some *twenty years* …"

and the other in I King 9:10,

"At the end of *twenty years*, in which Solomon had built the two houses, the house of the Lord and the King's house, …"

The recurring interval of years in which the ark was being moved from one location to another seems to have been some "twenty years." One may wonder if the moving of the sacred chest—the ark of the Covenant—from one location to another every twenty years was preserved in the oral tradition but its signification, after many centuries, had become obscure and then completely forgotten, but the ritualistic reenactment still remained.

Another unique aspect of *Ise* Shrine is its austere exterior appearance and the near-total absence of contents. A person fortunate enough to obtain official permission to visit *Ise* Shrine may be disappointed by the fact that this most sacred of all *shinto* shrines is a bare-wood structure, unpainted, with a primitive-looking thatched roof, and there are no visible objects of worship inside the sacred hall. There are no statues or images of gods, not even that of *Amaterasu O-Mikami*, the most revered of all deities in *Shinto* religion and to whom this *Ise* Shrine is exclusively dedicated.

However, this is precisely the most important distinction between a shrine and a temple. Shrine is a place for meditation on and reverence of *spirit* and, since spirit is invisible, there will be no icon of any sort to represent the spirit. In contrast, temple is the place for worshipping gods and deities who can be—and are always—represented as religious icons, such as statues or painted images.

Occasionally one may discover that a mirror is placed in a *shinto* shrine. This is often explained as relating to the mythological tale of *Amaterasu O-Mikami* conferring a mirror on her grandson when he was commanded to descend to the earth. The legend has it that the mirror was intended as a representation of *Amaterasu* herself, so that her grandson would contemplate on the reflection of her countenance in the mirror even when he was far away. Thus, it has been suggested that the mirror occasionally seen being prominently displayed in a *shinto* shrine symbolizes the presence of *Amaterasu*.

This, however convincing it may appear, is an inaccurate and even *erroneous* interpretation. The display of a mirror in some *shinto* shrines was the result of the influence of Buddhism after its introduction into Japan in about the late fifth century, when the new religion of Buddhism had counted among its converts a number of prominent members of the imperial household, the most famous of whom was Shitoku *Taishi* (Prince). Indeed, a mirror is often displayed in Buddhist temples; for instance, one may notice that *Kan-non*, or *Kwang-Yin Pu-Sa*, the goddess of mercy, is often depicted in Buddhist art and sculpture with a mirror. The fact that a mirror was never conceived as a sacred article in a *shinto* shrine can be atttested by the fact that a mirror is absent from all the *orthodox shinto* shrines, including the Grand Ise Shrine and the Great Izumo Shrine.

In this regard, it may be suggested that the word *temple* in Solomon's Temple may be inappropriate, since there was no image in that Temple that was intended as a visual representation of God. Unless (and perhaps it may be argued that) the ark of the Covenant and especially the Mercy Seat were regarded as the visual representation of the invisible God Yahweh. If this is so, then one may fear that the first and the most important of the Ten Commandments was defiled. For it is unequivocally stated that the people

"… Shall have no other gods before me"
and that they
"… shall not make yourself a graven image,
or any likeness of anything that is in heaven above,
or that is in the earth beneath, or that is in the water under the earth;
you shall not bow down to them or serve them;
for I the Lord your God am a jealous God …
(Exodus 20: 2-5)

The roof of *Ise* Shrine is also unique in its austere beauty: it is a thatched roof perhaps two to three feet thick and slightly tapered as the roof line ascends, without any curvature vertically or horizontally. The gables at both ends of the main roof (horizontal) beams are "tied" with two long and crossed *finials*, forming with the slant of the sides of the thatched roof line a large and nearly right-angled geometric figure of an "X." One should also notice that the finials are without any of the usual "Oriental" foliated ornaments, of the kind always found in temples. Moreover, the crossed roof timbers—the finials—are unproportionally long, straight posts with the simplest of 'ornamental' designs (carved holes with metal caps), protruding for at least six or eight feet or longer beyond the roof line (cf. Photo in **Figure 6**, courtesy of Japan Information Center).

Some scholars suggested that this unique roof style suggests the origin of (some stock of) early Japanese from the southeastern Pacific islands. One must mention, however, that, while thatched roofs with cross beams are a common feature in Southeast Asia and South-Sea island regions, it is also common in South-America and in Europe. There, however, the gable ends are always neatly sawn off, leaving no long protruding finials unsightly and unnecessarily extending beyond the main roof line. While long finials are seldom found in these above-mentioned regions, we may mention that they are more a distinctive feature of the dwellings of nomadic people, in the tents from the high plateaus of the far northeastern Eurasian continent (including Mongolia and Manchuria) to the steppes of Central Asia, in the grasslands of northern Africa to the deserts of the Near East. In other words, the *long finials are a distinctive architectural feature of tent dwellers and tabernacle-making people*. In fact, the architectures of the Inner Ise Shrine are not entirely all-too-different from the sizes and shapes of the structural feature for building the Tabernacle, essentially a tent, as suggested in the Lord's command for erecting the dwelling place for the Lord Himself and the ark (cf. Exodus 26-27).

With regard to a near total absence of any visible image of a deity in Ise Shrine, it is necessary that we make a brief inquiry into the *essence of shintoism*. First, it is of paramount importance to understand that *shinto* (or *shindo*) is not a religion, in the same sense that Buddhism or Catholicism is a religion. In fact the word *shinto* did not exist in the Japanese vocabulary—let alone being the distinct name of their national religion—until after the sixth century and more probably much later. The word *shinto* is a 'Chinese' reading (i.e., the *Chinese* monosyllabic word-reading) of the two Chinese characters—called ideograms—that the early Buddhist (Korean and Chinese) monks to Japan had used to represent the Japanese (spoken) words 'kami no michi.' Kami no michi literally means "the *way* of *gods*." However, this literal reading of kami-no-michi as "the ways of gods" is not altogether appropriate. In fact it may lead to misunderstanding of the true original intent of the expression. It is therefore necessary to clarify one of the most critically important points of conceptual significance of the Japanese *spoken* word '*kami*.'

Kami in spoken Japanese has multiple meanings, but in ancient times none of the meanings was used in referring to god or deity. In ancient writings (such as *Kojiki* and *Nihon Shoki*), *kami* was used consistently in reference to humans (of heroic character) and demigods (the personages in mythological tales), any person or persons who were worthy of respect. The use of this same spoken word *kami* to refer to gods was a result of the influence of Buddhism which arrived in Japan during the fifth and sixth centuries and, with it the introduction of Chinese literacy. Until then, Japan possessed no system of written language of its own, and the concept of deities such as of Buddhism or Christianity was alien to the ancient Japanese concept of spiritual beings.

It is necessary to mention briefly, here, that a uniquely Japanese system of alphabet—called *kana*—was not formulated until after the ninth century. (This aspect of Japanese language shall be pursued further later.) The "first connotation" (as in the dictionary definition of words) of the *spoken* word *kami* is "*high*" or "*above*"; it is an adjective used to refer to someone of *higher* position, a person in a more *senior* position in the family hierarchy. The word *kami* is even used to refer to someone else's wife (*e.g.* "*O-kami-san*" similar to "Mrs.) in showing a sense of respect, or to persons of position or authority, in office or in a societal caste system, and the same word is used to refer to a geographical location farther "up north." It was much later that the spoken word *kami* was also used to refer to deity.

In the most fundamental sense, *Shinto*-ism should be more correctly regarded as a belief in "reverence of the *ways of ancestors*" [and their *spirits* which reside in every signature of the great nature, in trees, brooks or waterfalls, mountain peaks, in cloud formations, in the fading light of the setting sun, or the first ray of the rising sun, *etc.*]. Hence, while we do observe the unique collective demeanor of Japanese people, we often fail to understand that, behind that graceful demeanor, there lies a national psyche that has been nurtured through countless generations in the course of history. It is nearly impossible to define or describe the collective psyche of the Japanese. For this study, may I offer the following: It is a belief that, in the transiency of life, *all manifestations of life and in nature*, however brief and fleeting—even as a cherry blossom petal making its brief and final journey from its mother branch to the soil below—and, indeed, *all things visible and invisible, are worthy of reflection, meditation and reverence*.

Shintoism may therefore be defined—and has often been categorized by Western writers and even specialist-scholars—as a *polytheism* or *animism*. But, like all things Asian and most especially with Japanese, their attitude, belief, and especially their *shinto* belief, defile any attempts of categorical labelling, especially when the labelling is more Western (*i.e.*, European) in concept than Eastern (*i.e.*, Indian, Chinese, Korean and Japanese). Instead of a categorization to conveniently refer to one thing with a name for another of similar or dissimilar nature, *shintoism* should be understood as an *attitude* born from the depth of Japan's collective posture, fathomed by its history and natural environments, an *attitude that regards life and nature—which are all inseparable, and thus regards and reveres all things visible and invisible, temporal and permanent, as sacred—kami*. And this attitude of virtuous reverence for all things is also the ways—the *michi*—of their ancestors—*kami*.

(It may be worthy also to point out that there are no plural forms in Japanese words. If the multiple-ness is to be emphasized, the same word is repeated twice, such as in *kami-gami* for "hosts of god" or *hito-bito* for "crowd of people." In repeating a word, the initial consonant of the second word is altered, referred to as *nigori*. This manner of repeating a word for emphasis or to mean the multiplicity or relative degree of comparison is also a unique aspect in Middle-Eastern languages. This word repetition is not only to express multiplicity but also for comparison. In the Semitic language, for example, there are no equivalents to "good, better, best" but, instead, the word "good" may be repeated to indicate its degree of superlativeness. One of the most notable examples of this, and familiar to many Christians, is the phrase "*holy, holy, holy*" to mean "the holiest" (*cf.* Isaiah 6:3), and "*amen-amen*" which is translated into English as "verily, verily"—to mean "most truly so.")

Shintoism, therefore, is an attitude or belief in revering the ancestral spirits and the lands they have inherited from their ancestors who also are their *kami*. Therefore, all that is within this land is worthy of remembrance and memorializing, especially the virtuous ways of the *kami*. It is therefore life's duty of all Japanese to care for the beauty of their lands where all the *kami* always reside. For all things reverence-worthy are *kami*. Hence, for countless generations and on every occasion when spiritual blessing was sought, ancient Japanese would invoke the phrase "*ya-yorozu no kami*" and wrote it on banners when going into battle. "*Ya-yorozu*" means eighty thousand. This offering of supplication to eighty-thousand *kami* may be seen as the most enigmatic expression of the Japanese collective attitude in regarding all venerable things both visible and invisible as *kami*.

In comparison to Buddhist temples, *shinto* shrines would inevitably instill in the mind of the worshippers a feeling of utter tranquility and celestial beauty, with their sheer austere solemnity. Nothing artificial or superficial, *shinto* shrines are all built with natural, unpainted *hinoki* (cypress wood). (This is in dramatic contrast to Buddhist temples everywhere—in China, Korea, Japan, and elsewhere—with all the walls, ceilings, posts and statues of Buddhas and Bodhisattvas in polychromia paint.) Therefore, while *Ise* Shrine is dedicated to the worship of *Amaterasu Omi-Kami* (who, in its Chinese ideographic connotation, means the Great God[dess] of Heavenly Illumination), there can be found not a single item in the entire shrine compound which can be regarded as a visible representation of this greatest *kami* in the entire *shinto* pantheon. Except one: the *Mitama-jiro* (literally the *representation of a divine spirit*), also known as *Kan-zane* (the *divine seeds*; see below).

It is generally acknowledged that there *are* sacred items reposited in *Ise* Shrine. In more recent publications on Ise Shrine are the photos of many ritual items used for ceremonial occasions. But, even with scouring through many bookstores in Tokyo, Kyoto and Nagoya, I have been utterly disappointed in not being able to find a single photo of *MiFune Shiro*. Clearly, this most revered of all *shinto* regalia will forever remain shrouded in mystery.

Still, it is an indisputable *fact* that there *is* a wooden chest stored deep inside the *Naigu* Shrine, behind the curtains and beyond the range of human stares.

This is verified in the official *record of inventory* of the Imperial household and of the *Ise* Shrine. This most sacred article of *shintoism*, essentially a dark-colored wooden receptacle *some* five feet in length by *about* two to three feet in both height and width (the size is an approximation, gauged from visual impression rather than actual measuring of the chest), is called *MiFune-Shiro* (or *Mi-Funa-Shiro*). And inside this *MiFune-Shiro* is placed *Mitama-jiro*, that is, *Kan-zane*.

"*Mi*" is the word of reverence. This Chinese ideogram is more often than not pronounced in Japanese as a short syllable of "*go*" or "*o*." However, it is pronounced "*mi*" (a more archaic pronunciation) when it is in reference to an imperial personage, or the articles belonging to the imperial family or its mythological lineage. "*Fune*" is a noun meaning a boat, large or small, while "*shiro*" refers to a thing that is a *replica* rather than the original article. Together, *MiFune-Shiro* literally means "*the Representation of the Divine Boat*." In other words, it is the *Replica of the Divine Ark*.

This same sacred regalia is also called *MiTama-Jiro* which literally means the *Representation* (*shiro* or, here, *jiro*) of a *Divine Spirit* (*Mi-Tamashii*). A greater interest is to be read into the other name for the same article: *Kan-Zane*. This name literally means the "*Divine Seeds*." This begs the question "the divine *seeds of what* or *whom*?" Does it mean the seeds of a plant (as *manna* is secretion from plant, described as like coliander *seeds*), or of a man?

One of the very few Westerners ever to have been given the privilege of viewing the sacred chest was Sir Ernest Mason Satow, *Esq*. The granting of this most unusual privilege, especially to a foreigner, must be appreciated in the context of the political climate in the last decades of the nineteenth century, during the period of Japan's transformation from the nearly millennia-old feudal society to a modern industrial nation under imperial reign. Satow first arrived in Japan in 1862, on the eve of the Meiji *Restoration* (*i.e.* of imperial power) as an *attache* of the British Consulate, spending over 21 years in diplomatic service in Japan and, from 1895 to 1900, was appointed the official British Envoy to Japan. (His Japanese wife, never officially married due to diplomatic regulations, bore him two sons.) Satow's many written works, including letters and journals, remain an important diplomatic reference even to this day.

This was the period of Emperor Meiji's ascendancy to the throne, and his vision of transforming Japan into a member of the (Western diplomatic) *League of Nations* was realized with the foresighted advice and decisive assistance of the new prime minister Hirobumi Ito, a Cambridge University educated intellectual and visionary politician. In particular, it was Ito who had advised Emperor Meiji to forge a close political alliance and military cooperation between Japan and England, and it was during these earlier formative years in Japan's new political period that Sir Satow visited Japan.

In 1872 Sir Satow was granted the unparalleled privilege to visit the Grand *Ise* Shrine. Two years later (on February 18, 1874), he presented a paper at the *Second Annual Meeting* of the *Asiatic Society of Japan* (held in Yokohama), in which he presented his own eye-witness accounts of the sacred regalia. Without the slightest of doubt, this is one of the most important sources and scarcest of information on *Ise* Shrine and on the divine regalia in particular:

"Each *mirror* is contained in a box of *hinoki*, furnished with eight handles, four on the box itself and four on the lid. The box rests on a low stand and is covered with a piece of cloth said to be white silk. *The mirror itself is wrapped in a brocade bag, which is never opened or renewed, but when it begins to fall to pieces from age, another bag is put on, so that the actual covering consists of numerous layers.* Over the whole is placed a sort of cage of unpainted wood with ornaments said to be of pure gold, and over this again is thrown a sort of curtain of course silk, descending to the floor on all sides. The *tamajiro* of the *aidono* are contained in similar boxes, without the outer cage, and of smaller size. The boxes, or rather their coverings, are all that can be seen when the shrines are opened at the various festivals."[9]

It should be noted also that even Sir Satow was not privileged to examine the sacred contents inside the wrappings. And we read in the same *Proceedings* that, following Sir Satow's presentation, the president of the Society expressed that "he had earnestly endeavored to find out *what there was in it*, but had long given it up, unable to find anything to reward his labor." In other words, *no one was ever permitted to untie and open the wrappings to ascertain the true identity of the alleged mirror.*

This most sacred wooden chest has been "lying in state" in the holy of holies of *Ise* Shrine for about two millennia, and is moved outside from one *Ise* Shrine into another, identically built Ise Shrine (therefore the shrine itself is a *replica* of the original earlier structure) only once every twenty years (or for certain special ritual occasions or historical events). During the procession of *sengu* (moving of sacred shrine) from the old to the newly constructed building in the adjacent lot, however, the chest is always covered with a heavy dark-colored drape, thus the sacred relic remains invisible to all those who line the short procession passage, standing in reverence, in darkness (for the event is conducted only in the night), and in total silence. It is a most solemn and mysterious procession, the likes of which is, arguably, not seen anywhere in the world.

This sacred *MiFune-Shiro* contains certain items of virtually equal importance with the chest, and the *Inventory Manual of Ise Shrine* lists these sacred articles as follows:

(1) *maga-tama* (crescent-shaped semi-precious stones and jedites);
(2) *tsurugi* (sword, with six branches); and
(3) *kangami* (mirror).

Together, these three are always referred to as a "set" called the *Sanpo* or *sanho*, or *Sanju no takara (i.e.,* the three treasures), and never as individual items separate from the others.

The *sanpo* is mentioned in many passages in the two ancient chronicles, *Kojiki* and *Nihon Shoki* (the latter also called *Nihon Gi*), always referred to as the imperial regalia, intimately associated with the symbolic representation and transfer of the imperial lineage from one reign to the next: *Kojiki* (translated herein as *Record of Ancient Affairs*, has been given various English titles such as *Record of Ancient Matters, Records of Antiquity* or even—but less correctly—as *Record of Ancient Things*), and *Nihon Shoki* or *Nihon-Gi* (rather uniformly as *Chronicle of Japan*). The writing of both of these was in the first quarter of the eighth century, and became the first "official" document on the history of Japan.

These two works were written entirely with Chinese ideograms. In the use of Chinese ideograms, however, there was one major difference between *Kojiki* and *Nihon Shoki*. In *Kojiki*, Chinese ideograms were used as if they were *phonetic symbols* (each of the written characters has but one syllabic sound but devoid of any connoted meaning), while in *Nihon Shoki* the same Chinese ideograms were used but with proper word meaning, instead of mere alphabet letters. It is in *Kojiki*'s most inappropriate and wholly erroneous use of Chinese ideograms that a considerable problem was created for later reading in deciphering and ascertaining the exact meaning of the significance of the names and events in Japan's historical past. Still, the particular difficulty in deciphering the meaning of the names of the personages and the geographical locations caused by improper use of Chinese ideograms in *Kojiki* was mostly left uncorrected in *Nihon Shoki*, for the exact meaning and original location associated with the names had been lost during the long course of oral transmission.

Much of the narratives about the personages and geographical locations in the earliest eras are mythological, with tales of gods and demigods gallivanting and carousing, fighting, murdering and vying for power, in a most 'human-like'—at times, most vulgar and even repulsive—manner, reminding one of some of the demigods' behavior in Greek mythology. In fact some of the Japanese mythological tales read like a direct quote or adaptation from Greek mythology (*e.g.*, the tales of Orpheus in Hades). And even concerning the events from the near-historical periods (*e.g.*, after the sixth century), the chronological sequence and dates are not always correct or reasonably reliable. Still, these two documents are the only "primary" written source material on the affairs—mainly surrounding the life of royal family members—from Japan's ancient bygone eras, and modern scholars still find them an inspiring—if often frustrating—source for discovering new information on and providing new perspectives into Japan's remote past.

At the same time, modern scholarship has made some measurable progresss in deciphering these ancient scripts. It has recognized, for example, the fact that, behind these seemingly outlandish tales of mythological personages, there are some fairly reliable historical bases, that they were events dressed in allegories, where people or tribes were often represented as named individuals, and drawn-out changes were nearly always figuratively retold as if they were single occurrences. (This approach in deciphering ancient writings is also used universally, for textual criticism and interpretive reading of ancient epic tales, including the books in the Old Testament.) Therefore, from the perspective of historical research into Japan's ancient events, *Kojiki* and *Nihon Shoki* will continue to serve as the principal and primary source document. It is, however, beyond the scope of this study to deal with this aspect more fully. Instead, we shall examine some unique and problematic aspects relative to Japanese *written* language, as well as problems that exist between the written and the *spoken* languages of Japan.

The unique difficulty in reading ancient Japanese history is due chiefly to a single cause: As mentioned above, Japanese did not possess a written language of its own until after the ninth century. It was during the period of importation of Buddhism from China, through Korea, in the fifth to the sixth centuries that Chinese script—called *ideo*grams because each of these written characters connoted specific meaning or *idea*—entered Japan. In this process of literacy adaptation, Japanese people were faced with a problem that was greater than that of the difference between any two languages. Although geographically adjacent, the two peoples spoke two fundamentally different languages of *incompatible linguistic lineages*, with the difference not of a sort between dialects (such as between northern and southern Chinese dialects) or even among adjacent European languages.

In fact the Japanese (spoken) language belongs to another, entirely different linguistic lineage; linguists classified it as belonging to the *Altaic-Tutonic* language lineage. *Proto-Japanese shares a common linguistic root with Finnish, Turkish and even Magyar languages, but nothing in common with the Sinitic (Chinese) tongue.* It is curious to realize that, even today, linguists are not altogether certain of the origin of the Japanese (and Korean) language, except to say that Japanese language is not related to Sinitic (Chinese) linguistic lineage (to which all other Far-Eastern Asian and South-Eastern Asian languages belong). In this regard, both Japanese and Indian languages are *non-Sinitic*.

One of the earliest scholars to make a philological comparison between Japanese and Chinese—and other languages that were thought to be the sources of what had become the modern-day Japanese language—was J. F. Edkins who was a missionary working in Beijing, China. In his paper presented at the first meeting of the Asiatic Society of Japan, Edkins declared that

"The Japanese then is not in immediate sisterly relation to the Chinese because it is *polysyllabic* and *places the verb at the end of the sentence*; nor is it Polynesian or Malaya because its adjectives do not follow their substantives; nor does it place the genitive after the nominative.... The *verb* [in Japanese language] *is rigidly attached to the end of the sentence* and marks the conclusion instead of the recommencement of action." [10]

On the other hand, the Chinese language, both spoken and written, is *monosyllabic* and *tonal*, and the slightest change in inflection will completely alter the meaning of that single syllabic sound. (By 'tonal' it refers to the inflectional contour in speech sounds, distinguishable as *rise, fall, down-and-up, etc.*, for example, that are inseparable from a single syllabic sound. This may be likened to the difference in expressing a questioning "Oh?"—with an upward inflection—as compared to an exclamatory "Oh!"—with downward and dynamically accented inflection.)

In direct contrast to the *monosyllabic* and *tonal* features of the Chinese spoken language, the basic linguistic features of spoken Japanese are *polysyllabic* and *non-tonal*. Hence, when Chinese ideograms were used in Japanese written documents, problems resulted: when several Chinese ideograms were used by Japanese as phonetic symbols in representing the sound of a polysyllabic Japanese word—much in the way of romanizing Japanese spoken language with Latin alphabet letters—an inevitable misinterpretation or misconception of meaning resulted. A famous example is the word "*hi-takami no kuni*": The written Chinese ideograms connote the "country of high-view of sun" (which was understood to mean a country on a "heavenly plain" and thus a celestial realm, *i.e.*, heaven), when the actual or more probable meaning which the spoken Japanese word "*kita-kami no kuni*" was intended to convey was simply a "country (*kuni*) in the *northern* (*kita*) *upper* (*kami*) *direction*." (Note: *kami* here means "upper" northern direction, and not as "deity.")

It was not until the late ninth century or early tenth century that Japanese finally created their own system of script for more accurately writing down their polysyllabic spoken language. This was the system of *kana*, literally means "*borrowed*" or "*false* name" ('name' referred to Chinese character or ideogram; 'false' implied the fact that in using the ideograms the originally connoted meaning of these ideograms was being ignored). Each of the fifty-one *kana* letters (as in alphabet letters) represented a single syllable sound (*e.g.*, pure vowel sounds, such as AH, OH or EH, or joining a consonant with a vowel, such as KAH, TOH or NEH; there were a few duplicated sounds or *kana* letters having identical syllabic sound).

Eventually, two versions of *kana* scripts were formulated: one is called *katakana* (which literally means "[from] the *partial* of false name") and the other is called *hira-gana* (which is a *script* form of the entire ideogram written out in a continually flowing or *fluid* manner). This second style was to become the favored script of poets, calligraphers, literati, artists, and especially a new caste of female writers and lady poets, since *hira-gana* also resembled the actual *calligraphic* writings of the Chinese literati. Eventually, the *hira-gana* became nearly the only version of written language during the later Kyoto period (*ca.* twelfth century) and well into the Edo era (from about the seventeenth to the mid-nineteenth century), relegating the stiff *kata-kana* script to the people of the lower caste (*e.g.,* the farmers) and the children of primary-school age.

Inherent in the laborious, tedious and not-always well systematized process of writing down the ancient oral history that produced the two official chronicles, are literacy (or textual criticism) problems which, to this day, have not been satisfactorily resolved. One is that many tales which originally were a part of the oral tradition were left out, due to "selective editorial priority" (for the self-serving purpose of the imperial house). Another is a considerable extent of misunderstanding of the original meaning associated with the names of persons or places in the oral history. This problem was in fact recognized soon after the issuance of *Kojiki* and *Ninon Shoki*, and in *Ko-go Shu-I* (*Remnant of Ancient Tales*, written in the early ninth century, several decades after the compilation of *Kojiki* and *Nihon Shoki*) we read the following in the opening paragraph:

> "[It is worth considering] the saying that
> 'In the remote ancient time when there was no writing,
> men of all castes and all ages alike had narrated and transmitted
> the sayings and deeds of [our] ancestors, and these tales were
> seldom forgotten.' Since [the oral traditions were] written down,
> people began to dislike hearing these ancient tales. [For the
> people have become more engaged in] vying for arrogance and
> vanity, increasingly despising the old people [who were the
> guardians and transmitters of these] ancient tales.'"
> (translation mine)

It was with this preface of nostalgia and indictment that the author of *Ko-go Shu-I* began narrating many intimate tales from the imperial household that were not found in *Kojiki* and *Nihon Shoki*. In short, *Ko-go Shu-I*, written under an imperial order, was intended as an *appendix* to *Kojiki* and *Ninon Shoki*. The above statement may also be taken to imply that, although often regarded as *the* historical documents, *Kojiki* and *Ninon Shoki*—the two "official" chronicles—in their written versions contain much misleading information and omission.

In more careful and critical reading of and research on *Kojiki* and *Ninon Shoki*, and with the help of more recent archaeological finds, scholars of Japan's ancient history have gained additional perspectives toward formulating a more holistic picture of Japan's ancient affairs. The matter of the *sanpo* is such a case. Apparently *sanpo* was used as the unequivocal symbol—the *regalia*—of the royal house, especially as a tangible seal of inheritance of the imperial throne long before the beginning of Japan's historical period. In *Nihon Shoki*, for example, there are references to the occasion of enthronements in 512 (of Emperor *Keidai*) and in 690 (of Empress *Jitoh*), when the subjects or members of the royal family submitted "the seal of the sword" or "the sword and the mirror" or all three—sword, mirror, and jewel. For example, earlier, it was mentioned that *Amaterasu O-Mikami* presented to *Ninigi no Mikoto*, her grandson and heir to the throne, "the jewel, the mirror, and the sword."[11] Another reference states that, in departing the celestial court, *Ninigi no Mikoto* received from *kami-gami* (gods) (but not from *Amaterasu OMikami*) the "*yasaka no magatama* (eight-foot crescent jewel; a *foot* here is approxixmately equivalent to modern 8 inches), *kangami* (mirror), and *kusanagi no tsurugi* (grass-cleaving sword)."

While there is yet no sufficient knowledge on how these three items had ever come to be regarded as the regalia (or the seal) of the imperial seat, there is nonetheless a strong likelihood that (the ritual conferring of) the *sanpo* was very much regarded as proof of the imperial lineage (at least) from the *Yayoi* period (300 to 100 B.C.), since many archaeological finds testify to the fact that the three same or similar articles were used to accompany the burial of chieftains of the *Yayoi* clan. The *Yayoi* clan had occupied a relatively large area of activities, from the plains of Edo (the present Tokyo; central eastern region of the Japanese main island of Honshu) to the northwestern region of *Izumo*, the site of *Izumo* Shrine. The shrine of Izumo is the oldest and most revered *shinto* shrine in Japan, next only to Grand *Ise* Shrine, with the architectural design—particularly the roof gable and the long finials protruding prominently over the roof line—resembling that of *Ise* Shrine. (The present building of *Izumo Shrine* was rebuilt in 1774 after a fire on its formal structure and, hence, it is believed that many of the contemporaneous Buddhist temple architectural characteristics of the sixth century were incorporated in the rebuilding of the shrine. The present *Izumo* Shrine is about 24 feet in height, as compared to the original shrine which was recorded as about 48 feet, twice the height of the present structure.) Still, it is a historically verifiable fact that *Izumo* was the earliest site of the gathering of *kami*, the chieftains of the earliest dominant clansmen who had arrived in Japan from Korea a few centuries before the Common Era. This *Izumo* Shrine was thus built as the memorial to the sacred site of the gathering of *kami*.

It was in *Izumo* and later in other geographical locations also in the area of *Yayoi* clan's activity that the tradition of *sanpo* as a symbol of imperial regalia was established. As mentioned, the *sanpo* consists of a divine mirror, a sword, and a string of jewels (semi-precious stones). And it is common knowledge that there are numerous copies (*replicas*) of the sword, the jewel string and mirror, reposed in many *Shinto* shrines throughout Japan, including the set in the shrine within the Imperial Palace in Tokyo.

There are, however, some puzzling issues in regards to the mirror. It is described (not by eye-witness account but by the description given by the priestly officials of the Shrine) that the item is fragile, that it required multiple wrappings of brocade and silk to prevent it from falling to pieces. This condition was noted in Sir Ernest Satow's presentation at the Asian Society, and is also noted as a *footnote* in Hadland Davis's book, *Japan: From the Age of the Gods to the Fall of Tsingtau*. David's statement is as follows:

"The Divine Mirror [called *kangami*] now reposes in *Ise* [Shrine]
… It is kept in a box of chamacyparis in the *Naiku* (the Inner Temple).
[It is said to be] wrapped in brocade, and when it begins to fall to
pieces it is … [further] covered with a fresh wrapping, so that the
precious relic is now protected with many layers of silk. The box
and its coverings are placed in a cage elaborately ornamented in gold,
and this again is covered with a silk cloth."[12]

The most puzzling and *illogical* point in the above statement is about the mirror being described as a "box," and that it was in danger of "fall[ing in-]to pieces" and, hence, this fragile box required layers of wrapping.

This statement is indeed strange, since ancient mirrors could never "fall into pieces." It is archaeological common knowledge that all ancient mirrors (before invention of glass capable of image reflection with a coating of mercury—or other metallic chemical—on the back side) were made of bronze (and, later, iron). Also, there are altogether too many archeological finds to refute the above statement. In fact, Davis also raised a question on this matter in *Myths and Legends of Japan* (*cf.* p. 190).

Specifically, ancient mirrors were metal plates (bronze or iron alloy) which had one smoothly polished side (smooth enough to reflect images and thus used as a mirror), with carved relief of ritual decorative figurations on the reverse side (*cf.* **Fig. 9**). This was the type of mirror prevalent throughout the ancient world, East and West, and a great quantity of these bronze mirrors has survived and been displayed in museums in China, Korea, Taiwan, Japan, as well as in Europe and the Middle East, nearly all of them in good condition. Such metal mirrors, created long before the importation of glass wares, glass mirrors, and lenses (that were imported to the East by way of "black-ships" of trading vessels from the European West in the sixteenth century), would not *break and fall into pieces*.

In my recent visit to *Atsuta* Shrine in Nagoya (Japan), I witnessed many *sacred* mirrors from Japan's historical past (as long as over a millennium ago), in sizes ranging from a few inches to nearly two feet (with handle), and with exquisite design of all sorts, all in perfect condition. And they are not concealed or protected with wrappings but, in stead, gloriously displayed for all to admire. Such mirrors, regardless of age, simply do not fall into pieces.

Could the above description, then, suggest that this *kangami* is not a mirror at all but, in fact, is something much more fragile, such as earthen ware, or wooden article? We may also notice that this same description of "falling into pieces" was never used in reference to the two other sacred relics, the sword—the *tsurugi* (also made with bronze or iron) (cf. **Fig.** 10), and the string of crescent-shaped, natural semi-precious stones—the *magatama* (cf. **Fig.** 11). We note here that stones as sacred ritual items in the Near East were nearly always of meteorites, the stones that *fell from heaven* and thus believed to possess *mystical power*.

It may be added that stones in Japanese legends were never associated with prayers. The ancient Japanese crescent-shaped *magatama* were the emblem of priests and priestesses (the *kami*), while the round-shaped prayer beads originated from the ritual items of Buddhism. Buddhism entered Japan in the sixth century, and quickly became the 'national religion' and vied with *shintoism* for imperial power and favor. It is therefore an interesting process of history that this and other *Shinto* and Buddhist practices had become commingled and indistinguishable during the ensuing periods. This coexistence and commingling of the two faiths is vividly described and eloquently portrayed in many passages in Japan's most famous historical tales, *Tales of Heike* [*The Tales of the House of Taira*] and *Tales of Genji* [*Tales of the House of Minamoto*].

What, then, is the real identity and factual description of these sacred treasure items?

The answer—or even a few possible clues to the answer—to this and other questions may be found by another careful and critical reading of the only ancient historical documents of Japan, the *Kojiki* and *Ninon Shoki*, as well as *Sendai Kyuji Honki* (or *Kuji Honki*; *The True Record of Ancient Affairs of Former Age*). This last chronicle, though not as popularly known, is actually recognized by the contemporary scholarship of ancient Japanese history as being more reliable of the three. The greater degree of credence of *Kyuji Honki* is due to an increased recognition among scholars that the two better known chronicles were commissioned by the imperial house to produce documentary proof to establish credence for claiming the imperial seat. In other words, *Kojiki* and *Ninon Shoki* were created by the imperial edict as documentation of autarchy (*i.e.*, autocracy). In contrast, *Kyuji Honki* was written as an objective narrative by one whose view of history was unbiased, uncoerced and untainted by the imperial authority. This will explain why *Kyuji Honki* was regarded as '*itan no setsu*'—a *heretical* viewpoint, particularly during the Edo period when the imperial household once again tried fiercely to reclaim its hereditary autarchical reign over the land.

Kojiki and *Nihon Shoki* are indeed the 'authorized version' of the history of ancient Japan, the *written version directly based on the oral narration* by one *Hiyeda no Are*. The name of this narrator is (now) known only as *Hiyeda*. In the most likelihood, he was a *katari-be* (*katari* means narrative or to narrate, and *be*—pronounced *beh* as in bet—refers to a person of official position), a "*reciter of orally transmitted history*" employed by the court, a man specifically recognized for his extraordinary memory and the ability to meticulously recite *verbatim* the long oral history with every detail. Such persons were an official member of the court in all ancient cultures, East and West, particularly before a literacy system was established. Japan did not have its own system of written language (the *kana* system) until about the tenth century. Therefore, in changing from pre-historic oral tradition to script-based historical chronicle, Japan had to engage Chinese ideograms to write out Japanese, beginning in the fifth century.

Herewith lies the great dilemma of *trans-literacy*. In transferring the story told in *Hiyeda*'s oral recitation into written script, the *polysyllabic* language of Japanese (which would require a system of "alphabet" in writing) was forced onto the script of a totally incompatible script system of Chinese, the *monosyllabic* ideograms (which did not require any system of alphabet). This resulted in what may be described as a case of (mis)appropriation of a wholly alien culture's written language in recording another nation's history.

The problem in misappropriating the written language of another culture was further compounded when two written records—*Kojiki* and *Nihon Shoki*—were produced. The two documents were created from one same oral narrative but used the ideograms in two different ways. When *Hiyeda* first recited the narratives, they were written down with Chinese ideograms by one *Yasumaro*, an excellent scholar of Chinese culture (and hence well versed in the system of Chinese ideogram). In *Kojiki* (written in 1712), *Yasumaro* used

Chinese ideograms as if they were alphabet letters to only represent the syllabic sounds, where the signification of the characters was not taken into consideration. But when the same narratives of Hiyeda were rewritten in 1720, with the new title *Nihon Shoki*, Yasumaro used Chinese ideograms correctly, in the learned manner of using Chinese ideograms as characters (that is, not as alphabets but individual words), each connoting specific literal meaning. The problems Yasumaro had thus created by using the Chinese ideograms in two different ways have lingered on ever since, and still cause issues for modern scholars in deciphering Japan's ancient history.

CHAPTER NINE

THE MYTHS AND LEGENDS IN JAPAN'S ANCIENT CHRONICLES

There is a fascinating creation story in *Nihon Shoki*. It tells that

> "Of old, heaven and earth were not separated.
> They formed a chaotic mass, the purer and transparent part
> of which rose up and formed heaven, while the heavier and
> opaque settled downwards and became the earth.
> The finer element easily became united, but the consolidation
> of the heavier was slow and difficult.
> Heaven was therefore formed first and the earth afterwards." [13]

The nature of this narrative may suggest the source of the original creation story to be of a far western region from Japan (the only geographical direction that any cultural influence could have come from). This is based on the fact that the essence in this narrative bears curious resemblance—even close parallel—with the creation story from the Vedic (Hindu) culture and of the Near East (*e.g.*, the Sumerian or the Egyptian mythology), from which also the creation story in the Old Testament (Genesis 1:1-10) is believed to have derived. (It may be noted also that there actually are two different creation stories in the Old Testament; the second one begins in Genesis 2:4, in which LORD God was described more like a person, who walked in the shade, and he created *adama* (*lit.* man; not a proper name) before he created other living things, even before he had caused the rain to fall and grass to grow. In fact there are two different names used in referring to God in the two creation stories: *Elohim*, translated in English as *God* in Chapter One, and *Yahweh*, translated as "LORD God" (in Chapter Two, vs. 4, *ff.*)

One needs only to remember that all the wisdom and knowledge that Moses possessed was from his Egyptian upbringing (in the Pharaoh's court and the educational curriculum there), that Moses was likely one of the very few literate persons—if not the only one—amidst the mostly illiterate Israelites. It was for this reason too that the authorship of the *Pentateuch* was often ascribed to Moses. (The more recent biblical scholarship dates the writing of the major portion of the Old Testament to the post-exilic period, after Persian king Cyrus permitted the Israelites to return to Jerusalem to rebuild the *second* temple to resume worship of God Yahweh. *Cf.* Ernest Wright, bibliography.) In any case, the two different versions of the creation story would imply that the authors of the Book of Genesis—whether by Moses as traditionally held, or by Levites and scribes of the post-exilic period—had at least two oral history sources, one from the land of Ur (of the Sumerian culture, from which Abraham had come), and the other from Egypt (the more enlightened of the two). To the Sumerian belongs Genesis' second creation story, and to the Egyptian the first creation story. It is in the Sumerian—more than the Egyptian—creation story that we find the interesting parallels and similarities in the creation story of many ancient cultures and particularly in Japan's *Nihon Shoki*.

Without a doubt the central and most prominent figure in mythological tales on the beginning of Japan and the Japanese is the sun goddess *Amaterasu O-Mikami*. *Amaterasu* was the daughter of *Izanagi* and *Izanami*, the brother-and-sister *kami* who were husband and wife. (In ancient Oriental tradition and in poetic expression even today, husband and wife are often referred to as brother and sister.) This *kami* pair is said to have "given birth" to the eight islands of the Japanese archipelago. Then Izanagi and Izanami descended to the island from *Ame no Takama ga Hara* ("high-view plain of heaven"), and gave birth to *Amaterasu*, the first of their heirs who would inherit and rule the terrestrial domain.

The Chinese ideograms for the names of these mythological personages and geographical locations would naturally give the literal meanings as connoted in the Chinese script (as shown in parentheses). However, one must remember that there was no written language in Japan prior to the writing of *Kojiki* and *Nihon Shoki*, that the Chiense ideograms were used as *ateji* (literally "ideograms to fit" the sound of spoken language). Hence it has become a nearly impossible task for the later readers of these ancient documents to ascertain if—whether, where and how—these *ateji* were used to refer to actual ideographic locations.

It is curious, for example, that the earliest *kami*—the word which, as has been explained, and as all modern scholars of Japanese history agree, simply means "honorable" or "reverence-worthy" *human beings,* rather than deities—had descended from the heavenly plains by boat. The fact that *kami* came to Japan by boat would suggest that the migration was a horizontal, seafaring journey, rather than a vertical, celestial-to-terrestrial descent. A number of Japanese scholars have already suggested convincingly that the often-used descriptive clause "*hi-takami-no-kuni*" (its ideogrammatic reading connotes "the country on elevated viewing of the sun") was actually another *bad* case of *ateji* resulting in heretofore an erroneous interpretive reading, that the "original" meaning of the name in the oral tradition was most probably "*kita-kami-no-kuni*" which simply meant "the country in the northern direction."

It is in this regard that the same critical textual scrutiny should be applied to examining the name of the great sun goddess *Amaterasu*, and the name of the mythological country of heavenly realm, the *Ame no Takama-ga-Hara*. Both Japanese and Western scholars agree that this approach to textual criticism is a critical necessity in order to make possible a more accurate inquiry into the origin of Japan's mythological tales.

Before examining a few of the most prominent names in *shinto* mythology, we may ask why and how it is important to demythologize these fantastic tales of the age of *kami*. In other words, couldn't we simply regard and let alone these mythological tales as *tales* like Greek mythology or Chinese creation tales of "*Bang Gu Kai Tian*" (*Bang Gu* Opens the Heaven)? To answer this question, I wish to cite the opinion of one of the most prominent and respected scholars of Japanese history, Prof. Robert Karl Reischauer, as a guiding principle in textual criticism. The following, rather lengthy citation is from his 1937 book *Early Japanese History*, which is still regarded as a ground-breaking work, possessing a most profound insight and objectivity, and persuasive eloquence, in discoursing the study of Japan's ancient history:

> ... The importance of these myths and legends does not depend primarily on whatever truth they may contain, but on the fact that they were believed and taught by the ruling classes, were accepted by the people as true, and thus had a profound influence on Japanese history. Hence no [study] of Japanese history would be complete without some reference to the myths and legends of "The Age of Deities and Legendary Heroes (*Kami*)."
> Some of these stories are probably attempts to record actual happenings, although in a somewhat garbled form. There is no clear distinction made between gods and men. The word *kami* (deity) simply meant anything extraordinary and hence was applied to noted human beings as well as to deities. Consequently it is

impossible to distinguish clearly between the two. In fact the same *kami* appear in some legends as ordinary humans, and in others as supernatural beings. That the Heaven-Shining-Great-August-Deity (*Amaterasu-Omikami*) was a Sun Goddess ... that Impetuous-Male Augustness (*Susano-o-no-Mikoto*) was a kind of Storm God, few will deny; but it is also quite likely that many legends grew up around the Great Sun Goddess that were stories about a real tribal chieftain or high priestess of antiquity who was the ancestor of the Japanese Sovereigns (*tenno*) and came to be identified with the Great Sun Goddess.... If one bears these possibilities in mind, these myths and legends take on added significance.

One soon notices that [the period and the area of the activity of these deities] can be localized roughly in four geographical areas:

    (1) the Plain of High Heaven (*Takama-ga-Hara*);

    (2) *Izumo-no-kuni*;

    (3) *Kyushu*; and

    (4) the central *Yamato-no-kuni* region.

This may be due to the fact that two or more cycles of legends belonging to different peoples were woven together to make the accounts found in the *Kojiki* and *Nihon Shoki*.

Each myth, therefore, must be sifted to find whatever factual element it may contain. That is difficult to do, but attempts have been made by eminent Japanese scholars to glean some knowledge of the early inhabitants of Japan, their history, and their customs from an analysis of these old myths and legends....

[The earliest of the cycle of myths such as the hiding of Amaterasu in the cave and her reemerging, and her brother's hideous acts, *etc.*] seem to be that of a mountain people and probably was developed in its final form by some tribe that lived in *Yamato-no-kuni*, because of the place names mentioned in these stories and many other reasons. It is, therefore, considered to be a more recent cycle of myths than the much more primitive stories about the creation of heaven and earth and the descendants of various *kami* from the Plain of High Heaven (*Takama-ga-Hara*), which deal with a seafaring people ... [The cycle of myths that deal with *Izumo-no-kuni*] centers around Impetuous-Male-Augustness (Susano-o-no-Mikoto) and his descendant.

... These were *kami* of waters, rains, thunder, and occult practices. *Izumo-no-kuni* appears to have been the home of a powerful caste of priests [and priestesses], which the worshippers of the Great Sun Goddess (Amaterasu-Omikami) in *Yamato-no-kuni* finally reduced to submission, but placated by making [the descendant of Susano-o-no-Mikoto] second in importance in the *Shinto* pantheon only to the Great Sun Goddess, and by leaving these priests [or priestesses] in charge of … worship …

When studying Japanese mythology one should also remember that it was written down in the Kojiki and Nihon Shoki by men who were using it to explain and to justify the dominant position in society that the Imperial Family and its allied clans had assumed. Myths that fitted in with this purpose of the two books were probably recorded without modification. However, other myths were quite possibly altered or left out altogether. In fact it is reasonable to believe that many genealogies and stories were fabricated by the central authorities in order to prove that privileged clans were entitled to their favored positions because their ancestors had held such, and to show that all the peoples' forefathers had accepted the rule of the Imperial Family. In connection with this, it is interesting to note how cleverly all the important kami in the different cycles of legends have been brought together in the genealogy of the Imperial Family.

There are many baffling problems growing out of these myths and legends that have intrigued some of the best scholars of Japan:

Was the Plain of High(-view) Heaven (Ame no Takama-ga-Hara) a real place from whence the Imperial Family and its allied clans issued forth to conquer Japan?

Why does the Imperial Family trace its ancestry back only to Amaterasu-Omikami and leave all the kami before her, including even Izanagi-no-Mikoto, out of consideration?

Does this prove that Amaterasu-Omikami, in addition to being the Great Sun Goddess, was probably a person as well as, say, a high priestess of the Great Sun Goddess, and that all the kami before her were never anything but mythical characters invented to explain the creation of heaven and earth, and the appearance of Amaterasu-Omikami herself?

Are *Amaterasu* and the *kami* Master-of-the-August-Center-of-Heaven (*Ame-no-Minakanushi-no-Kami*) the same [personage]? Do the myths concerning the creation of the earth, because they make no mention of land outside the Japanese islands, show that the people had been in Japan [for] so long they had forgotten there was any place else?

Does the fact that divisions of Shikoku and Kyushu (the two large islands south of the main island in Japan's archipelago), but not one of Honshu, prove that at first the Japanese were better acquainted with the two smaller islands than with the main island, and hence came to Japan from the southwest? What was the relationship between the people of *Izumo-no-kuni* and Korea?

Did the people of *Izumo-no-kuni* and those of *Yamato-no-kuni* belong to the same group of invaders? And,

Why did *Ninigi-no-Mikoto* descend in *Hyoga-no-kuni* while his brother, *Nigihayabi-no-Mikoto*, came down in *Yamato-no-kuni*? ...

These are but a few of the questions one should bear in mind when reading Japanese mythology.[14]

The very first problem Prof. Reischauer posed (suggesting thereby that the question is most important) in deciphering the myths and legends of ancient Japan

in *Kojiki* and *NihonShoki* is:
Whether '[*Ame no*] Takama-ga-Hara' is [the name of]
an actual historical geographic location.

We are reminded here that these names were a part of the earliest *oral*—rather than *written*—history of Japan, transmitted verbally for countless generations before they were finally put down in writing and, hence, the original meaning had most likely been lost and long forgotten. Another—and no less important—point to be considered is the fact that, in the course of committing these oral tales to writing, Chinese ideograms were used as *ateji* (*falsely appropriated* character), more to satisfy the intent of the imperial family who instigated and commissioned the writing of chronicles. Hence, as Reuschauer states, any "other mythological tales [which were regarded as not beneficial to the purpose] were either conveniently altered or simply left out altogether."

Herewith is the validity of Reischauer's questioning of the meaning in the name of the ancient Japanese country of origin: *Ame no Takama-ga-Hara*. In other words, putting aside the meaning connoted in the Chinese ideograms, is there any other meaning that might have been encrypted in the *phonematic elements* of "*AME no TAKAMA ga HARA*"?

CHAPTER TEN

AMATERASU AND *AME NO TAKAMA GA HARA*: DECIPHERING THE LOST ETYMOLOGY

The questions Prof. Reischauer raised in his book have been recognized—even by renowned Japanese scholars—to be some of the major issues in the study of Japan's ancient past. In my recent trip to Japan and in visiting many bookstores, I was amazed by the number of recent publications, all endeavoring to decipher and dispell the lingering mystery of Japan's origin. It is apparent that, even today, the questions of where did the proto-Japanese come from, who was the goddess *Amaterasu*, or where was the region of *Takama-ga-Hara*, have not been answered satisfactorily.

Indeed, among the issues which Reischauer listed is the question of whether *Takama-ga-Hara* (written in six ideograms as *Ame no Taka-ma ga Hara*, or in an abbreviated form in four ideograms as *Taka-ma ga Hara*) is the name of an actual geographical location. Curiously, Reischauer did not pose the same question about the name of *Amaterasu*, the name of the most revered Sun Goddess who is believed to be the ancestor of all the subsequent emperors of Japan.

It is somewhat puzzling also that no scholars of ancient Japanese history have posed serious question on whether *Amaterasu* is a personal name—of a historical or imaginary personage—or possibly a name that is a symbolic representation of an event or a cult. At the same time, there seems little question that *Ame no Takama-ga-Hara* is a locational name, perhaps the name of Japan's *origin of habitation*, while *Amaterasu* is a personal name intimately associated with a religious practice, perhaps of Japan's *origin of imperial* and/or *cultic lineage*. Perhaps these two names are closely related.

Fist, the name *Ame no Takama ga Hara*: The reading of the ideograms yields the meaning of "heaven" (*ame*), "high" (*taka*), "view" (*me* or *mi*), and "plain" or "field" (*hara*). Hence the name has been understood to mean a "high-viewing heavenly plain" or certain Plain (proper name) so high that it is on the celestial altitude.

84

There is another name with a similar historical connotation: *Takachiho no Sohori Yama*. This name appears in *Nihon Shoki* in referring to the high plateau from which Emperor *Jimmu* descended to arrive in the Japanese islands. The Chinese ideograms used for this name mean "*Sohori* Mountain of '*High Thousand Ear*'" (*e.g.*, ear of wheat). Apparently, this transliterated meaning of the phonetic sound of this name is all but incomprehensible. Hence it begs the question of what was *originally* implied in the name. One aspect that the Japanese historical archaeologists have become certain of is that *Sohori* is a Korean word and the name for the mountain near the present Korean capital city *Seoul*. Indeed, *sohori* in Korean language means 'the capital.' Hence this legend of gods descending from the high mountain of Sohori points to the coming through and descending from the high mountain plateau of the present capital of Korea during the course of the tribe's migratory journey.

Similarly, there are certain inherent problems associated with the pronunciation (in Japanese fashion) of the ideograms in the names of places or persons in *Kojiki* and *Nihon Shoki*. While the ideograms for heaven, high, and plain are nearly always pronounced in *old*-Japanese manner (or *OJ*, *polysyllabic*, in contrast to the *NJ* or *new*-Japanese, in the *Chinese monosyllable manner*) as *ama* or *ame*, *taka*, and *hara*, respectively, the ideogram for view (or to see) is never pronounced as *ma*. Hence it begs the question of whether *takama* was actually in reference to a place called *Takama* or another place with a similar phonemical sound. *Ama no takama ga Hara*, then, might have been intended to refer to an "extremely high plain of *Takama*" or "the plain of *Takama* that is as high as heaven."[15] If this is indeed a possible scenario, then it may require a search for a geographical name that has a similar phonemic with *Takama*, in a region far west of Japan, in Korea, China or Mongolia, or even further west, in the Middle East or beyond, that is on a high geological elevation.

Another problem is regarding the meaning associated with the name *Amaterasu O-Mikami*. In this *shinto* legend, the sun was represented by a female *kami*, a goddess, while moon is represented by a male *kami*, the brother of *Amaterasu*. This runs counter to the Oriental cultic perception of and reference to sun and moon. Sun was always associated with male gender, while moon was associated with female, and this is not only of the (Chinese) *ying-yang* doctrine of cosmic forces but also in Egypt, Sumer, and other cultures throughout much of the ancient world. Therefore, the fact that *Kojiki, Nihon Shoki* and *Kuji Honki*, as well as all the *shinto* traditions associate sun with the goddess *Amaterasu* (and moon with her next younger brother *Tsuki* which is the Japanese word for moon) would suggest that this cultic belief may not have originated in Asia. Instead, it had originated in a land further west of China, or that *Amaterasu* was not a goddess but most likely a title signifying the "lady in waiting"—*i.e.*, priestess—of a sun-worshipping cult. In considering the cult of sun worship, we find fascinating parallels and thus possible links between the cult of *Amaterasu* and the cult of *Mithras* in the ancient Persian Empire.

From about the fifth century B.C.E., Persia emerged as one of the greatest empires in the ancient Middle East, to the extent that historians would refer to Persia as one of the four major cultures in the entire human history. Specifically, not only did the Persian Empire replace the Babylonian empire but created what historians regard as

> "... one of the most enlightened governments the ancient world
> ever knew. *For the first time* [in human history] *the freedom and
> self-respect of local populations was fostered and not submerged.
> .* Captive people were *encouraged to* return to their former homes,
> if they wished to do so, and *pursue their religions life as they saw
> fit.* Permissin for Jewish exiles to return home [*or moving
> to other lands] was quite in line with official policy concerning all
> similar peoples.*"[16]

And it was within the vast Persian Empire that there flourished a cult known as *Mithraism* which was embraced by a large population living within that vast dominion. The central deity of *mythraism* was god Mithra or Mitra, the god of light and, hence, of the sun. The source of *mithraism* may be traced to the Canaanite religion (which in many ways had left imprints on the development of Judaism). In the earlier period, god Mithra was a male deity but, in due course and among popular cultic beliefs, it began to embrace female deity (either ministering priestess or shaman). There is no specific doctrinal catechism in *mithraism*, embracing only a vaguely conceived notion about the natural *spiritual* universe surrounding man, paralleling the doctrine in the dualism of *yang* and *yin*, light and dark, life and death, good and evil, *etc.* The two elements or the two forces, however, are believed to be not opposing or exclusive of each other but, rather, coexisting and complementary; one cannot exist without the other. If any label could be attached, it may be said that *mithraism* was a cult of nature worship, a reverence for all the visible and invisible spirits and forces therein.

The history of development of *mithraism* is complex and far reaching, to the extent that no religions major or minor during the pre- and early historical periods, can be said to not have been influnced by or had not made any influence on *mithraism*. Zoroastrianism, Hinduism and even Judaism are the case in point. And, as such, *mithraism* lingered long after the demise of the Persian Empire, and became also a major force in shaping religious cults of the common people during the Roman period. Suffice it to say, in brief, that *mithraism* worshipped the sun, and its faithful revered and followed god *Mithra's* earthly representative, the *priestess* or the *sun-goddess*. Here, however, it must be acknowledged that it is beyond the scope of the present study to expound on the impact and development of *mithraism*; suffice it to say only that the topic has been treated in great detail in many works, among them in particular the narratives in Jean Doresse's *Secret Books* (*cf.* Bibliography).

It is here, in enunciating the name *Mitra* or *Mithra*, that we find it difficult not to notice the phonetic similarity between *Mithras* and A-*materasu*. For this reason and in other respects also (see below), this *mithraism* may be seen as possibly the cult which had caused a rise of a cult or fathom a *sub*cult that subsequently entered Japan, reborn there as the cult of A-*Materasu*. Could it not be possible, then, that (A-)*materasu* was a slightly altered (*i.e.*, corrupted) pronunciation of the word *Mi-th(e)-ras*, that goddess A-*Materasu* was indeed the title for the chief priestess who ministered to the god of *Mithras* and, hence, yielded a considerable—but not absolute—authority over the faithful followers of this sun worshipping cult. If there is any validity to this hypothesis, then it will provide a substantially strong credence to further an anthropological and archaeological opinion that the proto-Japanese had originated from a country (or region) farther west of China, from beyond the Tibetan plateaus and Himalayan mountain ranges, quite possibly from Central Asia and the Middle Eastern region.

Specifically, the following aspects may be inquired into as potential topics for uncovering the identity and the possible origin of (one of the dominant ethnic stocks of) the proto-Japanese people:

1) who were the people who had come from an area of high geographical plateau;

2) what was the area which was known by the name of (or similar in sound to) *Takama;*

3) who were the people who followed the sun-worshipping cult; and

4) who was the female who served as the chief priestess of this cult and held a powerful sway.

In the ancient (pre-Christian era) Near- and Middle-Eastern worlds, there can be found only one location which meets all the criteria in this rather specific and narrowly defined bill, the name which lists many compound phonematic elements. It is the area called by the (ancient) name of *Tegarma* or *Togarmah*. The "country" of *Tegarma* or *Togarmah* is mentioned in biblical dictionaries as the land that existed as early as the fourteenth century B.C.E., an area that had existed even before the days of Moses. This was the area

> "lying between Carthemish and *Harran*, on a main trade route
> through southwestern *Armenia*. It was called *Tilgarimanu* in
> Assyrian times (Sargon and Sennacherib Annals) and was the
> capital of Kammanu on the border of Tabal."[17]

This location is in the area of western *Armenia* and eastern Turkey of today, an area of extremely high mountainous terrain notable by its proximity to the Mount of *Ararat*, famous as the site of the landing of Noah's ark of the biblical legend after the "universal" deluge. Into the historical periods, this entire region came within the vast Persian Empire. The Persians ruled the "entire known world" when, in the mid-sixteenth century B.C.E., King Cyrus had overrun the Babylonians (or Chaldeans who, earlier, had overrun the Assyrians who, in turn, had defeated the Israelite armies and devastated the whole of Jerusalem and the Temple).

In comparing the period of the history of the three great empires of the Middle East, the Assyrians, Babylonians (Chaldeans), and the Persians, the following scenario of migratory journey of Semitic tribe(s) carrying the stolen article(s) from the ark of the Covenant may be conjectured:

First, the ark was 'violated' some time between Joshua and Solomon, during the period of about four and a half centuries. More probably, the event occurred during the period of time when the ark was reposed in the tabernacle, essentially a tent. This "tabernacle of the Lord" was pitched by King David who assigned his soldiers to stand guard. We must also recall that David had "feared the Lord" and the ark (*cf.* II Sam.6:8-9, *ff*), and had kept it at a respectable distance. It is doubtful if David's posting guards at the tabernacle of the ark was a matter of priority to him or his soldiers. It may also be conjectured that the tabernacle was not much more than an ordinary tent, the kind the people and the soldiers would pitch out in the field (cf. II Sam. 11:11). It would not be a difficult task for anyone to attempt to invade the tabernacle to steal away the holy relics.

And there certainly was no shortage of candidates to invade the ark, to shame King David and the Israelites. There were people living in Jerusalem or even among David's armies who held deep hatred for the cruel and now arrogant king. The more notable among the people holding animosity against King

David were the Jebusites and Hittites, who had suffered gravely by the swords of David. The Hittites in particular had an ax to grind; Uriah, one of their tribal members who also was a general in David's army, had become the sacrificial lamb for David's carnal desire, and would have wanted to seek revenge on this terrible insult.

This period coincided with the height of the Assyrian Empire, known for its extreme cruelty toward the enemy. If a tribe—say, Hittites, Jebusites, or Edomites—was to escape from the oppression of the Israelis during its peak power period (*e.g.* of King David), they would certainly want to avoid the ruthless and brutal Assyrians. To do so, they would most likely choose their route northward, toward the high mountain regions near Mt. Ararat. A few centuries later, when the Assyrians were defeated and the Chaldeans came to power, these self-exiled people would likely have ventured out to the lower lands and began living in the plains area. Abandoning their nomadic life, these (self-)exiled people may even have learned farming skills, especially after the Chaldeans were quickly replaced by a much kindlier empire of King Cyrus of Persia.

The Persian Empire expanded its territory far and wide. Soon its domain stretched from Cashmir and Punjab districts (of northern India) in the east, to the Aral Sea and southern shores of the Caspian Sea and Black Sea to the north and west, including the eastern coastline of the Mediterranean Sea (including all of modern Palestine). The Persian territory even stretched to northern Africa (including Libya and Egypt) to include all the areas south of the "royal highway," the northern coastlines of the present Persian Gulf and Indian Ocean to the south. The city of *Harran* of the district of *Togarmah* in *Armenia* was about four hundred miles directly northeast of Jerusalem, within a relatively easy distance of a mere few months' journey.

One noteworthy act of the Persian lord, in dramatic contrast to the brutal acts of the Assyrians and Babylonians, was the accommodating attitude of King Cyrus toward the captured Jews. King Cyrus and the two kings after him, Darius and Artaxerxes I, had shown mercy to the Hebrites by returning to them all the precious sacred vessels (which the Babylonian king Nebuchadnezzar and his soldiers had looted) from the Temple of Solomon. The contrast in the treatment of the Israelites by Nebucadnezzar and Cyrus is vividly narrated in the closing passages of II Chronicles (*cf.* 36:17-21, *versus* 36:22-23) and continues into the Book of Ezra. The Persian king not only allowed the Israelites to return to their lands but also, in a gesture rarely witnessed in the cruel ancient world where massacre went hand in hand with military conquest, allowed the defeated people to rebuild the temple for worship of Yahweh, and granted them official protection from mistreatment in the restoration of Judaism (*e.g.*, under prophets Ezra and Nehemiah). (The kindlier deeds of the three Persian kings are duly recorded in the Book of Ezra.) Meanwhile, the Persian people and their religion are described in a bible dictionary as follows:

> "(the Persians) revered the gods of nature, fertility, and the heavens.
> The tribe of the Magi was nearly exclusively priests ...
> [and their chief deity *Ahura-mazda* was] represented by purifying
> fire and water."[18]

Although brief, this narrative is a succinct and significant reference to the general nature of the religion of the common people in the Persian Empire. Soon, however, *Ahura-Mazda* (who was also a deity in the Babylonian religion of Zoroaster) gave way to the increasingly more popular "folk cult" which worshipped the god of *Mithra* or *Mitras*. This god of Mithras was in fact derived from an earlier Aryan (*i.e.*, northern Indian) god of light, *Mit'ra* or *Mit'ras*. (It may be noted that *Mazda*, a well-known namesake of a Japanese auto maker today, is significantly one of the most common surnames of the Japanese people.) Therefore, it can be said that the main religion—actually more of a folk cult than a formalized national religion with a well-established creed—of the *common people* of Persia was *mithraism*.

In the ritual practice of *mithraism*, priestesses were the chief ministers and administered to the deity. It is worth noting that at the core of this Persian cult was an attitude of "reverence of *kami* (*gods, spirits*) *of nature*, fertility and heaven," and that the act of purification of the faithful, particularly that by water—in a form nearly indistinguishable from "baptism"—especially for the new initiates into the faith, was an all-important ritual. These two, it must be recognized, not only bear uncanny resemblance but in fact are identical to the belief and attitude of the *Shinto* faith and the Japanese people. (The rite of purification by water survives even to this day—and became a notable feature of Japanese life in the eyes of Westerners—as the daily *o-furo*. Although essentially a tub bathing, *o-furo* (or simply *furo*, without the reverential '*o*') is to Japanese not a mere hygienic exercise but an act of both bodily purification and spiritual rejuvenation. The word "*o-furo*" literally means "*revered open-air bathing*," paralleling the ritual of baptism in the open-air waterways—whether in the river or lake—as practiced by the followers of John the "baptizer" and then by all the followers of the Christian faith even to this day (*cf* "cleansing" later in this chapter).

In considering all the aspects mentioned above, it is tempting to conclude that there is more than a good measure of probability that *Togarmah* or *Tegarma* (hereafter only *Togarma* will be used) in ancient Armenia was the origin of the name *Takama*. Additionally, not only is there a close similarity between the sound of the names *Togarma* and *Takama*, there is also another uncanny similarity between the name *Haran* (the main city in the district of *Togarma*) and the Japanese word *Hara* (of the ideogram connoting "plain" or "field"). It should be added that a more correct pronunciation for reading the two ideograms of "*taka*" and "*ma*" would be "*taka*" and "*ama*." In other words, if the first two ideograms were to be more faithfully pronounced (as it might have originally been intended), the phonemic sound would or should be "taka-ama" (a double-A) or "takaAHma" (with an elongated AH). This reading would indeed render the *atiji* name a virtual double of Tog*AH*mah or Tog*AR*mah.

If the above scenario is to be surmised, then the word "*ame*" (with Chinese ideogram to signify "heaven" or "heavenly"), the word which often precedes *Takama-ga-hara*, can also be shown to yield additional support to the opinion that the proto-Japanese had come from a region in the Middle East or Central Asia. That is, if *Haran* (also spelled *Harran*) of *Togarma* was in the country of *Armenia*, then perhaps the Japanese word for heaven—*Ame*—may very well have been an abbreviated syllable in referring to the country of or a region in *Armenia*, the territory on high mountainous terrains that nearly "reached the celestial realm"—the hills of Mount Ararat. In other words, *Ame no Takama ga Hara* may well have been a name formed by linking the three factual historical geographical names, *Ame* (Armenia) no *Takama* (Togarma) ga *Hara* (Haran). Essentially, this was a made-up name, the name which the oracler of the legends could only recite, the name which was intended to identify or recall the land whence their forebearers had come, but the exact meaning and reference had long been lost and forgotten:

[**Hara**n, in the district of **Togarma,** in the country of **Arme**nia]

This deciphering of mythological names may provide a probable answer to the question of the origin of the Japanese people, the land from whence the ethnic and cultic stock had come and had subsequently entered the Japanese archipelago a few centuries before the Common Era. This will also help to resolve the problem inherent in the use of Chinese ideograms for ancient geographical and personal names in *Kojiki* and *Ninon Shoki*. Among them is the name of the most important personage not only in these ancient mythological legends of pantheon but also the central figure in the entire *shinto* faith: *Ama-Terasu O-Mi-Kami* (hyphenated here to show the sequence of the five ideograms).

O-Mi-Kami is clearly intended to convey the exalted state of the goddess. The specific meaning of the three ideograms is "Great, Divine" and "*kami*" which, as has been discussed, can be used in reference either to a deity or a human who is worthy of reverence.

The name *Ama-Terasu* itself presents a different sort of difficulty. First, a Chinese ideogram is seldom pronounced in the Japanese manner (the"old-Japanese" *polysyllabic* reading mentioned earlier) with *three syllables* unless it is an *ateji* which had come into practice much later. (*Mikoto*, as a generic title for a male *kami* or male member of imperial clans, is such an example among the few exceptions to the more common, *two-syllable* pronunciation of Chinese ideograms.) Could it be, then, that the three-syllable word *terasu* was an *ateji* in simulating the original one- or possibly *two-syllable* name? Or could it be the result of mis-grouping of yet another poly-syllabic word? (For *Mikado*, see "the tribe of Gad" in Chapter Sixteen, pp. 196–97.)

In identifying *Takama-ga-hara* as possibly a geographical reference to *Togarma* (in an ancient Armenia-Turk region) provides a significant ramification that the area was once a territory within the Persian Empire, and that *mithraism* was in fact a dominant religious cult of the Persian people of that historical period. If indeed the ancient Japanese sun-worshippers had come from a region within the Persian Empire, then the name *Amaterasu* could quite possibly be a modified or corrupt version of the name *mithra*. That is, *amaterasu* was a form of *ateji* for *Mit'ras* or *mithras*. If this possibility is to be acknowledged, then the name *Amaterasu Omikami* may indeed have been intended to refer to not only the hierarchical position of a particular individual priest(ess) of the cult but also a way of identifying the principal caste of priest(esses) within the cult. A slightly more in-depth look into a few aspects of Persia—the people and the empire, as well as the cult of *mithraism*—may be called for, in order to clarify related issues of importance to this study.

Persia was the name used until the early twentieth century when it was changed (in 1935) to Iran. The name change was for the purpose of more correctly identifying its ethnographic lineage with earlier people known as *Aryans*, who had migrated into the present Iran. The name *Iran* must therefore be recognized as a derivative of or identical with *Aryan*, the name of the ancient ethnic stock that had originally lived in the areas from southern Russia to northern India (into Indus valley). Around the mid-second millennium B.C.E., when the Aryan people began their migration from the original higher steppes plateau to more cultivatable low lands, one stock branched southward down to the Indus valley region and the other westward to the modern Iranian plateau. From an ethnographic point of view, the (present) Iranians are said to be directly related to the northern Indians; they are all of the same Aryan people. However, as such, Iranians or, earlier known for over three millennia as Persians, are themselves very much a mixed race, including the people of Turkish, Kurdish, Armenian, Assyrian, Dravidian and Afghan-Mongolian ethnic lineages.

Mention of the Aryans had appeared in ancient documents of the Hittites and Assyrians and even of the faraway people of Egypt, described as people of *mounted warriors*. Eventually the Aryan warriors began to spread, winning and taking territories and, on the backs of their galloping horses, the Aryan empire steadily grew. By the second half of the first millennium, B.C.E., its border had reached and covered the entire Semitic ("Palestinian") world. Hence, one would note that the name Persia (along with Assyria, *etc.*) was mentioned in the Old Testament as the doom and undoing of the dynasties of David and Solomon. However, the Persians were tolerant of other ethnic and cultic people and, historically, there had been little racial animosity. It is understandable, therefore, that a fair portion of Semitic people had adopted—or were adopted into—the Persian faith of *mithraism*, embracing the god Mithra as a merciful and, now, more victorious than God Yahweh.[19] Later, Alexander the Great conquered the Persian empire. By then, the new empire of the Macedonians and Romans covered nearly the entire eastern half of the Eurasian Continent, with the exception of the westernmost regions. Thus, the so-called the "first" great world empire under Alexander was created by uniting the Macedonian (Greek) and the Persian territories.

Here, it is of some interest to note also that, subsequent to conquering Persia, Alexander made himself not only the emperor but also declared himself god. Even in China, emperors did not dare declare themselves god. In China, an emperor was referred to as *Tian-Zhi*, a "son of god," meaning that he was appointed or annointed of god and, hence, had been given the "mandate of heaven" to rule. This mandate to rule the land could be—and on many instances, had been—taken away from him and given to another individual more worthy and acceptable in the sight of the populace. Not so with god himself, for it is impossible to usurp the power which rightfully belongs to god only, and to none other.

This *deifying* of a ruler even before his death was a common feature in certain mythical cultic beliefs, including those of the Aryans, who (such as the followers of the later Hindi religion) were *animistic* in their perception of the world and of the spirit. In this belief, all things in the great nature, visible and invisible, are worthy of reverence, and the person sanctified (as compared to merely being appointed) by the great spirit to rule over the land is certainly equal with that great spirit of (in Japanese terms) *kami*. Hence, probably taking from this particular cultic precept of the Aryan people who had now become a subject within his vast empire, Alexander the Great declared himself a god, even against the general opinion of the more rational-thinking Greeks. Subsequently, this arrogance of Alexander caused him to lose his life. Alas, he certainly was not *immortal*.

In Japan, until the end of World War II, the people had believed—or were made to believe—that their emperors were divine, *ara-hito-gami*, "gods manifested in human form." In other words, the Japanese believed that their emperor was god *incarnate*, god *indwelling in man*, or, in essence, the "*Emmanuel*." I recall several conversations I had with my Christian-minister father when I was in primary school, on the question of the divinity of Japan's Emperor. "My teacher said" I would tell my father, "that the Emperor was *kami*, a god; it is only that he is *ara-hito-gami*—'god in human form.'" The portrait of the emperor was everywhere in school offices and public buildings, to be seen and worshipped. At school, we would bow during the morning assembly every day to the direction of the emperor's palace and clapped our hands, the same ritual that was offered to the *shinto kami*. Then we would conclude the morning exercise with singing of "*Kimi ga Yo*"—the national anthem of Japan, the same song that is still sung today. This ancient patriotic poem states that,

> "The reign of the emperor would endure for a thousand
> and eight thousand generations,
> Until small pebbles grow to become great boulders
> and until moss adorns that great rock."
> (translation *mine*)

As a child I did not have any of the theological precepts, except to pose to my father the question: "who is greater, our (Christian) God or the Japanese emperor? Because at school we were taught to believe that Emperor Hirohito is *arahito-gami*. I could not recall how my father had replied; perhaps he had wisely circumvented a direct answer. Still, even as a child, I had some trouble wholly accepting this idea of deity of a human emperor. Nevertheless, the divinity of the emperor was never an issue in Japan, politically, religiously, or any other way. That was until noon of August 15, 1945. For the first time in the history of Japan, the emperor spoke to the whole nation. Over the radio waves, the emperor conceded defeat to the Allied Forces, and *inferred* that he was but a mere mortal.

One day during this period of arguably the gravest of political turmoil in Japan's history, many ultra-patriots and military personnel assembled in the outer courtyard of the imperial palace, outside the moat but with *Niju-bashi* (a "double-bridge" in visual impression) within their sight, and committed *seppuku* (or *harakiri*). (This event occurred following a *coup d'état* by a band of ultra conservative patriots who stormed the imperial palace and murdered a few cabinet chambers and military leaders in an attempt to remove the political party which favored surrender *per* the Potsdam declaration.) For these men who had never doubted that their emperor was divine, an honorable death was the only alternative to having to face the humiliation that their emperor was now *forced* to disavow his divinity.

During these same fateful days, there occurred within the imperial compound an event which, even to this day, had never been made common knowledge. On the eve of Japan's unconditional surrender to the Allied Forces, and even after two atomic bombs were dropped that had caused an unspeakable human tragedy, Emperor Hirohito was fearful of the prospect, even in the face of further loss of countless lives of the populace, that the imperial house may have to surrender the regalia as proof of its direct lineage of the mythological sun-goddess *Amaterasu Omikami*. For from secret *memoranda* of urgent meetings of the war cabinet during the darkest hour in Japan's history, there is a record to indicate that the emperor had devised a way to safeguard the *sanpo*—the three treasures of mirror, sword, and crescent-shaped precious stones—by gathering all these articles into his residence palace, instead of leaving them as they had been for centuries in different locations: the *magatama* (stones) in the palace; the *kangami* (mirror) in *Ise* Shrine; and *tsurugi* (sword) in yet another (*Atsuta*) shrine. In other words, even after being informed of the great human suffering in Hiroshima and Nagasaki, Emperor Hirohito had appeared to give greater concern to preserving his *kami* lineage and securing his throne by the safekeeping of the three regalia, more so than the concern for his country and his subjects. This act of Emperor Hirohito has been interpreted even by modern Japanese historians as his (last) effort to retain indisputable authority—as his grandfather Emperor Meiji had done in the closing decades of the nineteenth century—by eliminating all the other "feudal" powers in order to stake a claim on the absolute, indisputable and living *kami* regalia of the emperial throne.

There lies the mystique of the spirit of Japan, the *Yamato tamashii*, the spirit which also had given rise to all the unbelievable acts of *kamikaze* suicidal pilots. These were the best young pilots, many in their late teens, sworn to fight to the death for their divine emperor. Just before boarding their planes for the final flight (carrying only sufficient fuel for a *one-way* flight), these youthful pilots would face the direction of the imperial palace and sing "*Umi Yukaba*," an ancient patriotic song. Today, I am sure, this song "*Umi Yukaba*"* is no longer sung, and generations of postwar Japanese probably have never heard it.

But the singing this most famous and moving of Japan's patriotic verses even as a school-age child is still fresh in my memory. For the poem bespeaks of a Japanese man's sworn loyalty and unwavering dedication to his emperor, that to die for his emperor is the only unequivocal demonstration of his devotion to his *kami* and *O-Gimi*, the Great Lord and Master (English translation mine):

UMI YUKABA

(*The duet version was taught to me by my elder sister, then a high school student. I have not been able to identify the source of this duet setting.)

"Fighting in the seas, may my body rot and float on the waves;
Fighting in the mountains, may my body decay amidst the grasses;
For me to die at the foot of *O-Gimi*, my Great Lord,
I shall never regret."

The godhead of a human ruler is one of the characteristics of mythical and animistic cults which prevailed in the large Central Asian region, from western China (*e.g.*, Tibet) and western Mongolia all the way west to the regions of the Persian (*i.e.*, Iranian) steppes to Mount Ararat ranges, to the eastern shores of the Mediterranean and Red Seas. It was in this large region of the central

Eurasian Continent that the cult of *mithraism* had flourished. At the same time, this god is the *god of nature* and *one with nature*. Hence this god had given birth to islands and mountains, rivers and seas, and all living things within. It should be noted here, too, that this manner of storytelling about the creation of lands and seas, and the birth of all life forms, is consistent with and persistent in the mythological legend in Japan's *Kojiki*, *Nihon Shoki*, and *Kuji Honki*. In all this and in any study of Japanese culture, a good measure of understanding the *Yamato tamashii* (spirit of Japan) is quintessential. Without it, the history of Japan and the collective posture of the Japanese people would appear to the non-Japanese merely as curiously polite but still a wholly incomprehensible enigma.

The early people entering the Iranian steppes were Aryans who also brought with them *Mitra*, the god of light, who was more commonly associated with the other deities of ancient India (such as *Indra*). It was from this god of *Mitra* that the Persian god *Mithra* was derived. During the formative periods, even under the reign of King Xerxes, the older cults were beginning to be amalgamated into once the more folkish cult of (Indian) *mitra* and (Persian) *mithra*, a fire- and sun-god, one and the same. The quotation below, from *Encyclopedia Britannica*, may serve to elucidate the significant points regarding the rise of *mithraism* in the Persian Empire.

"… Whatever the exact form of the Persian religion, there is evidence that it was vigorously spread by the Iranians throughout the empire, especially in Armenia and Cappadocia, where the religion took deep root among the people, as also in Lydia and Lycia. Unlike Judaism, [the later] Zoroastrianism was not exclusive and intolerant, and it found little difficulty in recognizing other gods as subordinate to [its chief deity] Ahura Mazda. Consequently the foreign cults and creeds often reacted upon the Persian empire and strange syncretisms developed.

The unadulterated doctrine of Zoroaster could not become a permanent popular religion, for the masses could make little of its abstractions and its omnipotent, omnipresent deity; they needed concrete divine powers, standing nearer to themselves and their lot. Thus the old figures of the Aryan folk religions [*i.e.*, Mithra] returned to the foreground, there to be amalgamated with the Babylonian divinities. The goddess of springs and streams [Anahita but later emerged as Mithra] … [who also was the goddess] of all fertility … was endowed with the form of the Babylonian Istar and Belit. [Mithra] was now depicted as a beautiful and strong woman, with prominent breasts, a golden crown of stars and golden raiment. She was worshipped as the goddess of generation and all sexual life (whence the names and identities of Mithras and Anahita—or Anaitis—became interchangeable), and religious prostitution was transferred to her service [*i.e.*, temple prostitution]. At her side stood the sun-god Mithras, represented as a young and victorious hero. Both deities occupied the very first rank in the popular creed, while to the theologian they were the most potent of the good powers—*mithras* being the herald and propagator of the service of light and the mediator between man and Ahura Mazda, who faded more into the background.

Thus, in the subsequent period, the Persian religion appears purely as the religion of Mithras. The festival of Mithras was the chief festival of the empire, at which the king drank and became drunk, and danced the national dance."

(italics for emphasis mine)

Although ignored earlier by the staunch monotheistic Zoroastrians, the new cult of *mithraism* soon founded their major cult centers in many of the most important cultural and commercial districts within the Persian Empire, for example, at Acilisene in *Armenia*, as well as a larger metropolis in Cappadocia and Lydia. For the main appeal of this *mithraism*, arguably the most influential of all the Oriental mystery cults, was its accommodating posture of the belief, absent of any strictly defined catechism, which was especially attractive to the lowly and humble castes of the society, among them, the itinerant migrants. Subsequently, the status of this once folk cult was elevated to the state that the later kings such as Artaxerxes II and III would even invoke the name of the god(dess) Mithra—along with other deities who were once more powerful—in their royal inscriptions. Historians would therefore note the fact that the early cult of the (Aryan god) Mitra did not attract its western followers (*e.g.*, from west of Asia Minor) but, rather, it was an amalgam, essentially a new creation born of older and even rival cults, that increased its appeal during the early period of the Persian conquests, and subsequently became the virtual state religion of the Persian Empire.

The period of several centuries before the common era allowed a number of complex ethnographic and religious currents to play out, and to create what was to become *the* "Persian culture," the most enlightened of all ancient empires. This in turn served as a *peaceable* period which allowed the migrating nomadic tribes to find a land of respite, to absorb the culture and cultic beliefs of the new surroundings, and to reshape themselves. It may therefore be conjectured that the people of the ark of the Covenant had not only found solace in the strange land but saw it fit to accommodate and incorporate the local deities. For the ancient Hebrites were not always a people of monotheistic belief.[18] Hence, perhaps resurrecting an older *Mezzulash* cult (of the ancient Hittites) and embracing the *Mithra* cult of the land of their sojourn, a remnant of the Hebrites had fathomed, by necessity or by convenience, a new cult of proto-*A-Materasu* (the later *shintoism*). For *A-Materasu* is also a belief in a sun-god(dess), all beautiful, all powerful, and she, too, was a warrior and defender of all that is good as well as the destroyer of all that is evil. She also gave birth to life forms, and she was called by the likes of that Aryan name: (A)*Materasu*—*Mitras* or *Mithras*, and she reigned on the plain of celestial domain of *Takama* or *Togarma*. This *Shinto*, the cult of the *Ways of the Divine*, like *Mithraism*, also revered all things in nature and regard them *kami* worthy of deifying, and held the purification rite by water to be of supreme ritual importance.

As to the ritual of purification by fire, the scene from my childhood years of the *shinto* ritual on new year's eve, still vivid in my memory, should provide a significant perspective:

On the eve of *o-misoka*—the "great passover"—the worshippers dressed in traditional *kimono* and, wearing *geta* (wooden slippers), would enter the hallowed ground of the shrine. The faithful walk slowly and reverently in utter silence toward the front opening of the shrine ground. The forest and the entire surroundings of the shrine are dark except the passway leading to the shrine is faintly lit by fires on the stands lining both sides of the passage. On entering the holy ground, each person is handed a paper figurine cut in a human form. From the dark background behind the shrine (or from the shrine, I could not tell), *kan-nushi san*, the chief *shinto* priest, who was the father of my classmate Omura (and the counterpart—literally—of my own father, a Christian minister), dressed in his most formal priestly gown and wearing an *eboshi* (priestly cap) on his head, appears, briefly greets the worshippers, mostly in silence, and turns around to intone a solemn recitation in a deliberate and low monotone voice.

Then, on cue, the people, still kneeling, raise their right hand to wipe their body with the paper-cut figure, as if in cleansing. On the next cue, the people, slowly and reverently, raise themselves from the kneeled position, and walk to form lines to approach the bonfire in front of the shrine's main hall. Each one would toss the paper figure into the flame, then retire, and walk in silence out of the shrine ground.

I still remember how difficult it was for me to remain in a kneeled position for the duration of what seemed a long ritual. But the significance of this ritual, even to primary school children, had been explained clearly: that the paper figure was a *replica of the sacrificial offering* which, by wiping our body with it, would assume and take away our sin (*tsumi*, or *yogore*—filth) and, by burning it, each person is thus cleansed, purified, allowed to begin the new year without blemish.

More than a symbolic gesture, this is the ritual of purification by fire, the ritual of atonement of the sacrificial lamb of Judaism and the Christian faith of all denominations, as with the baptism or the "Lord's supper." It was most likely the same ritual that the faithful of Mithra had performed some three millennia ago, in the land of Armenia in the district of Togarma and other districts within the Persian Empire.

It may be worth adding here that *Togarma* is mentioned in ancient Chinese legends as the country from where the earliest knowledge of a music system had come. Arguably the earliest mention is in regard to Ling Lung, a minister of Huang Di, the legendary first emperor of China. Ling Lung was sent by Huang Di to the "land lying in the shadow (*i.e.*, the west) of Mount Kunlung, in the west of *Taxia* (pronounced Da-hsia, the *hsia* with a strong German glottal "h" sounds quite close to a soft glottal *gh*) to procure section(s) of bamboo in order to establish the system of ritual music." This country of *Taxia* is most likely a corrupted sound which, in turn, was written out in Chinese ideograms, for either *To-gar* (with *ma* being omitted) or *Da-Hae*. This statement is taken by modern Chinese musicologists as in reference to China's early importation of the system of tone generation from a land far west of China, possibly the land of the ancient Sumerians and Egyptians who were the first to establish the mathematical scheme for generation of musical tones. (This system employed the consecutive fifth generation, such as C to G to D to A, etc., the process which is often—but erroneously—referred to as *Pythagorean* tuning.) Later, on the spread of Buddhism in the early centuries of the Common Era to China and eventually to Korea and Japan, a country northwest of India and Tibet was referred to as *Da-Ruo-Jih Guo. Guo* means country, and the ideogramic meaning of the name of the tribe *Da-Ruo* (the character for *ruo* may appear as "moon" but is actually the ancient form of the character for flesh or meat, hence should be pronounced as *ruo*) and *jih* simply means people. The country of *Da Ruo-Jih* therefore may threfore be a reference to (the ancient) *Assyria* or *Syria* (see CHAPTER XIV).

The close parallels are also found in many other aspects of Persian and Japanese cultures, between *mithraism* and *shintoism*, such as in the names of the cult, in the practice of the cult and its festival, in the language and grammar, in the precepts and detail in mythological tales, in genetic and physical elements, and in the historical timetable when such migration, acculturation and final formation of the nation, the people, and their beliefs, had occurred.

The foregoing paragraphs suggest how the popular Persian folk cult of *mithraism* had quite possibly contributed to the shaping of a similar cult of the nomadic tribe(s) coming from the Semitic world; that these migrating (originally Semitic) stocks subsequently brought with them (the proto-) *shinto* cult into the Japanese archipelago (perhaps the cult which was already fairly well established before arriving in Japan, *e.g.*, while still sojourning in Korea); that, on arriving on the new and relatively uncontested and uncongested land and after (regional) conflicts toward unification, *Amaterasu* (of the similar namesake with *Mithras*) was worshipped as goddess supreme. In the foregoing chapters and sections, parallels and documentary evidences have been cited to support this postulate.

The parallels and evidences are not limited to these already cited, however. There are indeed many, many other equally peculiar parallels. Consider, for example, the regard for rock in *Mithraism* and *Shintoism*: *Mithra* was a sun god and was believed to have been born of a rock. When *Amaterasu* was shamed by her brother, she hid herself in the rock cave before reemerging as sun goddess to radiate the earth. The legend that Mithra, after accomplishing his good deeds of shooting an arrow at a cliff to bring forth water, and at killing and sacrificing a bull, was given a banquet in making an alliance with the sun god and hence becoming a sun god himself, would parallel with *Amaterasu*'s deeds and becoming the heaven-illuminating sun goddess. Both Mithra and *Amaterasu* were annointed the creator of life, and both were fierce defenders of their people against forces of evil. As one sees (*e.g.*, on photos of bronze or rock relief) the depiction of sun-god *Mithra*, shown with creatures such as a *lion* and raven, amidst the background of trees, *chrysanthemums* and other floral foliage, one may then become curious of the fact that a *lion* was once the emblem of Japan's imperial throne, and the sixteen-petal *chrysanthemum* the family crest of the imperial household. No lions had ever lived on the Japanese archipelago or on China's mainland (tigers had, and continued to live in the Asian continent), and chrysanthemum as emblem has always been portrayed as a twelve-petal flower. Then one becomes curious of another close parallel in the fact that, in ancient Persia as well as in Japan, both the *lion* and the *sixteen-petal chrysanthemum* were imperial insignia.

In the early years of the twentieth century, a team of archaeologists unearthed a stone column in Iran (*i.e.*, ancient Persia) which featured a sixteen-petal chrysanthemum on its top. This stone column was dated to be in the mid-ninth century B.C.E., during the height of the Israeli dynastic period. We may speculate that this was also the time when the bands of disillusioned ex-Semitic tribal people were sojourning in Persia, where they may have found *mythra* faith agreeable, and may have chosen to adopt many Persian cultural expressions, even the cultic symbols and emblems. For example, the raven or dove, too, although always representing a messenger, figured in the landscape of mythological legends of *Mithraism* and *Shintoism*, and, it might be added, in the Sumerian (and the Old Testament) stories as well.

The bird with outstretched wings (such as the two cherubims over the ark of the Covenant) is also the figure prominently displayed on the rooftop of *O-Mikoshi*, a small shrine that even today is the main feature in the wild procession of the summer Festival of *Gion* all across Japan. The procession concludes with carrying of *o-mikoshi* into a waterway. Having witnessed the *Festival of Gion* (November 6, 1928) firsthand, a certain Pennington, who was the correspondent for both the *London Times* and *New York Times* (as reported in *Tokyo Asahi Shinbun* [*Tokyo Morning News*] in its November 17 edition), sent a wire to both papers describing his impression of the *o-mikoshi* procession as follows:

> "... [the *O-Mikoshi* procession] *reminds one*
> *of the Biblical description of the Israelites crossing*
> *the Red Sea carrying the ark of the Covenant ...*"

No less significant than the Festival of Gion is the concept of and the attitude toward ritual cleansing, an aspect that is immediately noticed at entering every *shinto* shrine: the ever-present water basin for hand washing and mouth rinsing. Purification of the faithful by water and fire is a perpetual theme in both *shintoism* and *mithraism*. It is worth repeating that the greatest attraction of *mithraism* was to the people of lower castes who had little regard for established catechism or ritual prerequisites. The fact was that *mithraism* held no caste distinction, and this precept of ritual simplicity especially on matters spiritual was manifested in the simplicity of their temples and sanctuaries, in which both the priestly rank and the faithful joined to find joy and comfort in the modesty of circumstances. This simplicity of sanctuary of *mithraism* contrasted strongly with the temples of the Israelites and Egyptians.

This same simplicity in the sanctuary, in the ritual and in belief is quintessential to *Shintoism*. *Shinto* shrines are bare and austere inside and out, thereby manifesting a *zen*-like beauty of purity. (One may wonder why the philosophy of *zen* had never achieved any level of popularity in China where it had originated, but rather became in Japan the very *persona* of *Yamato tamashii*—the spirit of *Yamato, i.e.* Japan—and of *shintoism* in particular.) In the sacred ground, one sees no bright colors except that of the natural, and everything in the surroundings is in the natural form of rocks and trees and water. The faithful would come to worship and meditate in this surrounding of utter simplicity, but they recite no prescribed *mantra* (unless one is in the Buddhist temple). All that is "required" is that one behaves reverently, washes hands as a simple ritual of purification, then claps the hands to indicate that there is nothing in the worshipper's heart to interfere with communication with the spirit, and bows humbly. No creed, no caste distinctions, and no sacrificial offerings.

An itinerant tribe adopting the religious practices of the local people during the course of migration is a documentable fact of history. This was particularly so in the vast stretch of Central Asia where countless tribes roamed in all directions for countless centuries. That such is a fact of archaeological history has been meticulously researched and documented by scholars in the field, notably by Grousset in his *The Empire of the Steppes: A History of Central Asia*. It should be a reasonable assumption, therefore, that this same itinerant tribe would have incorporated elements of not only one particular religion but also *other* religions of other people along the long migratory journey. For the travel from one end to the other end of the Eurasian Continent would encompass several thousand miles of vast expanse of land, where countless tribes and empires rose and fell, gods and demigods created and morphed and were forgotten, like the mirages in the ever-shifting landscape of the deserts in Central Asia.

This scenario will gain an added element of credence when we examine the religion of the Hittites and compare it with *mithraism* of the Persians. For we will find that there are so many parallels not only between the religions of the Hittites, Persians and the Israelites but curiously also with *shintoism* of the Japanese. If indeed the proto-Japanese of (the later) *shinto* faith had traveled through the land previously occupied by the Hittites (in Asia Minor), and continued through the territory of the Persian Empire (from the eastern shores of the Mediterranean to the southwestern region of Central Asia), it may be assumed that the religion of these early Japanese people would have some features of the Persian religion *(e.g., mithraism)* and Hittite religion (of *mezzulash* worship); the latter shall be taken up in a later chapter. Suddenly, what may have appeared before as merely some rather unusual parallels—the *sanpo* and o-*mikoshi*, or the three treasures and the *Chest of Witness*, those few tangibles of *Shintoism* as possibly of the remnant lineage of the three sacred articles in the *ark of the Covenant* of the Israelites—may not now seem altogether too bizarre.

The story of the giant rock statues on Easter Island is familiar to many. The beginning of the end for the people on Easter Island was initiated when the last aged oraclers, the only men who still possessed the ability to decipher the cryptic pictograms carved on wooden planks—called "talking wood" by the natives—were taken captive by the Europeans as slaves. Until then, the marooned islanders still possessed their legends and hopes, even though the interpretation of the talking wood had become garbled and cryptic. Then, the Christian missionaries arrived on the Island on the heels of the slave traders and, in the name of obliterating all remnant of paganism, these overzealous men of God put all the sacred talking woods to the torch. Thence, there remains today only those giant rock statues with vacant gaze, too large to be destroyed or toppled even by those overzealous messengers of an alien god. Still standing in total silence, these giant rock faces could tell nothing about whence the ancestors of the Easter Islanders might have come from ages ago. For their oraclers and "oracle woods" were forever lost. Recent archaeological studies have identified some scientific evidences which seem to suggest that the Easter Islanders had originally come from the region of New Guinea, probably from the same ethnic stock who had peopled the Solomon Islands, some ten thousand ocean miles away to the west.

The people on the Japanese archipelago might have encountered the same fate as the Easter Islanders had they not had their oracles committed to writing for all posterity. We now know that the nearly insoluble problem was created when the ancient oracle was recorded with an alien script wholly incompatible with the spoken language of the oracler. Still, modern scholars believe that the phonetic sound of those ancient original names of personages and places of their ancestors were preserved even by way of *atiji* (false characters) in the chronicles. Thus scholars believe that the secret of these far-away ancestral lands of long ago may still be disclosed by careful and critical deciphering of the *ateji* names contained in the legends. For these chronicles are the only surviving "talking wood" about the history and story of the ancient Japanese.

There are, to be sure, much stronger evidences for the far-western origin of the proto-Japanese people than the far-western origin of the people of Easter Island. These evidences shall be presented in fuller detail in PART THREE.

CHAPTER ELEVEN

JAPAN'S EARLY "DOMINANT" TRIBES AND *SHINTOISM*

In many narratives in *Kojiki* and *Nihon Shoki*, there is a clear inference that the people of the sun-worshipping cult were not the earliest people to have entered the Japanese archipelago. For the people of Kojiki and Nihon Shoki are described to have encountered and subjugated the earlier inhabitants of the islands with considerable difficulty and bloodshed. *Kojiki* and *Nihon Shoki* named these earlier inhabitants of the islands as *Ezo* or *Iso* as well as *chigumo*, the latter meaning "earth spider" in reference to their cave dwelling, thus a spiteful name.

Ezo or *Iso* were described as wild and barbaric hunters, and with the physical characteristic nearly always as "extremely hairy." Eventually, the *Ezo* or *Iso* were vanquished; they were forced to retreat northward. Modern scholars of anthropology have identified that the modern *tribe* of Ainu living in the extreme northern region of the Japanese archipelago, on the island area of *Ezo* (also spelled as *Yezo*), the present Hokkaido and Karafuto, is the descendant of these *Ezo* or *Iso*. This tribal people once suffered most cruelly, being regarded as if they were subhumans or worse, until a relatively recent past. Today, they are recognized as a vanishing, *endangered race*, now numbering less than twenty thousand. Many attempts have been made by the modern government of Japan to pacify and repatriate this "lost tribe." This description "lost tribe" is neither new nor inappropriate, since anthropologists have not been able to identify the ethnic lineage of the Ainu, in spite of the many theories about their origin, ranging from Europeans (caucasians), Middle-Eastern, or Mongolian (but not Chinese). In terms of religion, these people were regarded as polytheistic and an animistic cult, although anthropologists have failed to identify many of their cultic practices, as they seem to defy any ordinary categorization. In terms of language, the Ainu tongue is also a "lost language," in that it does not seem to fit into any linguistic lineage, and the Ainu people never had any form of written language.

It is clear, from the narratives in *Kojiki* and *Nihon Shoki*, that *their* own people began their settlement by invading the island from the south (Kyushu) and northwest (the district of *Izumo*, most likely from South Korea), carried with them the belief in *kami* of nature and the cult of sun worship, that they bowed in worship toward the direction of the east, and exercised the important ritual of purification by fire and water. These new arrivals referred to themselves either as *Yayoi* or *Yamato*: *Yayoi* in reference to the people who were active in the *Izumo* district, while *Yamato* to the people who had first entered Kyushu Island from the south and subsequently moved up northward and occupied the central plains area of Honshu, the main island of Japan.

It is not clear, however, whether these two clans of later arrivals were of the same ethnic stock, or that they both had possessed sufficiently common shared ritual practice and beliefs. For *Sendai Kuji Honki* (the third Japanese chronicle written about three centuries later than *Kojiki* and *Nihon Shoki* which until the relative recent past was regarded as less credible) provides an imperial genealogy that differs from *Kojiki* and *Nihon Shoki*. However, recent scholarship tends to accord a greater degree of credence to *Kuji Honki*. At any rate, the two clans were subsequently enabled to unite as one people embracing the one "official" *shinto* belief. The prevailing opinion is that the *Yayoi* clan who were cult followers of the sun goddess arrived first, went ashore near the present Izumo (the area of the Grand *Izumo* Shrine), and the *Yamato* clan who were the mounted warriors arrived later, on the southern island of Kyushu. When the *Yamato* clan pushed northward and encountered the *Yayoi* clan, the gentler Yayoi clan yielded their rule to the *Yamato* clan who embraced the *Amaterasu* cult. Hence, the tone of the narratives in the chronicle shifts dramatically, from mythological tales of *kami* to narratives of human personages, identifying Jimmu (of the *Yamato* clan) as the first (human) emperor of Japan, who was cleverly woven into the *Yayoi* mythology as related to *Amaterasu*.

Specifically, contemporary scholarship of ancient Japanese history regards one of the major points of difference between the *Kojiki/Nihon Shoki* and *Kuji Honki* is in regard to *Amaterasu Omikami* and her relation to other *kami*. However, taken as a whole and in regard to the present study, this is a relatively minor point of dispute. For there seems to be little doubt that uniting of the *Yayoi* and *Yamato* clans created the dominant people of early Japan, in military might as well as in cultural impact and cultic persuasion. For, as mentioned, the narratives in *Kojiki* and *Nihon Shoki* as well as *Kuji Honki* had but one primary purpose for their being committed to writing as Japan's official chronicles. It was neither for preserving the accuracy of chronological sequence of personages and events in the genealogical lineage. Rather, it was for the sole purpose of creating a legitimacy of the *shinto* faith as the official faith of the land on one hand, and on the other, the priest, the faith, *and* the heir apparent of the imperial household—the two being the same—as the rightful guardian of the faith and ruler of the land.

In the course of compiling these two "historical" chronicles, therefore, their authors cleverly engaged whatever means to create a continuous tale to satisfy the mandate of the commissioner of the chronicle—the imperial household. Therefore the author(s) of these chronicles even engaged fabrication and falsification, with the result that whatever historical information there was in the original oracles became even more blurred and cryptic, due to deletion of aspects in the oral history which the imperial household regarded as unfavorable. Had the chronicle been fuller and more accurate in recording the oracle narrative, modern scholars would have a more reliable source to decipher the mystery surrounding the origin and antiquity of the Japanese people.

The methods of "fabrication and falsification" in creating what had become the official chronicle of Japan were a shared tenet of the view of history in the ancient world, the accepted method in chronicling the past events of a tribe and a nation. The chronicles of the ancient Israelites, for example, are no exception. In fact, it is virtually another identical case with the narratives in Japan's own "old testament"—*Kojiki* and *Nihon Shoki*. The following statements, from *The Ancient Historians* by an eminent historian Michael Grant, will suffice to shed light on the historicity and purpose of ancient chronicles:

"… On the southern borders of Phoenicia, at the turn of the millennium [B.C.E], the Jewish state was taking shape.…
But the writings of the Jews were wholly bound up with the purpose of Jehovah—interpreted as the sole god of their country, for, whereas the government and the Temple were often controlled by men prepared to worship other divinities in addition to Jehovah [*e.g.*, Baal], the Old Testament writers belonged to the rival school of thought which rejected this course …
To an unprecedented extent, therefore, the sacred literature of the Hebrews is a record and interpretation of bygone ages. Moreover, it tells of the relationship of God not only with a ruler as hitherto, but with an entire people. And nationalism turns into universality, because [Yahweh or Jehovah] is regarded as the God of all nations.…

Consequently, as G. R. Elton remarks,

> "… no other primitive sacred writings are so grimly chronological
> and historical as the Old Testament.' It selects from the course of
> events those facts and signs which seem relevant to the interpretation
> of God's Order, advancing from myth and legend to factual annals
> which selectively compile and edit earlier literary documents."

Grant further states, in regard to conflicting narratives on certain central personages in the Old Testament, such as King David, that

> "Passing through the semi-fabulous biographical tales of earlier
> personages … the accounts of the reigns [of these kings] far outdo,
> in literary eloquence, anything which has survived from earlier peoples
> or times.… These materials include a mass of detail from various
> sources. In particular, the anonymous and composite work known as
> the Second Book of Samuel, written in admirable Hebrew prose,
> provides full, frank and not wholly subjective historical narratives,
> based on information from an eyewitness or at least a contemporary …
> The principal compiler of the Book of Kings, which carries on the
> story, refers to the existence and availability of earlier royal
> chronicles."[20]

It was in this precisely same manner and attitude in creating the earliest chronicles of Japan that *shinto* as the national belief—even it is not wholly a religion—and the *authorized version* of the imperial lineage of *bansei ikkei* (ten thousand generations of emperors in one continuous and unbroken lineage) were fathomed. And the emblem or the regalia of the imperial seat to rule over the land and all the people within was always taken to be the *sanpo*, the set of three sacred treasures: string of semi-precious stones, the sword, and the mirror.

And it was in this course of the formulation of the early history of *the Japanese* people that the Ainu people, the earliest inhabitants of the Japanese islands, were conquered, subjugated, and pushed out of the central regions of Japan, up to the remote and desolate regions of northern Japan. In the narratives of the historical chronicles, the Ainu were first damned as barbaric, then abhored with spiteful names, banished and finally faded out of any mention in subsequent narratives in the chronicles. The present condition of their survival testifies to this fact; while the Ainu continue their subsistence, its condition is a heart-wrenching portrait of a vanishing human race. (The modern day parallel case to this is the place of American Indians. In chronicling the early history of the United States in both the factual and fabricated sequence of events, the Indians, the original inhabitants of America, were regarded with the same fate, with the consequent state of subsistence virtually identical with the tribes who were the original inhabitants of Japan.)

While the Japanese historical chronicles may have all but erased traces of the Ainu people, it is worth pointing out a very real and historical fact that the traces of their habitation in Japan are everywhere "written" in the *nomenclature* landscape of Japan. Japanese linguistic scholars agree that estimatedly nearly a half of all the traditional names of cities and villages, of mountains and rivers in the *Yamato* region of (central) Japan were the original Ainu names or derivatives of the names by which the Ainu people christened the land.[21]

The most famous of such examples is the name of the most revered sacred mountain of Japan, Mount *Fuji*. In modern factual references and in stories, the name of Mt. Fuji has various ideogrammatically written names, including the more poetic one that connotes "*never dying*" or "*no second*" (both to imply the ever living and incomparably beautiful mountain with gracious slopes and a snow-capped crown). These ideograms are in fact all *ateji* in simulating the sound of its original name "*huchi*" or "*fuchi*" which, in Ainu language, meant "the goddess of fire" in reference to the mountain's volcanic activity.[22] (The most recent eruption of Mt. Fuji occurred in 1707-08, covering the area sixty miles from the mountain with six inches of volcanic ash, including the entire city of Edo.) Even the name *Edo* or *Yedo* is believed to be of Ainu origin. (Edo was the older name for Tokyo that was used during the feudal era. The literal meaning of Tokyo is "Eastern Capital," in distinguishing it from the earlier capital Kyoto which simply means "*The* Capital.")

But, how about their original name of the tribe of *Ezo* or *Iso*? If the Ainu people had indeed left so much of the geographic names across the broad landscape of Japan, would it not be most likely also that this original name by which they were called by the newly arriving tribes of *Yayoi* and *Yamato* would contain some hint of their original ethnic lineage?

While anthropologists have yet to come to consensus on the origin or the ethnic lineage of Ainu, their unique physical features such as heavy bone structure and stocky built, heavy hair, beard and thick skin hair (hence the near derogatory reference of "the *hairy* Ainu") bear altogether close resemblance with certain Russian stocks. It is in fact possible to draw a line of probable migration route of the people of such physical characteristics from the region of Ainu in Japan westward, straight across northern (*i.e.*, outer) Mongolia and across nearly the entire width of the Eurasian Continent (avoiding the northern extreme and inhospitably cold plain of Siberia and treacherously mountainous and desolate region of the present Afghanistan, its bordering western countries) to arrive at the northern Near East, including the areas of the Dead Sea and Red Sea, the rugged mountainous region (peaks rising up to 3,500 feet). For this was the trans-Eurasian passage that was a part of the "king's highway" in ancient times and thus a trade route that connected the *western* and the *eastern* regions of the Eurasian Continent, serving as the migratory routes for various ethnic stocks on the continent. And the western end of this "king's highway" is also believed to be the early habitat of some of the semitic tribes such as the Edomites, the land which was later occupied by other nomadic tribes, forcing the Edomites and other less dominant tribes to emigrate eastward.

This possibility may be considered from the anthropological perspective that many of the earliest inhabitants of Japan came not only through the northern route but also by way of the "central" and "southern" routes. Anthropologists believe that while the *earliest* ethnic stock to Japan (the people of the *Jomon* and pre-*Jomon* era) appeared to have arrived there from the north (through the eastern end of present Russia and crossing the narrow strait of ocean to Kamchatka island, the northernmost island of the Japanese archipelago), the *later* west-east migration seemed to have taken a slightly southern route. These people—including the Ainu—more than likely have followed the "king's high-way" that eventually had become the earliest *trade route* for adventurers and daredevil merchants, somewhat along the same northern passages of what is now famously known, rather poetically, as the *Silk Road*. (There were in fact many silk-trading routes, including the ones through the southern provinces of China and present-day Malaysian regions, as well as by ocean route to southeast Asia, entering into the northern corridor of China through the "break" in the northwestern terrain of the Himalayan-Tibet range, continuing the eastward journey and down southward through the western shorelines of the Korean Peninsula, and finally arriving on the approximate area of *Izumo* in Japan.) It is also clear that many other tribes had similarly journeyed through much of the Eurasian Continent but came slightly more southward (through north-central China, as chronicled in the *History of Western Han*) to reach the northwestern shores of Kyushu after crossing the narrow strip of ocean between Japan and Korea or the northeastern shores of China.

Still, a question must be asked as to whether there are other evidences to support this anthropological view of cultural migration, that at least a few early Japanese stocks were offshoots of the Semitic people.

We will first note that listed among the early descendants of Abraham were a people of hairy hunters whose ancestor was *Esau*, the elder of the twin sons of Isaac. The duplicity of brother Jacob robbing Esau of his birthright, sowed thereby the enduring seed of hatred between the descendants of Esau and Jacob (the hatred that had never been resolved over the millennia and has now become the root cause of the conflict in the Middle East, with horrific and wholly incomprehensible tragedies that affect the entire world). This (perhaps the mythological legend of) Esau is referred to in the bible as the ancestor of Edom, the people called the Edomites. The bible also occasionally tells about the subsequent history of the Edomites, nearly always in negative perspectives relative to the Israelites. The Edomites were repeatedly humiliated by the armies led by Moses, Joshua and, still later and more atrociously, King David, and were subsequently forced out of their land. The same sad fate also befell other Semitic tribes, among them the Jebusites and Hittites who lived among others in the land.

Could it not be possible that the Ainu of Japan were the "lost" descendants of the hairy hunter Esau and the Edomites who were forced out of their land? For the Ainu were called *Ezo* or *Iso* (by the people of *Yayoi* and *Yamato)*, and the land they were now forced to live in has been called *Ezo* or *Yezo* since that ancient time. Anthropologists and archaeologists agree that the Ainu people do not share the same ethnic or genetic lineage of Mongolians or any other "Asian" (Sinitic, *i.e.* Chinese) racial or cultural stocks. Genealogically, the Ainu are much closer to Europeans and the Semitic people than Chinese or Korean. Could it not be possible, then, that the names *Ezo, Iso* and even *Izumo* and *Edo* were all derivative variants of *Esau* and *Edom*?

It is also a well-established opinion among cultural archaeologists that, around the late second millennium before the Common Era, bronze-age warriors of the Tungusic racial group (of the Altaic lineage) had invaded the northeastern region of the Eurasian Continent, and settled in the Manchurian and Korean territories and, there, mixed with the native inhabitants of Mongolian lineage. Hence, for example, while the Koreans today are nearly indistinguishable from Chinese, and the modern Korean language includes a substantial portion of Chinese language as well as Japanese languages (the latter due also to forty-years of Japanese occupation of Korea until the end of the World War II), the Koreans have derived their ancient mythology and their unique cultic practices (*e.g.*, shaminism) from the *non*-Chinese cultural-racial lineage of a much earlier period.[23] It was during this same period also that the Persians (including the Parthians, Medes and Scythians) who earlier were nomadic people known for their horse and cattle herding on the steppes of Central Asia, began to enter the Iranian plateau. However, these are learned opinions of linguists who had studied the larger picture and pattern of linguistic trends, particularly the cross current of linguistic migration of earlier times.

Edwin Reischauer and John Fairbank, in their book *East Asia, The Great Tradition*, offer the opinion that Japanese and Korean languages are of the Tungusic lineage and, at the most, to the Altaic "branch" of the Tungusic linguistic "block." Admitting the difficulty in even this generalized classification, these writers would only state that

> "Turkish, Mongolian and Tungusic are usually considered to be
> the three major Altaic language groups. Korean and Japanese,
> however, show close structural resemblances to the definitely
> Altaic language, and the Koreans and Japanese may, therefore,
> be two eastern extensions of Altaic-speaking peoples into
> predominantly agricultural areas."[24]

At the same time, what these and other writers on the subject seem to often leave out in formulating their studied opinion is the many "curious" elements which may be regarded as threads of cultural and cultic heritage of the *minority stock* which had succeeded in exerting a dominant influence over the earlier but weaker inhabitants. This has been sufficiently demonstrated in many parts of the world. Among the more immediately notable examples are the "Anglo-Saxon" strain of culture (and religion) in North America, and the "Spanish-Latin" strain of culture (and religion) in South America, where the Anglo-Saxon and Spanish-Latin stocks were of minority stock but with dominant cultural forces.

So it was with Japan (and, to a lesser extent, Korea). Indeed there is a sufficient amount of archaeological studies and reliable historical chronicles, the latter especially in Korea and China, that provide credible support to the view that the significant migration was eastward movement from the northwestern and western regions of the Eurasian Continent, that this ethnic movement was possibly from the regions that were within the powerful Hittite, Assyrian and Persian Empires of the last three millennia before the Common Era.

In light of the above anthropological opinions and the current knowledge on the history of cultic beliefs and practices, the present study proposes a more than probable scenario: That the nomadic people (some who are self-exiled Semitic stocks) had entered the territories of Armenia during the last millennium before the Common Era—the period of Assyrian, Chaldean and Persian empires—migrated further eastward, going through the Iranian steppes and Tibetan plateaus, and descended to the northern regions of China; that some had found settlement in the central plains region near China's major waterways (such as the Yellow River of China); that the main body of this migrant tribe continued their eastward movement and, through Korea, to finally arrive in Japan.

(To the foregoing narratives on the possible migration routes of the proto-Japanese stocks, it might be appended that the *south-to-north* migratory routes taken by other ethnic tribes were likely by way of "island hopping," from the southern coast of Southeast Asia, through the many island chain groups, including Java, Brunei, Sumatra, Philippines, Taiwan, and the Ryukyu Islands, arriving finally on the southern Japanese islands, most likely Kyushu. However, from the cultural point of view, the island people from Southeastern Asia had asserted much lesser influence and left only minor footprints in terms of the subsequent formation of the language, the culture and religion of Japan.)

Studying the narratives in *Kojiki* and *Nihon Shoki*, particularly in their earliest legends, it becomes clear that there were two "political" centers in early Japan: one is *Izumo*. *Susa-no-O no Mikoto*, the wild and unruly brother of *Amaterasu*, who was banished from the celestial realm for his misdeeds, first to Korea (in Silla) and, afterward, "descended"—that is, sailed—to *Izumo* (Japan), the land which his descendants came to occupy. Today one can still visit an impressive shrine called *Izumo no O-Yashiro*, the great fort of *Izumo*, which is dedicated to the worship of *Suna-no-O*. This district of Izumo is believed to be the land where the cult of Amaterasu had originated (see below).

The second political center was the mountainous province of Hyuga (or Hiuga), on Kyushu Island, the district where, as mentioned in *Kojiki*, *Amaterasu* had sent her grandson *Ninigi no Mikoto* to rule. It was to this *Ninigi no Mikoto* that the legend refers to as *Amaterasu* having given the imperial regalia of *sanpo*. However, from other documentary evidences, this story of transfer of the *shinto* regalia—or whatever the royal, cultic emblem—has lesser credibility. Modern scholars of Japanese history generally agree that Izumo—and not Hyuga—is the origin of *shintoism*. This is clearly implied in the story in the Chronicles of how *Amaterasu* herself had descended on Izumo to negotiate with the ruler(s) of Izumo *before* sending *Ninigi no Mikoto* to Kyushu (see below).

If the biblical narratives referred to above have any anthropological basis, and there is no evidence to dispute this line of historical archaeological opinions, then the following statements *derived from the Japanese chronicles* should lend additional measure of credence to the perspective that Semitic tribes had migrated and had settled into the farthest eastern shores of the Eurasian Continent.

1) That there were probably three (or more) identifiable "major" stocks of [nomadic] non-*Sinitic* people (in the context of the subsequent cultic history of Japan) coming into the archipelago during the period of (about the sixth or fifth to) the second century before the Common Era;

2) That (one of) the earliest were the people of *Ezo*, followed by the two later peoples who occupied the *Yayoi* and *Yamato* regions of central Japan (perhaps during the third or fourth to the second centuries before the Common Era);

3) But that these tribes may very well have been all related to the still earlier (Semitic) people in the Middle East; that the people arriving at *Izumo* district (called by the historians as *Yayoi*), and the people arriving a little later in Kyushu but subsequently moved northward to occupy the cenral plains region (called by historians as *Yamato*);

4) That the latter two had joined forces (perhaps during the last two centuries before the Common Era, during China's long Han dynastic period) and, by their more advanced cultural skills (including the knowledge of agriculture, of society and governing and, most importantly, the knowledge of effective warfare), created an united front to defeat the *Ezo*, forcing them to retreat to no-man's land in the extreme northern region of Japan.

Equally important, based on careful reading of *Kojiki* and *Nihon Shoki*, we can state with a measure of certainty that the *Yayoi* stock who had lived in the *Izumo* district were the people who brought the sun-worshipping cult, including the mythological legends of *Ame no Takama ga Hara* and the sun-goddess (*i.e.*, the chief priestess) *Amaterasu O-Mikami*, and established the *shinto* belief in Japan. That this *Yayoi* clan also created an early form of democratic governance of assembly of *kami* to discuss and implement rituals and rules of life of the people has also been acknowledged as a verifiable historical fact. For *Izumo*, as mentioned in the chronicles, was the site of the gathering of *"yayorozu no kami"*—eight million *kami*—i.e., the assemblage of all the chieftains from various tribes. It is also more than a possibility that these chieftains had all come from one or several home-bases in Korea. In other words, they were immigrants into Korea at still earlier times but later emigrated to Japan in an attempt to establish a nation uniquely their own. Having gone through and sojourned in Korea for several decades (as the ancient Israelites had wandered in the wilderness for forty years) or even as long as a century or two, these sojourners in Korea had no doubt absorbed much of both the cultural and ethnic elements of Korea. Still, never forgetting their migratory status or losing sight of the very purpose of their self-imposed exile, they would again gird up their loins and continue their journey toward the farthest eastern end of the land, toward the direction of the rising sun.[25]

It is one of the most significant passages in the Chronicles relating to the story of the *kami* of *Yayoi* submitting to the *kami* of *Yamato* all of its land and people. As briefly referred to earlier, the "historicity" of this story may be that it is an abbreviated and summary narrative in referring to an actual course of events leading to the merging of the two clans, the *Yamato* clan with superior warfare power, on one hand, and the *Yayoi* clan with a more established ritual and belief, on the other. Thus, it is not unreasonable to suggest that these two more recently arrived clans (as compared to Ainu and other arrivals) may have possessed some common cultural traits, even a cultic belief and ritual practice. For the narratives in the Chronicles suggesting that Korea was the common source of origin of both the *Yayoi* and *Yamato* clans is further substantiated by the narrative that when Emperor *Jimmu* arrived in Japan, a certain military general by the name of *Nigihayashi no Mikoto* had already been on the island of Kyushu, suggesting thereby that he was one of Jimmu's clansmen in Korea, that he was dispatched—as a front man—to scout the new frontier island. (Jimmu, the name which means a divine warrior or militant god, is not his personal name but, rather, a posthumous "political" title.) In the *kami*-era legends, *Jimmu* is described as the great grandson of *Ninigi*, this obviously as a way of establishing his legitimacy in the *imperial and ritual lineage*. At the same time, and unlike many other *kami*, Jimmu is regarded by most Japanese historians as the first historical—that is, human—military leader who eventually had unified and subjugated all other clans to form the first national polity, with himself as the first uncontested ruler of the land.

This series of probable historical events may indeed be regarded as the point which marks the founding of Japan as a unified and political cultural entity. That is, with the union of military power and religious authority, both *shintoism* and the throne were now firmly established. However, the writing of *Kojiki* and *Nihon Shoki* as the official chronicle did not become necessary because of any schism within *shintoism* or the imperial household. Rather, it became inevitable due to the rising religious conflict and competition for political power, caused by the introduction of a new faith: Buddhism.

Buddhism entered Japan in the fifth and sixth centuries, mainly from Korea. The new faith quickly gained converts who were ardent and dedicated, much more so than the *shinto* faithful who (even to this day) had no *mantra* to recite, no prayer beads to show their affiliation, and no ritual requisites to obey and follow. With the aid of holy writ and divine icons, Buddhism quickly gained a foothold and, soon, there were many followers. Hundreds of Buddhist temples were soon erected in the first capital city of Nara and then Kyoto, the second capital, and even the imperial family members had subscribed to the new faith and become converts. Among them was the most famous Prince Shotoku who relinquished his heritable right to the throne in order to follow the ways of enlightenment of Buddha.

But *shintoism* and the imperial throne possessed no tangible relics as a testimony of their religious and political lineage. It was in the face of this threat from Buddhism that the imperial edict was issued to create a holy writ of its own. The committing of the ancient oracles to writing even with fabricating the mythological lineage of *kami* using an alien script, became an urgent mandate. Thus was produced *Kojiki* and *Ninon Shoki* as the official chronicles, the absolute necessity for the survival of the imperial house and the preservation of the imperial cult of *shintoism*. The place of these chronicles may therefore be compared in historical importance not only to the *Pentateuch* and the other Old Testament books as a history of Israel as a nation and the story of their god, to serve as a declaration of their national and religious identity, but also to the declaration of a *constitution* at the founding of a political sovereignty (*i.e.*, that of the United States).

It is in this light of the need to affirm the authority of the imperial household that *sanpo*—the imperial regalia—was mentioned from early on and throughout the course of *Kojiki, Nihon Shoki* and *Kuji Honki.* The singular objective, of course, was to establish the credibility of *sanpo* as the indisputable *regalia* of the unbroken imperial lineage, beginning with the first ancestral *kami* of this *shinto* cult to Emperor Jimmu and all subsequent emperors. Historians agree on the perspectives that these chronicles and the mythology of *kami* had but with one central objective: to substantiate—by hook or crook—the claim of the imperial house that it only is the rightful inheritor of the sovereignty over the land and all its people.[26]

Meanwhile, a question in regard to the holy regalia still remains: why was the chest of receptacle called the "Replica of the divine *fune* (the boat or *ark*)" when the wooden chest resembled nothing like a boat? This also is at the core of the mystery.

CHAPTER TWELVE

THE *SHINTO* RITUALS
AND OTHER CUSTOMS

Besides the concerted assertion of the privilege of the imperial house and its unbroken lineage from *Amaterasu Omikami*, including also the reverence of all the *kami* of the imperial lineage and in nature, there is not much other doctrinal catechism or rituals of cultic requisite in the *shinto* belief. In fact, all *shinto* rituals that are performed today according to the officiating rules and calendar were established much later by the office of *shinto* rituals of the imperial household. It should be noted that, even today, the cost for maintaining the important *shinto* shrines in Japan is budgeted into and borne by the imperial household expenditure. During the feudal period in Japan's history, the districts of local *daimyo* (warlords) and the provinces of *shogunates* were also required to make annual "tithes" to help defray the costs associated with maintenance of and seasonal performance of rituals at the imperial *shinto* shrines. (This is reminiscent of the building of the Tabernacle and the Temple of the Lord in the history of the Israeli people, from the days of Moses down to King Solomon.) In turn, the imperial representatives, from the emperors down to the members of their household, would make offerings on behalf of the people as propitiation to the *kami* to bestow blessings of bountiful harvests of rice and protection from natural disasters and pestilence.

This, one of the most important of all *shinto* rituals, requires, even today, the very presence of the emperor, and is always performed at *Toyo-Uke Daijingu* (the great *jingu*—'sacred palace'—or shrine of "receiving of the '*toyo*'," *toyo* meaning 'bountiful,' almost always in reference to a rich harvest of rice), which is the *outer* building of the *Grand Ise Shrine*. It is worth special note that, in earlier times, one of the main ritual acts in this annual festival at *Toyo-Uke* Shrine was the scattering of rice over the postulating worshippers. This and other similar customs (such as the showering the newly-wed couple with rice as they emerge from the church now as husband and wife) can all be said to have their origin in the story of *manna* of the ancient Israelites, the "bread" falling from heaven to feed the hungry multitude during their wilderness wandering. And it may be well to remember that *manna* was a small white botanical substance. We shall consider the nature of the substance of *manna* later (*cf.* Chapter 17, the concluding paragraphs).

Earlier it was mentioned that the use of cypress or cedar wood was mandated in the construction of the Tabernacle and Temple, and the use of *hinoki* (Japanese cedar/cypress) for building all the *shinto* shrines as well as the chest for storing the *sanpo*. And we shall now note the scattering of rice in blessing the *shinto* faithful. If this *shinto* tradition of scattering rice over the faithful assembled in the courtyard of *Toyo-Uke* Shrine may seem a ritualistic reenactment of the legend of *manna* falling from the sky, perhaps it should be given another look and careful consideration, rather than summarily dismissing it as nothing more than a curious but isolated case of coincidence. For ritual symbols and gestures often possess a much deeper signification than may otherwise appear, for they are a part of the people's heritage that survives long after the original signification has been forgotten, especially when there is no written document to preserve the original ritual significance. It is well to remember, too, that both the ancient Israelites and ancient Japanese were illiterate people, not having had their own system of literacy, and when it was finally created, it came much later than the script system of their neighboring kingdoms; Israeli *versus* Egyptian, Babylonian, Assyrian or Phoenician, and Japanese, *versus* Chinese, Korean and Mongolian.

It is therefore of considerable interest to observe the following *shinto* festivals, to notice the extent of parallel features between *shinto* rituals and their Hebraic counterparts, and to consider that the extent of such close parallels may signify a relationship far beyond mere coincidence.

On July 17 every year, shrines in many cities of the Kanto (or Kwanto) district to Kansei (or Kwansei) district in Japan celebrate the summer festival called the *Feast of Gion* (pronounced with a *hard* G, as in *go* or *game*). The celebration lasts for a week, and the procession of *o-mikoshi* (literally translated to mean "the Divine Chest"; the word and etymological connotation, however, also signifies "the divine passing over" or *the passover of god*) is the central event which is the climax of the entire summer festival. Both the festival and more specifically the procession of *o-mikoshi* is also called *MiFune-matsuri*, the "feast (or celebration) of the Divine Boat."

The procession is one of the wildest festival scenes not only in Japan but perhaps in the world. In the procession, *the O-Mikoshi*—essentially a square box with ornamented roof (often with bird-like emblems perched on the roof-top, with its wings outspread)—is carried by four to eight (or more) young men (all *male*) wearing nothing but loin cloths and white headbands. These men neither walk in straight lines nor always forwardly but, rather, sway from side to side and forward and backward in most erratic ways, as if in the state of total stupor, all the while boisterously shouting "*wasshoi, wasshoi*" as they continue their wild procession. The crowd swells around, ahead and behind the *o-mikoshi*, swaying, dancing and shouting along with the men entranced with the spirit of *o-mikoshi*. The climax of the march of *o-mikoshi* would then come when these men wade into water (an ocean, lake, or river), still moving errati-cally but never capsizing the "ark" which they still carry on their shoulders. Western visitors observing the festival for the first time often express amaze-ment and total bewilderment over how and why the usually straight-faced and strict mannered Japanese men would behave in such a raucous and rowdy man-ner, particularly in a *shinto* festival supposedly solemn and with reverence.

Turning to the Old Testament, we read that Noah's ark came to rest on the top of the mountains of Ararat on the seventeenth day of July (*cf.* Genesis 8:3-4, *ff.*)—the same day of the Feast of Gion in Japan. We also recall the story of the procession of the ark of the Covenant when it was finally brought back to David's camp amidst wild pomp and circumstance. The procession of the ark must have been wild festivity, for the bible tells us that, when Michal—David's wife and the daughter of King Saul—saw her husband the king wearing only a loin cloth while "leaping and dancing" before (the ark of) the Lord and before all the people, "she despised him in her heart" (*cf.* II Samuel, 6:12-15; 16-23).

This same frenzied procession of the ark of the Covenant is vividly described by Hancock in his own eyewitness account of Apet ceremonies in Ethiopia, the Ceremony of the ark.

> "Here I found the reason for the curious stop-start, halting-lurching motion of the multitude. In the space ahead of the *tabot* [ark] several impromptu troupes of dancers had formed themselves … At the center of each of these groups was a drummer, his *kebero* slung around his neck, beating out an ancient and savage rhythm, whirling, jumping, turning and shouting while those around him exploded with energy, leaping and gyrating, clapping their hands, beating tambourines and cymbals, pouring with sweat as they capered and reeled.
> "Now, urged on by trumpet blasts and by shouts, by the thrum of a ten-stringed *begegna* and the haunting tones of a shepherd's flute, a young man … performed a wild solo dance while the priests stood

in their place stopping the eager crowd behind them and bearing
the sacred *tabot* aloft....
The youth seemed entranced. With all eyes upon him he circled the
pulsating *kebero*, pirouetting and swaying, shoulders jerking, head
bobbing, lost in his own inner rhythms, praising God with every limb,
with every ounce of his strength, with every particle of his being. And I
thought ... This was what it must have been like, three thousand years
ago at the gates of Jerusalem when
'David and all the house of Israel brought up the ark of the Lord
with shouting, and with the sound of the trumpet [and] played
before the Lord on all manner of instruments ... and David
danced before the Lord with all his might ... leaping and dancing
before the Lord.'"[27]

It is surprising to recognize that nearly every aspect of this celebration of the
Ethiopian festival of *Timkat*, also known as the Ceremony of the *ark* as well as
the Feast of *Zion* (more correctly pronounced as *Zee-on*), is reenacted nearly
verbatim in the Japanese festival of *Gion (pronounced Gee-on*, with **gee** as in
geese) celebrated all over Japan on the week of the seventeenth of July. It is well
to recall also that July 17th is mentioned in the bible as the day when Noah's ark
finally came to rest on the slopes of Mt. Ararat.

On new year's eve, Japanese in bygone eras (pre-twentieth century) celebrated the occasion with planting of greenery on the doorway, and with hanging of *coins* with *red taint (paint)* over the front door. The specific food items
served on new year's eve included *rice cake* made *without yeast* or any fillings,
and was served with (as many as seven different) *bitter herbs*. The new year in
the old Japanese *almanac* (or ritual calendar) falls in the month of March. (It
should be noted that March was the first month of a year in the ancient Near
East, the Greco-Roman Empire, and Europe until the Medieval period, and the
numbering of month sequence follows March. Hence, for example, the seventh
month of the year is called *Septe*mber, literally the "seventh" month counting
from March, and October the eighth, November the ninth and December the
tenth). Even today, the Japanese (and Korean) school year begins in the spring
(March or April). Also, new year's eve is called by Japanese as *o-misoka* which
literally means "the day of *crossing (the sea)*" or "the day of *passing over*."

Christians and Jews alike celebrate the Feast of *Passover* which falls in late
March (to April, within the month of the vernal equinox, the precise day being
determined by a ritual formula of Friday to Sunday after one *paschal* month—
full moon—after the day of the vernal equinox), which is familiar to mod-

ern people simply as Easter (Sunday). The traditional (*kosher*) food served at the Passover Feast includes *unleavened bread* (*without yeast*) and *bitter herbs*. For these two items were commanded by the Lord that the people "shall eat the ... *unleavened bread and bitter herbs*" on the eve of the Exodus (*cf.* Exodus 12:8). The people of Israel were also commanded to borrow *gold* and jewelry from their Egyptian neighbors and *paint their door posts with blood*. Blood (*red paint*) on the doorway, coins, unleavened bread (even the rice cake) and bitter herb, all these as symbolic requisites of the Passover feast, are the identical requisites of Japan's celebration of new year's eve (of the old calendar which is) in the month of March, coinciding with the period of the Passover—the first month of the Jewish year (of the *civic* calendar; *cf.* Exodus 12: 1-2). All of these are clearly narrated in Exodus (and elsewhere), that

> "The feast of unleavened bread you shall keep. Seven days you shall
> eat unleavened bread, as I commanded you, at the time appointed in
> the month [of] *Abib*; for in the month *Abib* you came out from Egypt."
> (Exodus 34:18-19)

It should be noted that the month of '*Abib* is the pre-exilic name for the month of *Nìsàn* (which is the later, post-exilic name for the period of March-April), the time of the Feast of Passover which is followed immediately by the Feast of Unleavened Bread.

There is a curious custom in the Feast of Unleavened Bread. As stated in Chapter 24 of Leviticus, the bread offered in the feast was to be eaten by the priest and his sons only. It would appear even more curious when one learns that, in Japan, a similar custom was observed until a not-so-too-distant past (before the World War II): The rice cake made without yeast and offered on *o-misoka*—the eve of the great passing over, that is, new year's eve—was to be eaten by the head of the household only.

The Book of Deuteronomy lists the three most important feast days in the Judaic calendar (*cf.* Deut.16:1-17, particularly verse 16): a) the *Feast of Passover* (March-April; the *civic* new year, in remembrance of the exodus from Egypt); b) the *Feast of Weeks* (mid-summer, for rejoicing and sharing, perhaps in memory of the thanksgiving rejoicing after Noah's ark came to rest on Mt. Ararat on July 17); and c) the *Feast of Booths* (harvest; thanksgiving and repentance; the *ritual* new year). Are these three not identical to the three feasts in the *shinto* calendar: a) the *O-Misoka* (new year "passing over" in March); b) the Feast of *Gion* (*Zion?*) (two weeks in July beginning on the 17th, featuring the wild procession of *O-Mikoshi*—an ark—wading into the water); and c) the emperor's annual blessing of rice and harvest in September, in the *gaiku* (outer shrine) of Grand *Ise* Shrine?

In the Judaic faith, cleansing is mandated not only with food but also in daily living. Observance of the sabbath, tithing, blessing of food (*kosher*), avoidance of unclean meat (*e.g*, pork) and, on the week of Jewish New Year (September) repentance and cleansing by sacrifice of the Paschal Lamb, *etc.* are all a part of ritual mandate.

In direct parallel, the rituals of cleansing—whether as formalized ritual acts or deeds in daily life—were of great importance to the Japanese. Nowhere in Asian countries is *furo*—the daily bath—as important as in Japan, and the sixteenth century Japanese regarded Western sailors and even the Jesuit priests as "unclean" and loathsome barbarians. (Until the end of World War II, Japanese also regarded Chinese as "pigs" because until then daily bathing was not a habit of common Chinese.) Until the period immediately preceding World War II, Japanese distanced themselves from eating pork, and thus abhorred Chinese with horror because they consumed coagulated blood (cooked in soup).

The ritual of cleansing was—and still is—the first act of reverence when a Japanese enters a *shinto* shrine. (This may be contrasted with the attitude and behavior of the faithful entering a Christian church or even Jewish synagogue; continuation of people's chattering shows little respect or no reverence to demonstrate any thought of being in the presence of god.) There, near the gate of *torii* is a small roofed stand where a well or water basin or an open bamboo pipe with flowing water is set for the faithful to wash their hands and rinse their mouth. In approaching the shrine and bowing the head in worship, the *shinto* faithful will clap their hands thereby expressing that "nothing lies between their heart and *kami*, that their mind is clean." And, on *o-misoka* (new year's eve), countless faithful would gather in the front courtyard of the shrine to perform the ritual of cleansing by wiping their body with a *kami*—which, here, has a double meaning as *paper* but also a surrogate *deity*, as in sacrificial lamb—and would then toss the paper figure into bonfire. The ritual signifies that *tsumi* (sin) or *yogore* (filth) of a person is being erased by *kami* through cleansing by burning. The eating of *unleavened rice cake* and *bitter herbs* also symbolizes an act of cleansing, here more of the spirit of repentance rather than for any special healthful diet.

In attending the *sumo*, the Japanese wrestling, Western visitors may have noticed and even wondered about a number of curious observables not seen in other sports events in Japan or elsewhere: One is the presence of *shinto* priests as officiating judge; second is the string of cut paper strips around the circular ground of contest; third is the wrestler's scattering of salt before each wrestling match. Little known to the Westerners (and perhaps many of the younger Japanese today), *sumo* is not a sports event in the usual sense of the term. Rather, it is reenactment of a mythological legend and, hence, a ritual, thus requiring the presence of an officiating *shinto* priest. The string of cut paper strips is a ritual symbol, a tie—a train—of *kami* (paper, but here, also signifying a boundary marked off by god) designed to ward off evil spirits. Scattering of salt also is for ritual cleansing of the ground on which the ritual of *sumo* is to take place.

These rituals in Japanese *sumo* find their literal counterparts in the Old Testament: It is in Jacob's wrestling with a deity (*cf.* Gen. 32:24-30; also see **Fig.** 12), and the scattering of salt (*e.g.,* in the temple or consecrated ground) as symbolizing a cleansing agent (*cf.* II King 2:19-22), to sanctify the ground of a divine encounter. Cleansing by water and by fire, or by any other ritual means, is inseparable from the *shinto* belief and the spirit of the people of *Yamato*. We are reminded again that cleanliness of both spirit and body is a mandated requisite for the Japanese people, whether in life or in death, in things great and small.

In reference to deities, Japanese would use the word "*hashira*" which literally means simply a column or pillar. Pillars—whether stone or wood—were found in Japan (and Korea) as the symbol of the dwelling or even the very presence of god (*cf. **Fig.** 13*). While this practice is not found in China, it is a parallel practice among the Semitic people. Indeed, there are so many references in the Old Testament, where stone pillars were erected to represent God or his dwelling place, or the place of his visit or to bear witness to an oath that had been given (*cf.* Gen. 28:12*ff*; 31:51*ff*; 35:6*ff*; Ex.23:24; Joshua 24:26*ff*; and Deut. 16:22, *etc.*). These stones are natural stones, and not carved stone images. For such will be regarded as the "graven images," an abomination to the Lord

In the immediate premises of a *shinto shrine*, the faithful would be hard pressed to see *kannushi*—priests. If a *kannushi* is spotted, he would be in his white priestly garb with a double-folded breast piece. In bygone eras, this priestly garb also had small bells attached to its sleeves or skirts. It may be amazing to note also that these distinctive features of double-breasted gown (often with small stones attached) and bells attached on the skirt of the priestly garb are the same also on the priestly robe of the Levites of the Israelis, the features which have been meticulously described in the Old Testament (*cf.* Exodus 39:9-11 and 25-26; also Exodus 28: 15*ff* for double-folded breastplate, and Exodus 28:33b-35 for bells).

Japanese respect of and steadfast regard for cleanliness is legendary, and this same regard for cleanliness is maintained also in their homes. Entering a Japanese house, even a dilapidated farm house, a visitor would first take off his shoes. This is not so much for keeping the house clean but, rather, an act of reverence, of not wishing to defile the *kami* of the residence, to keep it symbolically and ritually "clean." There is an unmistakable parallel between the act of taking off one's shoes when entering a house and the Lord's command that Moses must take off his shoes because he was standing on "holy ground" (*cf.* Ex. 3:5).

Indeed, when Japanese refer to their country as the *shinkoku* or *kami no kuni*—the country of *kami*, or the sacred land—it is not only in reference to the land which was given by and inherited from the *kami* of the mythological age but, more profoundly, to the land where everything—from a rock to a tree, from a brook to a mountain peak, from the cloud to the wind blowing through the pine branches—is *kami*, individually and collectively. This, also, is quintessential to *Yamato tamashii*.

Besides the ritual customs, many parallels in the folk customs of the Semitic and Japanese people, though perhaps of lesser significance when compared to the ritual customs, can also be observed. One is the custom of carrying a heavy load on the head. This custom of carrying a water barrel or farm produce burden on women's heads (but seldom on men's heads) is a common sight in rural Japan (and Korea) but not observed in China. Another is (or, was, until the end of World War II) the prohibition of a husband entering the kitchen area; the area for food and especially meat preparation was regarded as *unclean*. And men whose life obligation was to serve their godhead emperor must not be contaminated, by food, blood, or women. I recall that my mother never walked past above my head when I was lying in bed (*tatami*, or straw mat floor); for I as her son was dedicated for the emperor's service and should not be "subjugated" below woman, even my own mother. I am tempted to see a parallel attitude between the mother of a Japanese son dedicated to the service of their *kami* the emperor, and the mother of a Jewish son dedicated to the service of *their kami*, God Yahweh (*cf.* mother of Samuel the prophet).

FIGURES

FIGURE 1   The cover of Oyabe's book, featuring the seal of the *Star of David*.

FIGURE 2   The inspector's office seal and inscription of censor

ORIGIN OF JAPAN AND JAPANESE

By

Jenichiro Oyabe, M.A,PH.D.

頭山滿 大人題字
竹越與三郎先生序
小谷部全一郎著

日本及日本國民之起原

發兌

東京 出版圖書 厚生閣

FIGURE 3　　The inside cover of Oyabe's book showing the title and the author's
name in both (Chinese) ideograms and English.

FIGURE 4   The Star of David on Oyabe's book cover (enlarged to show the
                Hebrew script "*The Voice of God*")

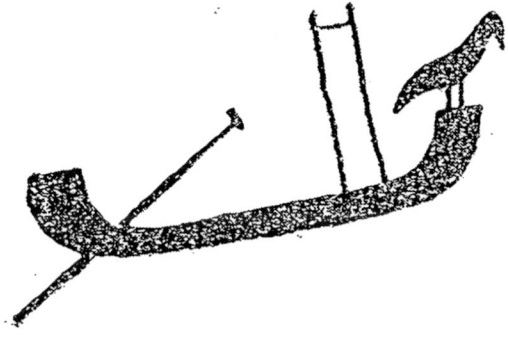

FIGURE 5   The "ark" and the "boat": A sixth century cave painting in
             Japan (Mezurashi Zuka, Fukuoka Prefecture), showing a
             large ship figure with shields and a large bird (a stylized
             icon) pitched atop, and the sun on the left of the bird figure
             (indicating the direction of the sea voyage?). The small ship
             below the sun (bottom figure, enlarged to show detail), with
             a bird figure on the ship's helm, resembles the funeral boat
             of ancient Egypt. (*Cf.* also FIGURE 19: *O-Mikoshi*, the "Divine
             Chest.") There is an intimate relationship between this
             and other cave art depicting ships and the shape of coffins
             unearthed from Japan's *kofun* (ancient tombs); the shape of
             coffins changed from the earlier ship-like to a more chest-like
             square form, from one reminiscent of the funeral boat to a
             more familiar chest-shaped sarcophagus of ancient Egypt.

FIGURE 6   The Grand *Ise* Shrine (The hall of the "holy of holies").
The shrine ground, fenced off with high wooden walls is
off limits to all visitors except the ministering priests, and
imperial entourage on special ritual-festival occasions.
Cf. also FIGURE 7

FIGURE 7   An aerial view of Ise Shrine, the *Naigu*—"Inner Shrine," which is equivalent to the Holy of Holies of Solomon's Temple, never approached by common visitors and outsiders.

FIGURE **8**   The *Izumo* Shrine, the most ancient of all Shinto shrines, at or near
the site where the earliest arrival of followers of the Amaterasu
cult is believed to have taken place on the shores of the Japanese
archipelago.

FIGURE 9   *Kagami* (ancient sacred mirror), one of the *sanpo* items.
Numerous such bronze mirrors of various sizes and shapes and
from different (mostly feudal) periods are reposited in the Shinto
shrines all across Japan.

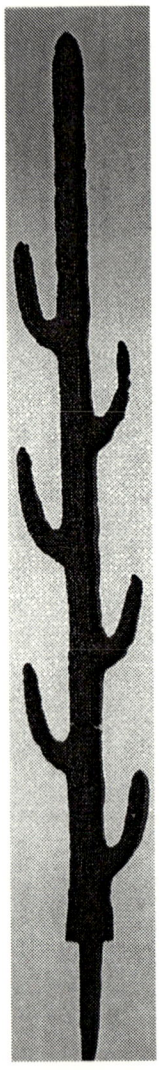

FIGURE 10   *Tsurugi* (sword), one of the *Sanpo* items. Here the figure shows the
'seven-branch' sword—the *Shichi-shi To*. Atsuta Shrine (Nagoya)
and Ishikami Shrine (Nara) are dedicated to (this) divine sword.
In both of these shrines are reposited also many swords from the
feudal eras, along with other 'divine' relics such as bronze mirrors of
various sizes from various periods.

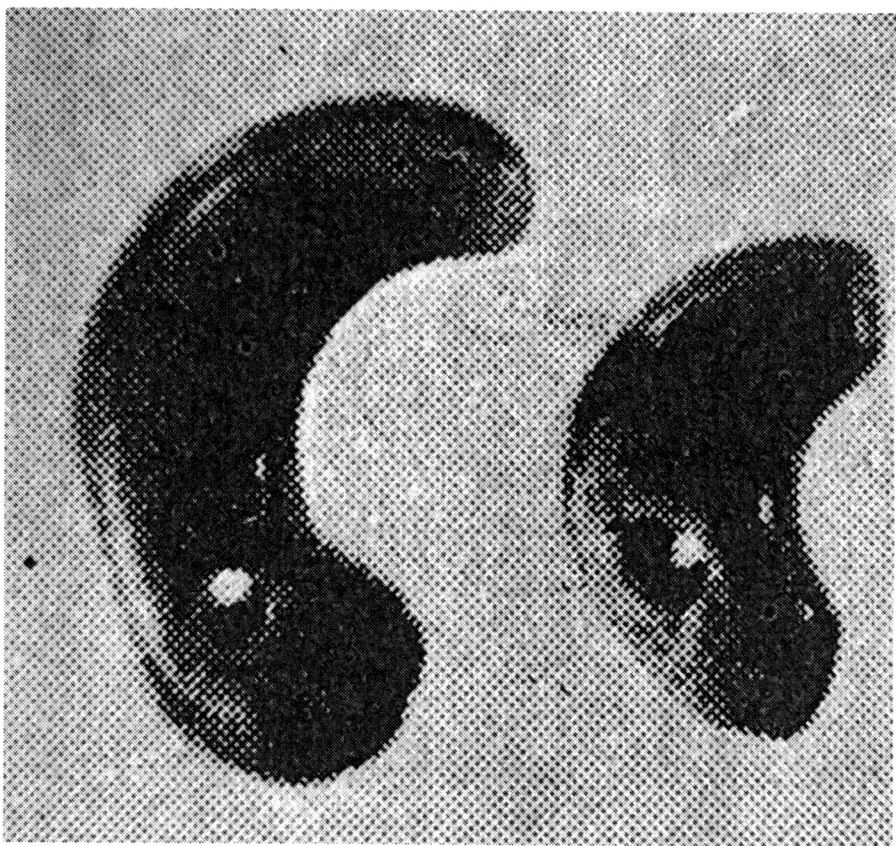

FIGURE 11   *Maga-tama* (crescent-shaped stones), one of the *Sanpo* items. Such crescent-shaped stones have been unearthed in great numbers from ancient tombs, indicating that they were ornamental of the people of high castes such as military and cult leaders.

FIGURE 12   *Sumo* wrestling (ritual wrestling): The drawing on the right shows the ritual vessel with two wrestlers (from Iraq, c. 2300 B.C.E). The picture on the left is from the Greek period, when wrestling became a popular sport and hence may or may not have carried ritual significance.

FIGURE 13   Pillar (stone) as memorial of divine visit or sacred
oath (covenant). The memorial shown here is from
(the southernmost region of) Korea, where there were
considerable cultural and commercial exchanges and
military engagements between Korea and Japan.

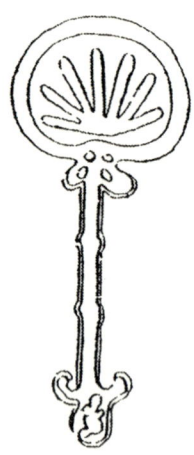  

FIGURE 14   *Menorah*, the *Tree of Life*, in various manifestations (*cf. **Fig**.* 10):
Shown on the center is the more familiar Jewish *menorah*. The
figure on the right is a 7th century B.C. Assyrian stamp seal.
The figure on the left is the 6th century cave painting in Kura-te
District of Fukuoka Prefecture in Kyushu Island, Japan; it shows the
figuration similar to the *menorah* figure that may be intended to
symbolize the *Shichi-shi To*, the "seven-branch sword" said to repose
in the Ishikami Shrine in Nara (*cf. Nazo no Nihon Tanjo*, p. 117). Cf.
also ***Figure*** 15.

FIGURE 15   The cave painting in Kyushu Island (*cf. **Fig.** 14*) dated to be from the pre-sixth century era. Framed by the two *menorah*-like figures are animals and a human figure in the costume (outline) which is identical with the mounted warrior clay figure found in abundant number from ancient tombs throughout central and southern Japan.

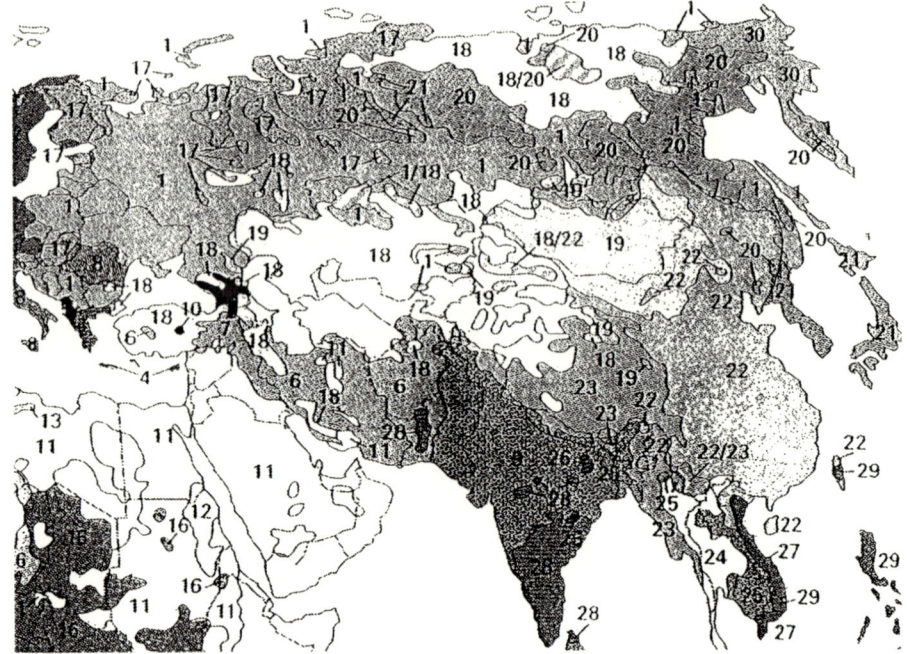

FIGURE 16   A map of World Language Distribution.
Notice the isolation of language No. 21, the "orphan language" (Japanese
Island and Korean Peninsula), alone with other unrelated surrounding
language. The nearest region where *language No.21* is found is in the
farthest northwest part of Central Asia. The origins of Japanese people and
its *proto language* (*i.e.*, No. 21) are traceable to at least seven distinctive
ethnic and linguistic lineages.

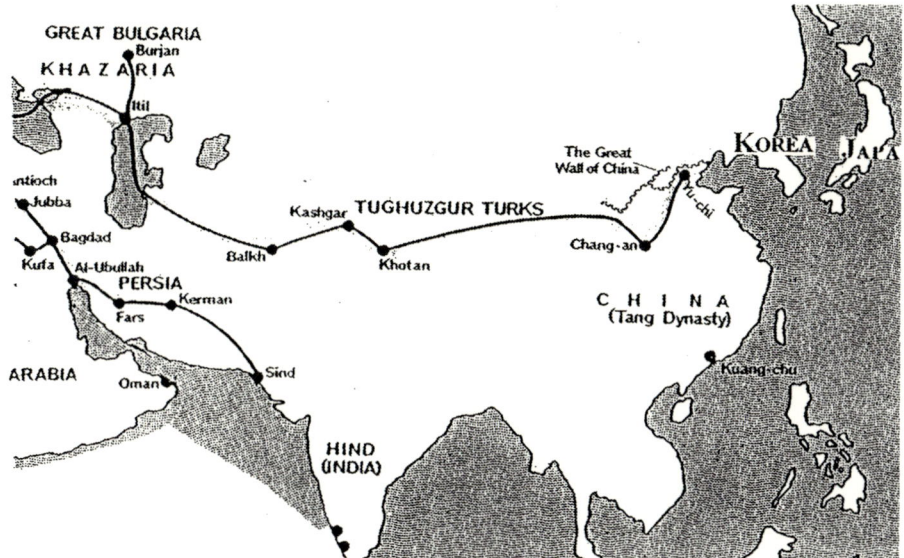

FIGURE 17   A *speculative* migratory route of Semitic tribe(s) from Palestine to
China, and (lines not shown) through Korea and, finally, to the Japanese
archipelago (to Izumo first and, later, to Kyushu). The route shown is
actually that taken much later by Jewish traders during the period of c. 800
to 900, C.E. However, the route was essentially the same general passage
taken by traders for at least a millennium before, and eventually became
the "official" *Silk Road* (the name coined much later) established during
the Western Han Dynasty, where both the Chinese and Romans had posted
garrisons to secure the first East-West communication "highway." This
also was the route believed to have been taken by Jewish refugees earlier,
following the Jewish revolt (against their Persian overlords) in the mid-
fourth century B.C.E.

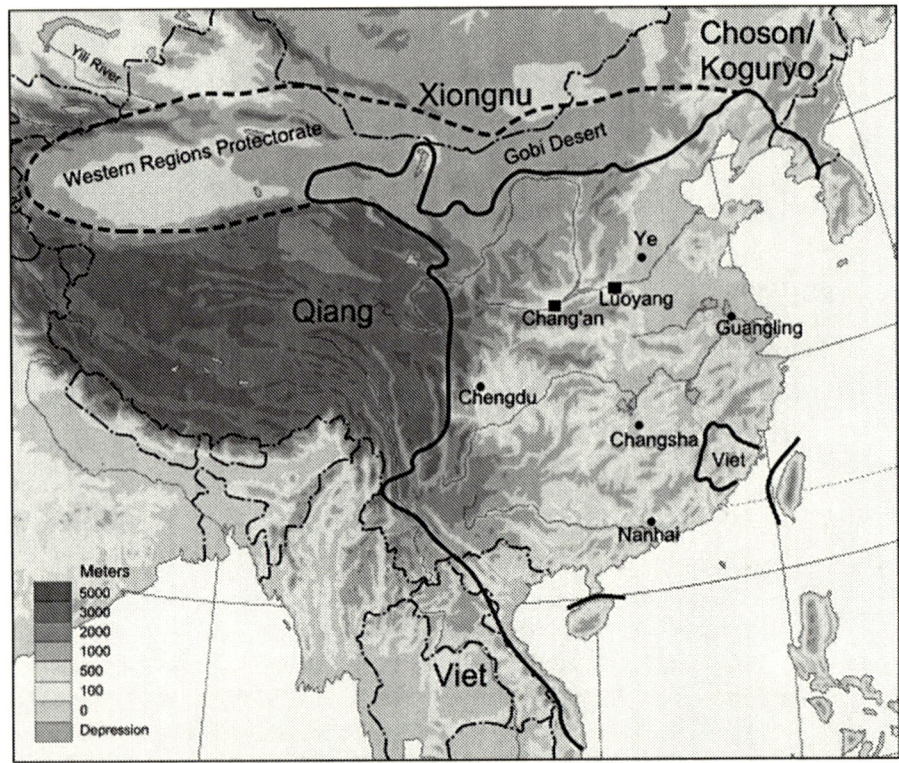

FIG. 18   The Map of Western Han Dynasty at Its Most Powerful Period, under
Emperor Wu (Han Wu Di). The dynastic boundary extended to include the
northern two-thirds of Korean Peninsula to the east, to regions bordering the
Black Sea to the west, the (present) Inner Mongolia and Qinghai Province
(China) to the north and northwest, and parts of Vietnam and Thailand to
the south. The vastly stretched east-westerly dimension of the Han dynastic
territory ushered in the period of unprecedented communication between
the far western and the far eastern regions of the Eurasian Continent, in
commerce, Political and military alliances, creating a relatively peaceable
landscape on the continent in the few centuries before and after the Common
Era. (The lower left inset map shows the boundary of Qin Dynasty which
preceded the Han Dynasty.)

FIGURE 19   A pre-World War II photo of the *O-Mikoshi* procession at the culmination of the *Festival of Gion* (Feast of Zion?). The festival and the O-Mikoshi procession are observed every July throughout Japan.

FIGURE 20   A parallel folk custom of Middle Eastern and Japanese women carrying loads on their heads. (The photo is from pre-World War II era, taken on Izu O-Shima (The Greater Izu Island).

FIGURE 21   The *Sengu* procession (the moving of *Ise* Shrine), from right
(previously built) to left (newly built). The next move, exactly
twenty years after the last, will be from left to right (to yet an-other
newly and identically built shrine).

PART THREE

IN SEARCH OF THE CLUE

CHAPTER THIRTEEN

On the Migratory Journey of the 'Tribe of Knife's Cult'

Between the Semitic world and the region of Far-East Asia, there lies the "heartland" of the Eurasian Continent, the greatest stretch of land mass in the world. This vast land covers the distance of about seven thousand miles, slightly shy of one-third of the circumference of the world at its widest (the equator). And the vast "middle" territory between these two westernmost and easternmost geographic and cultural regions is the still vast area of mostly unforgiving terrains broadly called Central Asia. This is the area which saw the greatest migration of various people and tribes in the ancient world, the territory which, today, is known as the Turkistan-Mongolian-Iranian plateaus and steppes. Even today, historians and anthropologists are still not altogether certain of how to decipher the enigma of the complex crosscurrents of ancient migratory movements in this stretch of land lying between the ancient Mesopotamian civilization and the Far-Eastern civilization.

One of the major studies on the history of tribal and ethnic migration and acculturation within the heart of the Eurasian Continent is *The Empire of the Steppes: A History of Central Asia* by René Grousset (*cf.* Bibliography; English translation by Naomi Walford). In the *Introduction* and Chapter One, Grousset devotes a considerable space in discussing the patterns and influences on the ethnic migration in Central Asia during the prehistoric and early historic times. One of the important insights articulated by Grousset particularly as related to the present study is that, in direct contrast to the ethnic migratory movements since the beginning of the Christian era which were from east to west,

> "In the [pre-]historic period, *the movements must have been more often in the opposite direction* [*i.e. from west to east*]," and that "one gains the impression that nomads of Iranian—that is,

151

Indo-European—stocks, called Scythians and Sarmatians by Greek historians and identified as Saka by Iranian inscriptions, must have penetrated a long way to the northeast, to the region of Pazyryk and Minusinsk, *while other Indo-Europeans populated the Tarim oases, from Kashgar to Kucha, Kara Shahr, and Turfan, perhaps even as far as Kansu* [province in the central plains of China].

> (Grousset, *The Empire of the Steppes:*
> *A History of Central Asia.* "Introduction"
> p. xxiii; *italics mine*)

Additionally, Grousset asserts the credible archaeological finds that testify to the fact that these same routes which were trekked by numberless and nameless tribes and ethnic peoples had been in existence from the long prehistoric past, much more ancient than we could imagine:

"The *first known Eurasian route is that of the northern steppes.* By this trail, *in paleolithic times*, the Aurignacian culture spread through Siberia … and *thence into northern China.*

"… In *the neolithic period*, and more precisely toward its close, the Siberian steppe route was also the route by which comb ware (*i.e.*, pottery decorated by "combed" lines) found its way into Asia … *so gradually influenced the proto-Chinese ceramics of the Ch'in-chia-p'ing in Kansu* [province, central western China].

> (p. 3, Chapter I, Sec. 1,
> "Early History of the Steppes";
> *italics mine*)

All this gives evidence to the fact that the history of ethnic migration in Central Asia was far more colorful than the arid and rugged landscape suggests, and probably more dramatic than—or at least as dramatic as—the processes of acculturation in other regions of the ancient world. For, in spite of its unforgiving terrain and climate change and, no less dangerous, with the ever-present threats from roaming bandits and warring tribes, the peoples in the western regions of the Eurasian Continent had become aware of, and made attempts to reach, the land in the "far east," the land where there was a promise or even just a hope of more peaceable and abundant life. This desire—or need—to open the earliest East-West communication route was instigated, from at least three millennia, B.C.E., by the tales of silk in the farthest north-east-east of the "known world," the rarest of commodities which was valued in its weight in gold. Hence, as Grousset would describe in *The Empire of the Steppes*,

> "This route of the steppe by the desert gave a particularly decisive turn to the history of the Tarim basin, in what is now Chinese Turkistan … this area acquired the urban, commercial character of the oases of the caravan routes and, by the chain of these oases, formed a line of communication between … the West—those of the Mediterranean world, of Iran, and of India—and that of the Far East, namely, China. A double trail was laid in a double curve north and south of the dying Tarim River; the northern route ran through Dunhuang, Hami, … the Fergana basin, and Transoxiana; the southern, by way of Dunghuang,…. the Pamiar valleys, and Bactria. This slender dual thread that crosses the desert and peaks by turns, frail as a winding, long-drawn-out line of ants moving crosscountry, was strong enough nevertheless to ensure that our planet [the Eurasian Continent in particular] should consist of a single world and not of two separate ones, and to maintain a minimum degree of contact between the anthill of China and the Indo-European anthills. It was the *Silk* [*Routes*] and the road of pilgrimage, along which traveled trade and religion [and migration of countless ethnic tribes], the Greek art of Alexander's successors and Buddhist missionaries from Afghanistan. By this route the Greco-Roman merchants mentioned by Ptolemy struggled to obtain access to the bales of silk from [China], and Chinese generals of the second [or the Western] Han dynasty sought to establish communication with the Iranian world and the Roman Orient. The maintenance of this great route of world commerce was, from the Han to Kublai Khan, an age-long principle of Chinese policy.
> (*Introduction*, pp. xxii-xxiii)

It is not difficult to picture how painstakingly slow these ancient migrations must have been. Unlike population shifts from war-ravaged lands, or the forced exodus (*e.g.*, of the ten lost tribes of Israel from Jerusalem to Babylon or the Hebrites returning to the land of their ancestors after World War II), these bands of vagrant people *had* to move steadily but very slowly, for the sake of the children, women and the aged among them. We are indeed all too familiar with the story of the Israelites wandering in the Sinai Desert, yet we may not fully appreciate how and why it took the vagrant people forty years to travel across the relatively short distance. It was due primarily to the need to survive the journey while still remaining as one people. To do so, it was necessary that they would negotiate the unfamiliar terrains and climates but also to adopt and conform with the life style of the host tribes along the journey, even by subscribing to their religious beliefs. As Grousset narrates,

> "In some instances these alternating movements [of ethnic and tribal migration] took centuries to complete owing to the vast distances involved, to which everything about these people—their physical build and their way of life—had become adapted. Of these unceasing wanderings between the Yellow Rive [north-central Chinese plains region] and Budapest [Asia Minor], history ... had retained but little, and then only such events as affected themselves."
>
> (p. xxiv)

There, in the heartland of China, is a Jewish community, in the city of Kaifen, on the banks of the Yellow River. Known to local Chinese by the notoriety of their practice of "the cult of knife" (*i.e.*, circumcision), these people, in all appearance are now indistinguishable from the locals, could still recite the *Torah*. These remnants of the "wandering Jews" from an unknown past, may have lost all the outward features of their original ethnic identity, for, through the long journey, they had "successfully" adapted themselves to customs, costumes, language, and physical features, quite possibly by intermarrying. Yet they are still unmistakably Jew, with their religious belief and practice. We shall examine in a greater detail in the next chapter the transient journey of this itinerant tribe through the heartland of China.

I remember that, even as a child, I had wondered why the ancient Japanese—the personages in the *kami* mythology and especially the armies of Jimmu Tenno (Emperor Jimmu, the first historical leader/emperor of Japan, though the name is fictitious)—were always portrayed in children's books as wearing baggy clothes with waistbands over loose slacks which, in turn, were tied with ropes around their knees and ankles, as if readying for horse riding. And men were nearly always depicted as heavy bearded. It is from reading historical works such as that of Grousset that the portrayal of ancient Japanese people finally became meaningfully enlightening:

"… the steppe is the land of the horse. the man of the steppe is a horseman born. Whether an Iranian of the west of a Turko-Mongol of the east, it was he who invented the *riding dress … substituting trousers for robes.*"

(p. xxvi)

For "… the *northern nomads*—whether of Iranian stock like the Scythian or of Turko-Mongol like the Huns—*lived their steppe life on horseback*, engaged in chasing herds of deer or wild asses and watching wolves hunt antelope over the boundless plains …"

(p. 12)

And these people were "*bearded* [and wore] *roomy garments—tunic and wide trousers—common to the Saka and to their Median and Persian cousins.*"

(p.7)

This historical-anthropological explanation of the role of animal hunting also helps to shed light on the strange animal figures in the otherwise ritualistic cave painting in Kura-te District (Kurate *Gun*) of Fukuoka Prefecture in Kyushu, (the large southern island of) Japan, depicting two *menorah* figures framing the animal and human figures. Could this not be an image or remembrance of ritual incantation for a good hunt in the wilds of the steppes of Central Asia? Indeed, animal motifs occupy a uniquely prominent place in ancient Japanese legends and mythological tales; the depiction of lions and other animals which are not native to Japan appears in drawings and on military helmets, as well as in many encounters in *kami* stories (*i.e.*, in *Kojiki*). It is worth noting that Kyushu and Fukuoka Prefecture is where the legends have it as the location of the descent (arrival) of Emperor Jimmu, the first identifiable human emperor and military leader of Japan.

During this long period of wandering, the migrant tribe would absorb the lifestyle, religion, and even the language of the other people along the way. Whatever their original tongue, the decades or even a century-long coexistence with the peoples of Central Asia would alter their "mother tongue" to the extent that the resultant language may have become what modern linguists would regard as an "orphan language"—possessing similar linguistic features but fundamentally different and unidentifiable with any major linguistic lineage. On this, Grousset further comments that

"Modern linguists believe that the Scythians should be classified as an Iranian people—an Indo-European family, of the Indo-Iranian or Aryan group. [However,] their way of life was very similar to that of the Hunnic tribes of Turko-Mongol stock which ... became active at the other side of the steppes, on the borders of China.
(pp. 7-8)

In other words, complex crosscurrents and continuous acculturation of these tribes, in languages, beliefs and cultural elements, including garments and rides, produced yet another unique cultural entity. Grousset cites a particularly elucidating example of cultural imprint on a migratory tribe:

"... it is very probable that it was during the wanderings across Western Asia in the seventh century [B.C.E.] that the Scythians completed their transition from the bronze to the iron age ...
"There is irrefutable evidence of the direct influence exerted by Assyrian-Babylonian Mesopotamia on the first Scythian works of art: the iron and gold ax of Kelermes in Kuban (from about 6th century B.C.E). *This ax displays the old Assyro-Babylonian—and Luristanian —theme of two ibexes standing about the tree of life, together with some fine deer.*
(Grousset, pp.11-12)

The imprint of *mithraism* of the Persian folk cult that could possibly be detected in the names of *kami* and features of *shintoism* has been discussed. There, the possible connection of the name of the great Sun-goddess *Amaterasu,* the most revered of all *shinto kami* and its phonetic similarity with the sun-goddess (or priestess) of *Mithras,* has been mentioned. Such similarity goes beyond the mere phonetics of the two names of the divinity personages; in beliefs and in rituals, there are also parallels. If indeed an itinerant Semitic people carrying a ritual regalia of the ark, the chest of promise, on their long migration which may possibly have taken decades or even a century or more, across the vast stretch of Central Asia, would it not be possible that imprints of much earlier cultic practices and beliefs be found among the more recent posture and symbolism of *shintoism*? In other words, are there other remnants of cultic and cultural imprints of ancient Central Asian people still detectable on this itinerant tribe which is now beholden to the *shinto* cult?

Indeed, there are. First, we will begin tracing the possible cultural lineage by examining the ancient Hittites who had established one of the most powerful empire in the early centuries of the second millennium, B.C.E. This Hittites were a Semitic people who also had numerous historical interactions with the Israelis who were a cultural latecomer.

The bible relates that Abraham had lived among the Hittites, and dealt with them in acquiring a piece of land for the burial of Sarah, his wife. Esau also had a share of his life with the Hittites: he took in two Hittite women for wives. The Hittites (also known as *Hatti* to biblical writers, and *Khatti, Khitta* or *Kheta* to others, *e.g.*, Egyptians, after the name of the earlier inhabitants of the land) had once established a powerful empire, occupying the land in the present Asia Minor (the area northeast of the Mediterranean Sea and south of the Black Sea), and had established a considerable cultural monument (*e.g.*, writing and architecture, civic law and government system). After flourishing for some six centuries, the kingdom of the Hittites declined, invaded by armies from the west (Israelites?) and forces coming from the sea (*i.e.*, the Mediterranean), and the Hittite people scattered. Since then, Hittites became "mixed" with Amorites and Jebusites, and one stock came to live in the area later called Jerusalem. In biblical patriarchal times, the "Hittites of Canaan" were inhabitants in the district of Hebron, Judah, and it was there that Abraham had sojourned among them. Later, Hittites suffered greatly when David eventually overtook the fort, and renamed it (rather ironically) the "City of Peace" ("Jeru-*salem*") as well as for his own vainglory (the City of David). Still, among the generals of David's armies were a number of Hittites; the most famous being Uriah the Hittite who, evidently, was a Jerusalemite. The narrative in the Second Book of Samuel (Ch. 11) tells the story of Uriah's misfortune of having a beautiful wife who lived in a house near King David's court, far too close for comfort, so much so that the king appropriated Bathsheba, Uriah's wife, and sent the hapless husband into battle to die.

To the present study, however, the more important aspect of Hittite culture is the fact that there are so many aspects of its religion which bear curious parallel with the beliefs of *shinto* and the mythology of its *kami* (gods). Situated in the bordering land of Central Asia, the Hittites in Asia Minor possessed a religion that was also uniquely different from the monotheistic religion of the Israeli people. This is due, no doubt, to the fact that Sumerians, Hittites, Assyrians, Babylonians and Persians had occupied the same region of the land northeast of the Mediterranean Sea and southeast of the Black Sea. To wit, "Hittite" (variously known; such as Khatti) was also the name Syria and Assyria was referred by. The more notable parallels and similarities listed below should serve as a sufficiently persuasive testimony in evidencing the more than probable historical relationship between the Hittite religion and the Japanese *shinto*:

FIRST, among Hittite deities, the weather god and sun *goddess* were the chief divinities. This was (and is) true also in *Shintoism*. While universally the sun was always represented by a male deity, it was deified as the most revered goddess in Hittite and *shinto* religions. (This also was true with mithraism of Persia, where the sun was administered by *priestesses*.)

SECOND, the Hittite pantheon recognized all "possible gods," domestic and foreign, a thousand gods. On important political events and ritual occasions, these myriads of gods were summoned to bear witness. This summoning of thousands—even "eight thousand"—of gods was a part of the ritual practice in Japan from time immemorial, and the summon was announced by the call to the "*ya-yorozu no kami*"—literally eight thousand gods.

THIRD, one notable feature regarding the Hittite deities is their polysyllabic names, some as long as over half a dozen syllables in a single name. This feature is also true of nearly all the original names of *kami* (gods) in shinto mythology (as in *Kojiki*). It should be noticed also that so many Hittite deity names close with a particular consonance—"*sh*"—or its variant or similar phonemes such as ji, gi, ni, *etc*. This, too, is true with many *kami* names in *shinto* mythology. Specifically, so many *shinto kami* names end with "-*NUSHI*" (meaning "lord"). For example, the first three names to be mentioned in ***Kojiki***, the "trinity" who had opened the heaven and earth are called by the following names: AME-NO-MINAKA-*NUSHI*; TAKAMI M*USUHI*, and KAMI-M*USUHI*. (For names of Hittite deities with similar phoneme endings, see below.)

FOURTH, while the similarity or even a virtual identity in the phonemes of the deity names in the Hittite and *shinto* religions is duly noted, the similarity between the names of the sun-goddess must be recognized as possessing a far greater significance. For the sun goddess ruled supreme and commanded the greatest of reverence in worship, and the name itself is regarded as holy and invariable (unchangeable):
the name of the Hittite sun-goddess is: ***Mezzullash***,
the name of the *shinto* sun-goddess is: (A-)***Matelasu***
In further examining the aspect of phonemes of the name of deities, the final syllable of the names of the following Hittite weather gods may also be noted :
god Ne***rig***; god Khattush***ashi***; storm god Telepi***nush***, and
god ***Inarash*** (who was related to god Âl*ash* and goddess Al*âsh*).
On the parallel of other phonetic endings between the Hittite and *shinto* deities such as "-*gi*," "-*ji*" and "-*mi*," one only needs to recall the two *shinto* mythological names of great importance: Izana*gi* and Izana*mi* (the brother-sister deities).

FIFTH, the faithful of the Hittite religion also worshipped gods—or spirits—of the Heavens, the Earth, mountains, rivers, wells, winds and clouds. This also was—and still is—an identical posture of *shinto* and the attitudes of its faithful. As mentioned, the word *kami* refers to not only *shinto* deities but also any person or thing, animate or inanimate. Hence, as there was in the Hittite religion even a deity of fields and fruits (named Khalkish—notice the phonetic ending "*ish*"), so do Japanese people. In other words, Mesopotamian deities, the numerous *nature deities* in the Hittite pantheon, seem always to find their worthy counterparts—or "siblings"—in the myriads of *kami* in *Shinto* religion (as named in *Kojiki*). It is here that the lineage of personification of nature *kami* in *shinto*'s belief in nature *Kami* can be traced to its possible original source—in the divinities in the folk cult of Sumeria-Babylonia: heaven god, earth god, sea god, moon god, god of underworld (as related to goddess *Ish*tar and war god *Ish*khara, *etc.*).

SIXTH, among the chief features of Hittite rituals, purification by water and fire, and human or animal sacrifices ranked as the most important. In this regard, many connections with and borrowings from Babylonian religious beliefs can be established. Then we note that these features are identical with those in the *shinto* rituals. Purification by water, as has been noted previously, is the absolute requisite in entering a *shinto* shrine. On the other hand, while animal sacrifice is nearly a universal religious custom, human sacrifice is not, and this latter is a distinguishing feature in the Hittite religion as well as *shinto* ritual. To wit: one cannot help being amazed by the frequency of ritual and sacrificial deaths mentioned in the *Kojiki* narratives. Even as late as the feudal period, human sacrifice was deemed necessary and honorable in appeasing gods of nature (mountains, volcanoes, rivers, seas), and ritual sacrifice of humans was often required on completing the building a new castle, or constructing a major bridgeway. (It may be noted—aside—that the phrase "My fair lady" in the children's ditty "*London Bridge is Falling Down*" was originally in reference to (but later suppressed) the legends that the fair maiden who was sacrificed to ensure the safety of the bridge—by burying her alive under the bridge—was, alas, rumored NOT to be a virgin. The angry River god would certainly not accept such a defiled offering, and the bridge is therefore not guaranteed and thus was "falling down.")

This same spirit and concept of *shinto* human sacrifice was manifest in so many incidents found in the pages of Japanese history, with the final page in the closing months of the World War II, in the infamous *kami-kaze* whose youthful pilots gladly and honorably gave their lives for their emperor *Arahito-gami*—god *Kami* in human form (as in "Emmanuel").

And, finally, although not a religious perspective, a reference should be made on an aspect of "cultural temperament" which, in this writer's view, may be seen as an ethnic *persona* of the Japanese people. It is an appearance of "lax" social code of sexual conduct. Linguistic anthropologists of Hittite history have noted that there is a markedly lax attitude toward sexual crime and sexual "impropriety" of its citizenry, in otherwise stringent civic and government laws of the ancient Hittites. The Hittite Empire of the second millennium B.C.E was among the earliest to create a system of writing (cuneiform), and the archeological finds have provided sufficient evidence to indicate that the Hittite society was among the most developed of the ancient Mesopotamian civilizations, equal in many respects with the Egyptians and Babylonians of the contemporaneous period. Yet, in the area of their laws regulating sexual conduct, Hittites were obviously—that is, being noted as—*lascivious*.

This fact seems also to provide a secondary perspective to support a possible cultural connection between the ancient Hittite people and the people of Japan. The civil laws in Japan, as in its neighboring nations such as China and Korea, were most stringent from its earliest history. This, no doubt, reflects the wholesale subscription of the legal system of the ancient dynastic period of China (from the Han to the Tang-Song eras). That is, Japan and Korea had not only adopted the entire legal system of the Chinese society, but also subscribed to China's system of government and education, art and literature, as well as social code of ethics and morality (*e.g.*, Confucianism). It would seem strange, therefore, that, in regard to codes of conduct between man and woman and the penal codes on sexual misconduct, Japan has been—and still is—decidedly lax.

Soon after arriving in Japan, Francis Xavier, the first (Jesuit) missionary to the Far East, had noticed the abominable sins of the Japanese people. The abominations that Xavier had named were all *carnal* sins: infanticide (especially same-sex twins, believed to be the reincarnation of double-suicided same-sex lovers) sodomy (same-sex affairs), polygamy (including harboring of mistresses), and the like. And Xavier was most unreserved in uttering his condemnation, on the street corners and even in the presence of *daimyos* (warlords). (It was said that the reason Xavier was never condemned to immediate death for his rude behavior and outbursts was due to his wholly unintelligible Japanese, and the *daimyos* regarded his demeanor curious, even comical, and dismissed his wild mannerism.)

When this writer was in Tokyo for some six weeks over two decades ago, he was struck by signs everywhere of society's permissive attitude toward sexual promiscuity; in publication, in provocative graffiti "posted" in public and not so public places, in such graphic detail that would make even the most free-spirited youths of the Western hemisphere blush. And when one realizes that this sort of depiction of—and invitation to—the "affairs of the chamber" was not a modern, postwar phenomenon, but had been a trait of Japan's collective *persona* for many centuries, through all the feudal periods, as so graphically depicted in the 'underground' *ukiyo-e* (pictures of "floating world"), one could not help but wonder if this is not a reflection of an aspect of "ethnic tempera-ment" of the Japanese people, as it also was of the ancient Hittites.

It is worth mentioning that, in the ancient world, many religious beliefs and cultic practices contained implicit and explicit sexual elements. The amaz-ingly—even shockingly—explicit reliefs of Hindu temple grounds graphically portraying numerous sexual coupleting positions are but one of the more explicit manifestation of ancient Middle-Eastern and Central Asian religious practices. And while the "orthodox" Jews regarded such practices as abomina-tion, the existence of the business of temple prostitution in Egypt, Greece and Palestine (*e.g.,* Jerusalem) has long been known to scholars. Indeed, there are biblical references to support the opinion that practices of such abominable heathens were already a part of Temple worship in Jerusalem before the *dias-pora*. It is well recorded that Kings David and Solomon yielded to the demands of thier many foreign wives and erected temples for the worship of foreign gods. This is clearly inferred in the writings of prophet Ezekiel. Although writ-ing in Babylonia as a captive, Ezekiel saw in his visions horrendously profane practices even in the holy of holies in the Temple. In Chapter 8, Ezekiel makes mention of Jaazaniah (v. 11, who had offered incense to idols in Jerusalem), of "women weeping for Tammuz" (v. 14, Tammuz is the Greek god Adonis and associated with Aphrodite and thus, by inference, to a phallic cult; *cf. Scoffield* Bible commentary note), and of "their faces toward the east; and they wor-shipped the sun toward the east" (v. 16, in reference to nature worship).

There is no doubt that the displaced Hebrites in Babylon and Persia had come to subscribe to such practices which, although abominable to Yahweh, were common among the people of Central Asia. And it is precisely in these aspects also that we identify common threads in the cultic practices of Hittites worship of *Mezzullash*, Persian worhip of *Mitras* or *Mithras*, the Roman *Helios* rituals, and the Japanese *shinto* worhip of *Amaterasu*: the worship of sun and nature, the dominance of priestesses, sexual overtones in the cult, and in names of their deity.

It must be added in haste here that this association of laxity of moral code and thus the appearance of the society's collective posture of condoning sexual promiscuity notable in ancient Hittite culture and observable in the traditional Japanese culture is not in any way an ethical or moral judgment (as it was from the harsh lips of Xavier). This, in fact, is a phenomenon common to all ancient societies where fertility rites were an essential part. In ancient agrarian society, people believed that cosmos was controlled by forces of *ying* and *yang*, or female and male, and the *union*—in other words, the *copulation*—of male and female, was a ritual representation of procreation of life and all the products therein. Therefore, this belief was so graphically manifested in all the likes of Hindu temples. Recently, this author had observed the same graphic representation of sexual acts—some in what may be regarded as outlandish postures—in the terra cotta figurines of the ancient Incas in Andean mountains. Thus an appearance of sexual laxity is another point among the many curious parallels and similarities found in this study between the religious and ethnic-cultural attitudes of ancient Hittites and the (modern) Japanese, the parallels and similarities that are far too deeply and broadly based to be dismissed simply as another feature in a long series of most curious coincidences.

CHAPTER FOURTEEN

IN THE FULLNESS OF TIME:
THE *SECOND EXODUS* TOWARD *NEW CANAAN*

When King Cyrus defeated the mighty armies of the Babylonian Empire and founded the Persian Empire, he adopted a kindlier posture toward the people displaced from Palestine. Eventually, Cyrus not only allowed the captured Israelites to restore worshipping of God Yahweh but also allowed them to return to Jerusalem, now within the new and vast Persian Empire, and to rebuild the ruined Temple. However, in this *Second* Temple, and in spite of the repeated call for its search and return, the ark of the Covenant was never recovered.

To be sure, the history and chronology of the Jewish *diaspora* (*i.e.* dispersal) was far more complex than what the above statements imply. For the remnants from the diaspora into Babylon and Persia were not always submissive, as, for example, history records that the Jewish populace had revolted against Persian authority. Such unrest among the dispersed people would certainly have caused internal strife, and subsequent to the diaspora might be waves of both westward and eastward to northeastward migrations, the latter to the regions beyond the Caspian Sea. Perhaps a brief summary of various stages of the notable diaspora may be appropriate here to provide a general geographical context for understanding how the divided or at least not-wholly concerted migrations of the Hebrew tribes took place during the Persian Empire, with the probability of some of them migrating eastward and, traveling through the China plains region, eventually arriving as far as the Japanese archipelago.

First, the early diaspora following the Assyrian and Babylonian conquests in 772 and 586 founded settlements in Antioch, Aleppo, Pethor and Haran to Halah and along the Euphrates down to Mahoza and Cutha, Babylon and Sura, to the eastern banks of the Tigris, in the cities of Nineveh, Resen, Calah and Ashur.

After the Jewish revolts in Persia in 359 to 338, the Jews (were) further dispersed in two main directions: one to the [mountainous] regions [west] of the Caspian Sea, the other further down southeastward from the Tigris River, to Susiana and beyond.

The later fourth century B.C.E. period saw the demise of the Persian Empire and, contemporaneous with the eastern conquests of Alexander the Great (ended in 323), the rise of the Roman Empire. It is during this period of a century or so after the beginning of the eastern conquest of Alexander, that the first great *international* power in the Far East rose up: the Western Han Dynasty (206-88 B.C.E.). And it was during the reign of Emperor Wu Di (the fifth emperor of Western Han) that communication "highways" between China and all the lands and political powers of Central Asia, the Middle East, and West—the Roman Empire—were established (see below).

(It is noteworthy also the fact that the Jewish diaspora did not stop after the revolt. After a relatively short period of inertia, another wave of eastward Jewish migration took place between 200 and 100 C.E. (*i.e.* AD). It was during this later period of diaspora lasting as long as a milennium that resulted in many Jewish traders from Turkistan and refugees from Persia to settle in China and the outlying regions. By 1200, many towns in China had small Jewish communities, and historians believe that many of these had certainly been founded over five centuries earlier. Even Marco Polo had noted in 1286 that there was a strong commercial and political influence of the Jewish communities in China. However, by 1650, the Jews in Kaifen—which, by the late nineteenth century, there were only about 200 families left, still clinging to the Jewish heritage— were the only surviving Jewish community in the entire China.)

It is safe to assume that not all the descendants of the first diaspora into Babylon who later lived under Persian rule were restless, scheming to return either to Jerusalem or to seek yet another new "home"-land. After a prolonged period of captivity, many Israelites have become relatively comfortable living "among strangers" and, equally probably, chose not to return westward to the land of Judah, to a life of uncertainty and turmoil. (As it was during the first Exodus, when on many turns of events the Israelites murmured and outwardly complained about life in the wilderness, wishing rather to have remained in Egypt for a life of relative comfort and security.) For those who chose to remain in and under the new and kindlier rulers of Persia, they too were allowed some freedom to practice their old religious belief.

It was under such condition and environment, as this study proposes, that the old Hittite belief (in the sun goddess *Mezzullash*) was gradually morphosed into one which would also accommodate elements of the Persian folk cult of (sun goddess) *Mithras* and, thereby, eventually creating the mythology of (what eventually was written into *Kojiki* as) *A-Materasu*. Whatever the persuasion of the newly fathomed cult, the followers of this belief possessed—or, more likely, concealed in their midst—the secret holy relics from the ark of the Covenant, now stored in a *replica* of the holy Chest of Witness—the *ark*, which continued to serve as the enduring witness to the fidelity of their heritage. This *Replica of the Holy ark*, the chest, is *Mi-Fune Shiro*.

If this scenario has some validity, then it begs the question as to why this tribe, living in relative comfort for a considerable length of time, would now decide to take up a journey into the wild and uncharted unknown, to begin— as it were—the second exodus.

In the late fourth century B.C.E., there arose in the west of Persia one of the greatest empires in human history—the Hellenic/Roman Empire. The Roman armies overthrew the Persians in 331 after the most devastating battles. And the new ruler proved to be as cruel as the Babylonians. The Israelites were once again treated with life worse than a second-class citizen, and their religious freedom was fundamentally threatened. For the new rulers had exhorted their new gods over all other gods.

It was during this same general period from the late fourth through the next century or two (*cf.* to the Jewish revolt against the Persians as mentioned earlier), it may be surmised, that this tribe of the Replica of the ark of Witness had taken up another exodus, in order to be as far away as possible from the Persians and the new Roman Empire, moving into mountainous plateaus and steppes. Here, it worth noting: in the aftermath of the failed revolt, some Jews took refuge northeastward to the mountainous area east of the Caspian Sea, in the region of Mt. Ararat, not far northeast of Haran in the district of Togarma.

However, this was in the period when east of the Caspian Sea and the mountainous plateau further east was still unsafe by the threatening rampage of the Xiung-nus. The people of the Replica of the ark would have to wait for the fullness of time when the way of the Lord shall be prepared, making it

> "straight in the desert a highway for" the Glory (or the Replica
> of the ark) of the Lord, when the "valleys shall be exalted, and
> every mountain and hill shall be made low; and the crooked shall
> be made straight, and the rough places plain: and the Glory of
> the Lord [the ark] shall be revealed"
>   (Isaiah 40:3-5)

for the *second exodus to a new Canaan*, in the archipelago off the farthest eastern shores of the Eurasian Continent.

History testifies to the fact that this general period (the third century B.C.E to the first century C.E) also coincided with one of the greatest changes in the landscape of Central and Far-Eastern Asia. This was the beginning of a new dynasty of Han, one of the most powerful periods in the entire history of China, one that was to rival the great Roman Empire of the same period (*cf. National Geographic* Magazine, Feb. 2004).

Alexander the Great (and later the Roman Empire) had extended the boundary of its conquered and secured territory eastward to include the southern regions of Central Asia (including India), and ultimately to what he and his armies had believed to be the "end of the world"—the Hindu Kush and Himalayan mountain ranges. The Macedonians had no knowledge that beyond the impenetrable cliffs was an empire far greater than any the West had ever known. And they also were not aware of the fact that *that* Eastern empire was also expanding its own conquered and secured territory *westward*. In less than a century, China's territory will greatly expand, to include the whole of Tibet and *Da-xia* (which was *Da-hae* or *Da'Ae*, the district northeast to the Caspian Sea). Eventually China's protectorates will extend as far as Turkistan, and will establish communication and alliance with the countries as far as the Middle East, including present-day Iran and to the shores of the Persian Sea, and regions under Roman authority. (*NB. Da-xia* should not be confused with *Tahghar* or *Ta-Ruo-jih*, or with *Togar*(-*ma*) which is *Takama* in Japanese chronicles).[28]

In 221 B.C.E, the king of Qin methodically eliminated all other regional kings, ending the period in China's history as the Period of Warring States and, for the first time, unified the entire country of China. He thus crowned himself *Xi Huang Di* (*lit.* the "*founding Emperor*) of the Qin, the first Chinese dynasty. The unification of the vast territory of China was not only in terms of political rule: Xi Huang opened channels and riverways, set standards for measurements and even the width of highways to accommodate the wheel axil of chariots, and also unified the language and the system of written script. The dynasty ended in 206 B.C.E. Soon after the death of Qin Xi Huang Di, Liu Bang overthrew the cruel reign of Qin with the assassination of Xi Huang's inept son. Liu Bang was made a *King* of Han (province) in 206 B.C.E. and subsequently claimed himself *Emperor* in 202 B.C.E., after defeating Xiang Yü, the renowned but less cunning general. The house of Liu (*i.e.*, the Han reign) lasted for more than four centuries. However, historians divide the Han dynasty into two periods: the Western (or the Earlier) Han, and the Eastern (or the Later) Han, the two periods being separated by two-and-a half decades of 'Wu usurpation.' (The prefixes *western* and *eastern* are in reference to the location of their respective capital cities of Xi-An or also called Chang-An, being in the west of Lo-Yang, of the earlier and the later Han courts, respectively.)

The Han Dynasty was one of the two or three most powerful, enduring and influential dynastic periods in the entire history of China (*i.e.*, along with Tang and Song dynasties, and perhaps the early years of the Ming dynasty), to the extent that the name *Han* was to be associated ever since with Chinese people and their culture: *Han-ren* (Chinese people/person); *Han wen-hua* (Chinese culture); *Han-wen* (Chinese writing); and *Han-zih* (Chinese ideogram). At its peak, the borders of the mighty Han Dynasty reached (and included) Korea to the east, and to the northwest far beyond Tibet and (the present) Xinjiang (Sinkiang) provinces, to districts in *Xi-yü, i.e., the Region of the West* (see below), and, to the south, beyond the Yangtze River and as far to the present Fujiang, Guangdong, and Yunnan regions, even to the present-day Vietnam (*cf.* **Fig. 18,** the **Map of Western Han Dynasty** at its peak period). Particularly noteworthy is the long, northwestern stretch of territory covering northern Hindu Kush to the Takla Makan Desert on both banks of the Tarim River and up northwest to Ssyrdarya, north of the upper Indus River region.

This vastly expanded territory of the Han Dynasty, larger than any other dynastic periods in the political history of China except the Yuan (the Mongol), was attained during the reign of *Wu Di*, the greatest of Han emperors and one of the most illustrious of all Chinese emperors. While the earlier years of the new regime followed in the feudal system of administration established by the Qin emperor, it was during the long, fifty-four year reign (140-87 B.C.E.) and brilliant political maneuver of the Han's fifth emperor Wu Di that the dynasty effectuated both its political vision and military might, wielding its influence far and wide, thereby establishing the Han dynasty as China's first truly *international* dominion. This historical achievement was due principally to two administrative decisions of Wu Di, giving rise to China's dominance and influence throughout *Far* Eastern and *Central* and *Middle Eastern* Asia, as far as the Roman Empire region.

The first was the conquest of the *Xiung-Nus* (later known as and dreaded by the West as the *Huns*, a large number of them subsequently settled in present *Hung*ary). Xiung-Nus, originally also a sibling tribe of the Chinese, had ruled the northern Chinese territory in a pre-Qin period and, for centuries, menaced the Chinese populace on the bordering areas especially during the winter period when hunts for survival of their nomadic life were meager. For the Chinese living in the moderate climate, fending and *fencing* off the Xiung-Nus was a major political undertaking and thus began the building of segments of defensive walls. Subsequently, it was Qin Xi Huang-Di who saw the advantage in connecting the preexisting walls to form one continuous "Great" Wall that meanders over the hills and plains for over three thousand miles. (Some fifteen centuries later, further reinforcement of the Wall was undertaken during the early years of the Ming dynasty). Xiung-Nus continued its sporadic harassment on the border populace during the reigns of Han's earlier emperors, which gave Wu Di a resolve to rid his dynasty of the cause of this perennial unrest.

Among Wu Di's generals was one Wei Ching who, in spite of his relative youth and inexperience, soon proved himself a skillful strategist and tactician. And it was under the leadership and strategic maneuvering of Wei Ching and his much younger nephew Huan Chühbing that enabled the Han armies to render a decisive defeat to the mounted warriors of Xiung-Nus, pushing and containing them beyond the Gobi Desert, in the area known today as *Outer Mongolia*.

This successful military campaign not only stopped the intrusion of nomadic bandits from the north but also effectively removed the thorn which had plagued China for many centuries. For the first time in China's history, Xiung-Nus was subjugated and became one of the "subsidiary regions"—essentially a colony—of the Han Dynasty, bearing annual tributes to the Han court, and cementing the allegiance with political marriages. The subjugation of the Xiung-Nus also reaped one significant bonanza: the securing of the northern trade routes which, precarious at best for many centuries, connected China to her far western neighbors, famously known since the most ancient time and to the West as the *Silk Road*. (Actually the term *Seidenstrasse* was coined by the German geographer Ferdinand von Richthofen in his 1877 book on *China*.) To be sure, there were other silk routes, some by southern land passages and the other by the seaways, for example, from the Arabian Sea, around the Indian Ocean, to finally coming ashore off the South China Sea, near present Guangzhou (which has continued to serve as one of the major trade ports until the present). Thus the two silk routes had given rise to two different names for China in ancient Greek literature: *Seres* (literally means "silk" in Greek), the northern China reachable by the overland route; and *Sinae*, the southern China reachable by the southern sea route.

The second crucial administrative act of Wu Di was the dispatching of Zhang Qian (variously spelled as Chang Chien or others) as an official envoy to *Xi-yü*. *Xi-yü*, literally meaning the "western territory," was in reference to the then still unknown regions far beyond the present-day Xinjiang (Uygur) and Xizang (Tibet) Provinces, the two most western provinces of China, and beyond the present-day Afghanistan. Essentially, the name *Xi-yü* refers to the vast geographical territory of the Eurasian Continent known today as Central Asia and the Middle East. And this vast area of the central Eurasian Continent was the stage for the most significant political and cultural interplays during the last two to three centuries B.C.E., unmatched in the entire cultural history of the world before or since.

The westward expansion of the Han territory began with an event of no particular significance, one that otherwise would have only become a small footnote in the court chronicle. Once, among the gifts to Wu Di, was a sword said to have belonged to a Xiung-Nu king, which was smuggled out by a "patriotic" Chinese engaged in trading of goods between China and its northern neighboring tribes of the Xiung-Nus. Wu Di, a military man himself, wanted to see how superior this gift was as compared to the Chinese sword, and quickly discovered that the blade of this black sword was so hard yet flexible that the Chinese sword was cut to pieces when the blades were crossed as in combat. Wu Di immediately recognized the military impact of the *steel* sword. However, hearing that even the Xiung-Nus did not know the secret of forging such a metal, Wu Di commissioned Zhang Qian (who was the tutoring companion during Wu Di's childhood schooling years) on a fact-finding mission, to inquire about and obtain the secret of producing *jing-gang tieh* (steel).

In 138, Zhang Qian left for *Xi-yü* with one hundred military escorts, and traveled beyond Bactria (a district further west of China's Tibetan border). Zhang Qian's trip took twelve years, and he did not return to the court until 126 B.C.E. For, *en route*, the Xiung-Nu soldiers fell on the Chinese envoy and, for six years, Zhang became Xiung-Nu's captive. During the confinement, Zhang was given a nomadic maiden for a wife who bore him a son. In 126 B.C.E, Zhang Qian finally returned to China, now accompanied only by Gang-Fu (and along with his Xiung-Nu wife and a son). It was this Gang-Fu, Zhang's immediate assistant and an excellent archer, and the son of a former servant to a Xiung-Nu king, who had sustained Zhang in surviving the long and arduous journey through the unimaginably desperate situations (*e.g.*, the two captures by Xiung-Nus) during the twelve-year journey.

Upon his return, Zhang Qian provided Wu Di with not only the information on the secret of steel forging but also valuable information of the geography, people, and travel routes from China to *Xi-yü*. Indeed, Zhang Qian was the Marco Polo of China, predating the young Venetian's adventure to the land of Cathay by some sixteen centuries. It was about this time also that Korea was subjugated by Wen Man, a northeastern Chinese chieftain, and subsequently became a political colony of the Han dynasty.

It was through Zhang Qian's knowledge of travel to and from the Middle East, *i.e. Xi-yü*, that Wu Di also recognized the great political and military implication, and mobilized all resources toward opening and securing the trade routes between China and *Xi-yü*. This was the beginning of the "official" *Silk Road*, a royal highway on which Wu Di also posted garrisons to ensure the safety of the communication routes between the far-eastern and far-western territories of the Eurasian Continent. History would witness the fact that Wu Di (and, at the other end, the Romans) would provide military guards and escorts to sustain the secured flow of trade caravans in both directions between China and the regions of the Persians and Romans. As the result of increased communication between the Far East and the Far West of the Eurasian Continent, diplomatic and military alliances were established among the governments of this vast region.

Was it necessary, and politically and militarily feasible, that Wu Di's effort went beyond obtaining knowledge of the technique of steel forging, to such an extent of providing massive military forces to secure the Silk Road and expanding the western territory of his regime, far more than any other dynasties before (and after)? At the heart of all the massive undertaking of Wu Di was still the singular objective: to control the Xiung-Nus. For not only did the emperor learn of the source of steel sword forging, but also was informed of the fact that the people of *Ruo-jih Guo* living in the western land (*i.e. Xi-yü*) had long been known as a sworn enemy of the Xiung-Nus.

Wu Di had learned from a Xiung-Nu captive that, centuries earlier, Xiung-Nus had defeated *Ruo-jih*, decapitated a Ruo-jih king and used his skull as a wine goblet for *Maodun Dan-Yü*, a Xiung-Nu king (*Dan-Yü* is the Xiung-Nu title for chieftain or king). After the defeat by the Xiung-Nus, the Ruo-jih tribe had retreated to the western plateaus of Central Asia and became cattle herders and farmers, but had not given up the vow of revenge. Wu Di thereby recognized that, through establishing alliance with the militia of *Ruo-jih* and other peoples in the Central Asian plateaus, China would be certain, for the first time, to contain the Xiung-Nus, thus minimizing future threats to China.

Following Zhang Qian's travel and Wu Di's military alliance with the major polities in Central Asia, commercial exchanges flourished. Chinese silk and *china* (porcelain) goods began to appear in quantity in the Mediterranean regions and as far as European countries, and Chinese currencies were circulated in Roman territories. New art forms began to emerge in China, and art historians recognize several of the new art forms as possibly influenced by contacts with Central Asia and the Middle East, Persian and even the Hellenistic-Roman cultures. (This was a parallel case with Indian art; the fluid style of

Indian Buddhist art forms most evident in painting and sculpture were the result of cultural exchanges prompted by the conquest of Alexander the Great.) Agricultural products such as grapes, walnuts, pomegranates, and carrots, none of which were native to Asia, were introduced to China during this period. In 81 C.E. (during the Later or Eastern Han period), an official Chinese embassy was established in *Xi-yü* and court officer Ban Gu became China's first embassador to the Roman region, serving in this capacity for thirty years until his death.

But exactly where were the lands of *Ruo-jih*, the area vaguely known to ancient Chinese and called also as *Da-Xia* which was more in reference to the land of great warriors whose fame and fear had spread to the farthest reaches of the Eurasian Continent? Based on the travelogue of Zhang Qian and the description of the distance of travel, of the landscape, the agricultural products and the customs of the people today, the regions of Zhang Qian's journey have been fairly accurately identified (see below).

A few years after Zhang Qian's return to the Han court, Wu Di commanded him on another journey to *Xi-yü*. In 121 Zhang Qian left with an envoy of several hundred soldiers, ministers, and men and women servants. During this period and upon Zhang's recommendation, Wu Di also sent royal princes in political marriages in order to further consolidate alliance with the *Xi-yü* powers, and exchanges of ministers and government officials between Han and countries in Central Asia became frequent affairs.

Finally, Zhang returned to the Han Court in 114 B.C.E., having completed the task of establishing official protocols (ambassadorial offices) in nearly a dozen countries and districts in Central Asia, covering virtually the entire Central Asia and well into the regions of the Persian Gulf and northern Africa, the latter within the (Eastern) Roman Empire. Today, not only the exact extent of the Silk Routes but also the precise lands and the routes Zhang Qian's journey had covered have been accurately identified. (This historical work was largely achieved through the effort of the modern archaeological studies particularly under the auspicies of The Division of Cultural History, The Chinese Academy of Science, formerly *Academia Sinica*). Below are the ten major districts and countries in *Xi-yü* that Zhang Qian visited and the official protocols established, shown in both the Chinese names (in *italics*) as recorded in the Han chronicles, and the present-day (political) names:

Da-Xia: for *DA'Æ* (variously as *Da-Hae* or *Da-Ha, i.e., Da-Hsia*) area west of the Kunlun Mountains (the plateau of Tibet) *i.e.*, Afghanistan

Wu-Sun:	Kazakstan and Kyrgystan
Kang-jü:	(*Kang-ghi*): Tajikistan
Shen-du:	for *Hin-du*, *i.e.*, India
Da-Rwan:	Uzbekistan
Da-Ruo-jih:	Turkmenistan
An-xi:	Iran (including part of Iraq)
Xian-Du:	Pakistan
Da-Qin:	Eastern Rome (including Turkey and Iraq)
Tiau-ji:	The Persian Gulf [coast] to (north-)East Africa

With the military alliance established and the border lands and trade routes secured by Chinese (and Roman) garrisons, the exchanges in scientific knowledge—including mathematical, calendrical, and technological information—were also increased. And, it was with these countless caravans traveling on the Silk Road in both directions that people of various religions had brought and propagated their faith. The extent and frequency of the caravan and migratory movements can be gauged in even the brief description found in the Han chronicle, such as the following:

"[the caravans] ranged in size from the largest of several hundreds to the smallest of over a hundred; each year, such traveling [caravans] numbered from over a dozen to half a dozen or so ..."

Buddhism arrived in China (first century C.E.), and members of the imperial household were converted to Buddhism. Soon thereafter, religious rituals in the imperial court shifted between or concurrently in Buddhism and Daoism, the latter being the 'orthodox' religious belief of the Han people. (This very same scenario was to be repeated in Japan from the early sixth century, when Buddhism was introduced to the imperial capitals of Heian and Nara, and Shintoism and Buddhism began to vie for supremacy.)

Thus this also was the fullness of time when the people of the Replica of the ark and of the "knife's cult" have very possibly made the eastward journey, coming down from the mountainous areas west of the Caspian Sea, and traveled eastward through the full length of the Silk Road, to enter the plains of China, and continued further toward the rising sun. Indeed, this was the fullness of time when, as the prophet Isaiah had seen in his vision, "the mountains, valleys and hills were made plain and the passsages made straight for the Glory of the Lord" which was the ark, even its *Replica*.

Among Emperor Wu's other achievements should be mentioned the establishment of a civic examination system. This national, or more commonly known as the *civic* examination system—later exclusively held in the nation's capital, hence referred to as *jing-shih, i.e.,* examination of the capital—was for identifying a person of caliber and ability (as opposed to basing it on aristocratic lineage or social caste) for consideration worthy of appointment to government offices. Scholars and historians now view this system as one which helped also to bring about a sense of true national unity, peace, social growth and prosperity in the Han dynasty, when common people could—and indeed did—attain positions of influence, power and authority. (The founding emperor of the Han dynasty was himself of common birth, and was the first emperor of China to rise to the throne from a non-aristocratic lineage.) During his long reign, Wu Di not only expanded the country's territorial boundary (*e.g.* conquered and subjugated the northern two-thirds of the Korean peninsula in 110 B.C.E.) and secured the borders but also, within the boundary, encouraged art and literature, and promoted general education for commoners.

Of particular significance among the new category of literary work was historiography. This was the beginning of China's court chronicling which was to continue uninterrupted for more than two millennia. The official chronicle of the Chinese court was unique, in that every official event at the court and every word uttered by the emperor and officials in attendance was recorded *factually*, for the singular purpose of preserving an accurate record for all perpetuity, and even the emperor was not permitted to examine the document, let alone being allowed to alter or edit.

The one work from the Western Han period is particularly noteworthy: the monumental *Chronicle of History (Shi-Ji)* by Ssu-Ma Qian and his father (Ssu-Ma is the surname), the book which scholars regard as the first *universal history* in the world. The credence of this work rests on the fact that the younger Ssu-Ma was most meticulous in the accuracy of his recording not only of events and personages but also the time, sequence of events and geographical locations, as well as causal effect of historical events. Included in his narratives also are aspects of the society, customs, as well as minority tribes within China's border, including, it might be added, their migratory movements.

However, Ssu-Ma Qian's work was not to become the *official* chronicle. For Wu Di regarded the author's opinion too harshly critical of his deeds (*e.g.,* in the author's opinion, unwarranted cruelty toward ministers and imperial family members suspected by Wu Di as being disloyal or disobedient). Once Ssu-Ma Qian had defended Li Ling, a general of Wu Di. Li Ling's army was defeated by Xiung-Nus due to a breakdown in reinforcements. The angry Wu Di thereby had put Li's entire family—all the members within the "ninth distant kin"—to death. Ssu Ma Qian had pleaded the case on behalf of General Li which angered the Emperor, and Ssu-Ma was put to *fu-xing*, the "punishment of decay" (*i.e.,* castration). In spite of this extreme and unjust penalty put on him, Ssu-Ma eventually succeeded in completing the work. Wu Di permitted the work to stand as written, with an edict that the work was to be regarded merely as *yieh-shi* (unsanctioned history), *i.e.,* "the voice of one historian." In its place, *Han-Shu*, the *Chronicle of Han Dynasty*, written by Bang Gu (mentioned earlier as the first embassador to the West, after Wu Di's reign), became Han's official chronicle. Ssu-Ma Qian's work, however, continues to command respect and preferential reference even today. *Shi-Ji* consists of one hundred thirty *pian* (chapters); over 520 thousand words, supplemented with charts and diagrams for greater clarification of relative position of time and personage.

It was during the Han Dynasty also that paper (made of wood fiber, instead of marsh sedge or *papyrus* as in the Middle East) was invented in China in the early years of the second century C.E., thus contributing greatly to propagation of literature, literacy, and general education. (Prior to invention of paper, documents in China were written on cloths or bamboo reeds.) For Wu Di also promoted opening of schools throughout his dominion, and he established in 124 the Imperial Academy to educate the new generation of court officials and for government appointment throughout the dominion. And it is in (the modern editions of) these historical documents written on bamboo, silk (cloth) and, later, paper that students and scholars today could still find reliable information on events that occurred more than two millennia ago. And it is here that we shall identify two testimonials that are crucial to the present study of historical intrigue. Both are related to the early Japanese people, one as an established polity, the other as an itinerant tribe.

The first is in the *Chronicle of Eastern* (or the *Later*) *Han* dynasty (25-219 C.E.) that we find a passage which mentions for the first time the name of a country heretofore never mentioned in China's court record: *Wei-Ren Guo*— the "Country of the *Dwarfs*." It is recorded that

> "In [57 C.E.] the Country of *Wei People* made tributes to the throne, and the Emperor conferred on [the ambassador] the seal "King of *Han-Wei* of the *subjugate* Country."

This country of *Han-Wei*, otherwise known as *Wei-Guo*, was the earliest recorded and the *official* name for the country of Japan. It needs to be mentioned that the act of bringing tributes to the throne and being conferred a seal of the regional king represented the signature gesture that the territory now officially had become the protectorate of the ruling dynasty (the Han throne) under its military power.

This narrative in the Han court chronicle bears witness beyond any doubt that, before the first century B.C.E. or no later than the first century C.E., the people on the archipelago of Japan were already functioning as a unified society, with a form of government and social order. That there were already some cultural and commercial exchanges and mutual recognition between China and her two eastern subjugate countries (Korea and Japan) is a well recognized historical fact. And, in spite of the fundamental difference in language, both Koreans and Japanese had somehow sufficiently adapted in engaging Chinese ideograms as their official script. Hence, shortly after entering China (in the early years of the first century, C.E.), Buddhism also spread to Korea (in the following century), and reached Japan (in the late fifth to the early sixth century) from Korea with the help of Buddhist scriptures written in Chinese.

The second is in the official *Chronicle of History* (*Shi-shu*), in the Book (Section) on the "Western Han Dynasty" (*Xi Han Shi*), where we find the passage on the itinerant people:

"[during the Han dynasty] a people [practicing the] knife's cult coming from the west, [passed through China] and continued their migratory journey toward the east"

This period of about three to four centuries was truly one of the "fullness of time" in the history of Central and Far Eastern Asia. Even while waves of military campaigns continued to ebb and flow westward and eastward on the steppes of Central Asia, an era of a peaceable kingdom began to dawn over the horizons of the Eurasian Continent. Following the period of relative stability under the rule of the Persian Empire (500-331 B.C.E), and following the eastern conquests of Alexander of Macedon, the Roman armies went on to put under control any remnant regional militia, and the *royal* highways stretched from Europe, past the Caspian Sea, to reach the western hills of the Himalayan "Hump" (*i.e.* the Hindu Kush, northwestern India). These 'highways' and trade routes were now guarded by both the eastern (*i.e.*, Chinese) and western (*i.e.*, Persian and, later, Roman) garrisons, positioned to maintain the artery that not only sustained the communication but also enlivened it and enriched the life and culture of various ethnic peoples, from the central plains of China to the western lands beyond the Tibet and Afghanistan all the way to the Persian and Roman Empires.

The establishment of communication highways and byways between the Far West and the Far East was a historical precedent, for the alien peoples living in the Eastern Empire (China) and Western Empire (Persia and Rome) began to "know" one another. Essentially, this period marked the "fullness of time," when the entire Eurasian Continent became, for the first time in human history, one multi-ethnic, multi-cultural and multi-lingual tapestry, with neighboring peoples becoming more intimately aware and understanding of one another. And the history of the very first dawning of East-West cultural communication is nowhere more vividly recorded, not in any written chronicles, but in the over four hundred caves on the ancient riverbed cliff walls near the town of Dunhuang on the far northeast of China (in the far northeastern corner of the present-day Gansu Province, bordering Xingjiang Province).

The town of Dunhuang sits on an oasis junction on the Silk Road, a trail that was trekked out by ancient caravans that had traveled some four thousand and five hundred miles between China and the Mediterranean regions. This ancient highway(s) served not only for commercial purposes but, far more significant, also for exchange of human ideals as well as religious beliefs, and cultural and artistic ideas. By the 4th century AD, the Silk Road had brought Dunhuang both commercial prosperity and a growing Buddhist community. Some fifteen miles southeast of Dunhuang, at the edge of the Mingsha Shan (a.k.a. *Dunes of the Singing Sands*) lay a dried river bed, carved out into a deep and long cliff over millennia. It was here, in the year 366 AD, that a local monk set about carving out a cave for solitary meditation. Over the next millennium, hundreds of similar caves were cut into the same rock face, giving birth to one of the richest "living" archives of cultural expression of our ancient ancestors.

Historians have identified four of the greatest cultures in human history: Chinese, Indian, Persian, and Greco-Roman (Hellenistic). And it is only in many of these Dunhuang caves that we witness the harmonious coming-together of all these religious, cultural and artistic ideas (*e.g.*, Caves No. 234, 323, 428, *etc.*). Of all these caves, the most dramatic manifestation of the fruit of the 'harmony' of these four human cultural lineages can still be witnessed in Cave No. 285: here is the truest portrait of *pantheon*, where painted statues of deities and religious personages from all four major human cultures—of China (Daoist monk Yü-ren), India (Shiba), Persia and Greco-Roman (the moon-goddess Diana)—pose side by side, as if they were siblings of one human family, where there is no distinction between East and West, sacred and profane.

It was precisely during this (general) period of the great Han Dynasty (a few centuries before the creation of the Dunhuang caves) that the people of the "knife's cult" had begun their travel, in different waves and at different times, slowly migrating through the full expanse of the Eurasian Continent, always moving toward the rising sun. The charted and now secured trade routes enabled them to move in relative ease, crossing the treacherous rocky and mountainous routes and through the northern "lower" passages of the Himalaya ranges, always under the watchful eyes of Roman and Chinese garrisons, to finally descend and enter into the north central plains region of China. From there, they continued their eastward journey to enter the Korean Peninsula which was by then also fully under Han rule. After a period of sojourning in Korea, they finally left the soil of the Eurasian Continent and, crossing the strait of Japan as their forefathers had crossed the Jordan River, finally arrived at the land of their new Canaan, the Japan archipelago. And they still carried with them the *Replica of the ark of Promise*, or *the Chest of Witness*, or *the Replica of the Divine Boat*.

We can never know the exact or even attempt to fathom a likely scenario or a plausible time and itinerant routes of the people of the 'knife's cult.' But, from the court chronicles of the Han Dynasty, this much we can ascertain: that,

1) during the Western Han period, the people who practiced circumcision as religious ritual had come from western Central Asia, passed through the plains region of China, and continued their eastward migratory journey through the Korean Peninsula, and settled in the Japanese archipelago;

2) they had entered the (main) island in at least two main waves of migratory movements, and subsequently they had succeeded in merging the two factions to create a unified society, sufficiently homogeneous enough to undertake diplomatic exchanges with China (and Korea) during the Eastern Han period, with official protocol; and

3) the united people had embraced (or continue to uphold) the cultic belief in the sun-goddess *Amaterasu* who was (regarded as) the supreme *kami* of the (later) *shinto* faith.

Based on the historical facts that have emerged from the scholarly studies, and in light of the timing of the birth of a new government on the Japan archipelago which claimed to be the possessor of a *replica of the divine ark* with the *contents* which bear altogether curious similarity to the holy regalia in the ark of the Covenant of ancient Israel, the following suggestions may indeed not be entirely incredulous:

1) The people of the "knife's cult" had tarried within the Persian Empire region for a considerable length of time, during which a cult that merged their old (pre-Yahweh) religion of *Mezzullash* worship with Persia's folk religion of *Mithra* worship, creating a cult of the sun-goddess later called *a-Materasu*, that they had chosen rather to remain in Persia instead of returning to Jerusalem

with the more zealous and orthodox worshippers of God Yahweh when King Cyrus had given the captive people a choice;

2) However, due perhaps to the demise of the Persian Empire by the newly emerging Hellenistic Roman forces (Alexander the Great), or after the 'Jewish revolt' during the late Persian rule, this tribe had come to realize that the *adopted* land would never be their homeland forever, that they must seek a virgin land which could become their "New Canaan," where they could safely and freely worship their sun goddess symbolized by the replica of the ark. This second exodus and second diaspora, in waves and at different times, took place sometime during the fourth to second century B.C.E.;

3) The people of the first migratory wave, probably represented in the mythology as more peaceable and agrarian-oriented *kami*—demigod and hero personages—who followed "female" *kami* (including *Amaterasu*), eventually arrived in Korea and sojourned there for yet another period of transient settlement where they had learned the agricultural life style and rice cultivation (this may be evidenced by the fact that Korean folklore, mythological tales and names of Korean places are found in Japanese mythological tales, as well as in the similarity in the linguistic elements between Proto-Japanese and Korean spoken languages, and in more recent genetic studies that show close kinship between the Japanese and Korean people);

4) It should be noted also that modern Japanese historians and archaeological anthropologists are in general agreement that there were two main waves of migration entering Japan from the Korean Peninsula (the chief proponent being Prof. Egami Namio) during the last few centuries before the Common Era. The earlier wave of a more peaceable tribe beholden to the *Amaterasu* lore with other deities symbolizing natural phenomena such as sun, moon, water, fire, animals, *etc.*, thus was symptomatic of agrarian society which also practiced shamanistic rituals. This was followed by the later wave of a militant, mounted warrior tribe (who had led the 'Jewish revolt'?) who was beholden to the *Takama ga Hara* legends of the *kami*, descending from high mountains down into Japan to wage military campaigns of conquest and unification (*cf.* (6) below);

5) The time of arrival of the people of proto-*shintoism* (the *Izumo* clan carrying the replica of the ark), coming ashore near the site of Izumo Shrine, is estimated by Japanese historians to be about the third century B.C.E or earlier, coinciding with the end of the Persian Empire and beginning of the Greco-Roman period, and also the beginning of the Western Han dynasty which had established for the first time an earnest cultural communication and political-military alliance with the West, the countries in *Xi-yü*, *i.e.*, the Middle East region;

6) Jimmu (represented in the mythology as a male warrior-*kami*), regarded by modern scholars as a factual historical personage (though the name was post-humous), entered Japan from Kyushu (the southern island of the archipelago) possibly in the second century B.C.E. (*i.e.*, perhaps a century or more after the *Izumo* clan), waged the "eastern campaign" of unification and ultimately joined with the *Izumo* clan by subjugating the peaceable tribe in exchange for subscribing their (proto-)*shinto* cult and *Mi-Fune Shiro* and *sanpo* as Jimmu's imperial regalia;

7) Both the agrarian and militant tribes had come from eastern Central Asia (the region of Togarma, Haran of then the Persian Empire), past the Caspian Sea and through important cities along the royal highway connecting China and Central Asia—Balkan (Bactria), to Kashgar, to Khotan then finally enter-ing China and into Chang-An (the ancient capital), possibly through Loh-Yang, then turning northeast to Yuchi, to enter the Korean Peninsula. For this route was by then established and secured by the Han garrisons (the remains of garrison watchtowers still stand). It may be worth repeating that the Caspian Sea was in the east of the region of Mt. Ararat, close also to Haran, in the dis-trict of Togarma (*cf. Takama-ga-Hara* of the "homeland" of the sun-goddess *Amaterasu*).

A brief historical appendix may be appropriate here:

These same routes, more famously known as the Silk Road(s), had changed little over the centuries, and were to be used extensively by all traders and migrant tribes throughout the following centuries. While there is no one par-ticular route that can be called *the* Silk Road, the main trade artery can be described as that which connected Balkh (within the territory of Babylonia, Assyria, Persia and, later Rome) to Kashgar to Khotan, and finally to the mod-ern city of Xi-An (called Chang-An in the ancient time) in the central China plains region, and then to Yu-chi in the eastern end of the Great Wall, nearly to the southeastern border of Korea. And it is this route that it is believed the later Jewish migrants such as those whose descendants still live in Kaifen traveled from the Middle East and Central Asia to China. (The other main trade routes are by the waterways of Persian, Indian, and southern China Seas, arriving on shore at Guangzhou of today). After the fall of the Roman Empire, Jewish mer-chants had played dominant parts in the East-West trades, prompting a Persian writer to note in about 850 C.E that a Jewish entrepreneur adventurer known only as Radanites had extensive trading between China and Europe over both the land and sea routes. The name *Radanites* is believed to be of Persian origin, meaning "One Who Knows the Way"—*i.e.*, the *way of the Silk Roads*.

Such a scenario may indeed very well have been the **Second Exodus**, the journey of the remnants of the first exodus and the exile, in going through the vast stretch of Central Asia. These journeys followed the routes that were opened and garrisoned by China's Han dynasty armies, enabling the migrants to enter China's plains region and, continuing eastward to and through Korea, to finally arrive on the Japanese archipelago, their new land of Canaan, where they will indeed forever dwell, virtually free from all outside invasions.

In the mythological tales in *Kojiki* and *Nihon Shoki*, evidence to the above (left from the original oral tales) is everywhere. However, such evidence may not be immediately noticeable, and undoubtedly much of the details had been lost, due to the fact that the oral tradition of a polysyllabic and non-tonal language of proto-Japanese had been transcribed phonetically into another, altogether incongruous script of Chinese monosyllabic and tonal language. Why, then, did the imperial house feel compelled in the eighth century to commit their mythological oracles into writing, in the strange language of the people of another culture?

The answer lies in the fact that the followers of the worship of the sun-goddess and the believers in the sanctity of the Replica of the ark and its contents were threatened by the arrival of Buddhism in the early sixth century. The pace of spread of Buddhism and the rise of its power and influence soon after its introduction to Japan was an eminent and present danger to the Imperial house. The rapid rise of Buddhism can still be witnessed today in the countless Buddhist architectures built during the early centuries within and surrounding the city of Nara and Kyoto. The rising power of Buddhism became even more pronounced when a few prominent members of the imperial household (notably the Grand Prince Shotoku) were converted to Buddhism and enthusiastically promoted the faith inside and outside the imperial family, resulting in people within and outside the imperial household embracing the new faith. No doubt the advisers to the emperor and imperial household who were the guardians of the *Replica of the ark* and of the *Amaterasu* cult felt an encroachment or, worse, the possible demise of the *Amaterasu* cult. It was for this reason that the Amaterasu legends were put into writing (as if to rival the Buddhist scriptures now brought to Japan). It is also quite understandable, therefore, that the Grand Ise Shrine was not (re-)built in either Nara or Kyoto but was erected in (or moved from an earlier site to) the lonely and isolated hillside on the northeastern shore of Ise Peninsula.

Thus the writing of *Kojiki* and *Nihon Shoki* was commissioned by the imperial house, for the singular purpose of providing an official documentation, a histographical proof, as it were, on the legitimacy of the imperial lineage, and for sanctioning of the emperor's right and privilege to rule over the land and its people. The guardian of the descendants of the tribes who were itinerant several times over during the course of history, did not wish that their god or goddess would be once again forced to be replaced or minimized, thus forced to relinquish the seat of power, or to pick up the ark for another exile.

This same concern has been with the Imperial House for all subsequent generations of Japanese emperors for over a millennium and a half, and was to be replayed in a most dramatic situation in the summer of 1945. On the eve of Japan's surrender, when militant factions of the Imperial Army schemed to revolt and invade the Imperial Palace, when the invasion of the Allied Forces into Japan was all but certain, the foremost concern of Emperor Hirohito was not the safety of the Japanese masses or his now defunct Imperial Army. Rather, it was the security and safety of the *sanpo*, the *three sacred regalia* of the Replica of *the Ark of Witness*, the *Shirushi no Mi-Hako*.

CHAPTER FIFTEEN

THE GENETIC AND LINGUISTIC EVIDENCE

The authors of *Japan: Its History and Culture* state unequivocally that

> "the Ainu are [ethnically] of Caucasian type, and that while the
> Japanese ... are of Mongolian race ... [one can distinguish] within
> the Mongolian family at least two more exact areas of origin ... for
> those people who mingled to form the Japanese race: the first is
> Central Asia; the evidence for this is to be found not only in the
> physical type [but also in language].[29]

The ramification from this statement is that what may be summarily dismissed
as mere myths and folklore may be proven to contain some clues which veil the
complex threads of the early ethnic lineage.

It has been pointed out that one of the more indicative aspects in the Japanese
kami legends is the regard of the female goddess as the sun, and her brother
as the moon. Further reading of *shinto* mythology as presented in the three
chronicles will make it clear that while the male *kami* had the military authority, it was always the female *kami* who had the more significant cultic—and
cultural—impacts. The near-equal partnership between the female and male
kami in Japan's mythological tales may also help us understand why Japan was
the first nation in the East, if not the world, to have female emperors, and why
Japan can also boast having some of the earliest and noteworthy literary works
by female writers, that history of Japan is made more colorful by the many contributions of female personages in the arena that in other cultures elsewhere
were dominated by males. There were, for example, *Himiko*, claimed to be the
direct descendant of the sun goddess, who had ruled the region of Yamato, and
Empress *Jito* (*Jito Tenno*) who reigned over Japan from 686 to 697, and Chinese
court chronicles duly took note of these "unusual" facts of female reign.

In direct contrast, this dominance or at least the partnership of female with male is not at all the norm in China (which had only one female empress—but never so officially recognized—Wu Zhetian, in its five-millennia history), or in the narrow strip of land on the far-western side of the same continent (the Semitic world), except in Central Asia. This was the land where the Sumerians had lived, where Noah's ark had come to rest on the top of Mt. Ararat, and where the "legends" of both Helen of Troy and the fierce female warrior tribe of the Amazons (see below) had left a most memorable historical impression, all proven now to be historical facts through archaeological research during recent decades. This area includes modern-day Turkey and Armenia in the west to the western border of the Altaic mountains (the westernmost Mongolia), far from the Far East.

All through the history from the Greek period to the nineteenth century, the story of Helen of Troy, the legend orally transmitted since the tenth century B.C.E. and finally compiled and written down by Homer in his *Iliad*, had long been believed to be a mere poetic fiction, a folklore. In the late nineteenth century, however, a German amateur archaeologist Heinrich Schliemann believed in Homer's story enough to undertake archaeological excavations, and provided the first evidence of historicity to the legend of Helen. Subsequent research confirmed that Helen was a Spartan sorceress, became the wife of a Greek general (her first husband), and then "eloped" with a Trojan prince (her second husband and true lover) to Troy, leaving historians to debate whether Helen went to Troy willingly or by abduction. It was against this fortified port city of Troy that the story of Homer tells how Greek armies held a long siege with a "thousand ships" and, failing to bring it down, schemed the famous Trojan horse that enabled Greek soldiers to penetrate the indomitable Troy, and brought it and all its inhabitants to utter destruction. In Homer's tale, Helen's life was spared by her former Greek husband, and, once again back to Greece, where she once again became a priestess. Today, on the top of a hill, there still stands a shrine dedicated to Helen.

The story of Helen traces the passage from the Greek islands to Troy located in the far northeastern corner of the Mediterranean Sea, which is also the territory of modern-day Turkey, on the western slopes of the plateau often associated with Mount Ararat. The whole area, especially the southern regions, was under the powerful influence of Hittites, a great empire in Asia Minor that flourished for nearly a thousand years from the early second millennium B.C.E., that also had non-invasion treatises with Troy. Nearby, up north from Troy, is Istanbul. For centuries it had served as the gateway from the West (*i.e.*, the *Near* East) to the East (*e.g.*, *Central* Asia or *Middle* East) and farther eastward, to the *Far* East.

This route runs more or less parallel to the "king's highway" (or the "royal highway"); this was the main trade route for several millennia before the Common Era and, during the period of about two millennia before the Common Era, saw the busiest traffic of ethnic migration. This period also coincides with the "age of the heroes and heroines" of Greek mythology, of the age of Helen of Troy. Amazingly, the legend of the female warriors of the *Amazons* also has been proven to be from this period and from this region of the Eurasian Continent.

In 1994, the anthropological study of Jeanine Davis-Kampbell and her Russian associate unearthed a tomb of a female warrior, high on the western Mongolian steppes. Until then, they had been researching about the historical credibility of the legend of the Amazons mentioned by ancient Greek historians. Herodotus, the Greek historian, had mentioned that there was a female clan, tall, blond and fiercely combatant. They were mounted warriors, and they were called by the name *Amazon* (*i.e.*, "without breast") in reference to a story that these female warriors cut off their right breast in order that they could more effectively pull the bow to shoot the arrow.

The purpose of Davis-Kampbell's research was to find sufficient evidence to substantiate her opinion that this ancient Greek mythological tale is not mere folklore but has factual basis in history. During the course of the final phase of her research, Davis-Kampbell had also engaged the assistance of Joachim Burger, a German geneticist, Vincent Brinkman, Munich Antique Museum, as well as the scientists of the genetics lab at Wiesbaden police headquarters. Finally she was able to establish that, about 500-400 B.C.E., there actually was a fiercely independent female tribe of mounted warriors that lived in the Near East region. Homer's tale also lends support to this historical perspective, in that bands of female warriors had in fact given military support to the forces in Troy on the eastern shores of the Mediterranean Sea. Eventually, these female warriors were defeated by the Greek fighters, and had retreated to the Kozakstan mountain regions and, pushing further toward the east, arrived on the wide open grassland of the western Mongolian steppes and found a safe haven there.

The most remarkable part of Miss Davis-Kampbell's research is her discovery that individuals who are the direct descendants of the ancient female Amazon warriors are still living in this western Mongolian area, near the Altai mountain areas, in the capital city of Orgiy, who belong to the nomadic Kazak tribe. Eventually Davis-Kampbell found a few individuals who still carry the genetic code that is identical to that of the legendary female warriors who had lived twenty-five centuries ago. That is, even with the separation of long historical periods and in spite of a complex admixture of migratory tides and currents, the descendants of once legendary Amazon people are still alive, and they possess lighter complexion and blondish hair, with facial features that are more "European" and not at all typical of the Mongolian characteristics. A young girl of nine (in 1994) named Mirangu, and her mother, had been scientifically proven to carry the same genetic code as that of the single female warrior unearthed from a tomb where she was laid to rest in ritual fashion some 2,500 years ago, in her burial posture and in the shape of her thigh bones, indicating that she was a mounted rider and a warrior of high position.

On the Greek red clay potteries unearthed in the area and carbon dated to be from about 500 B.C.E., slightly before the time of the writing of Heroditus's legend, are the depiction of these legendary Amazon female warriors, often wearing loose gowns and ornaments such as sea shells and tall pointed hats. Clearly, these tall and blond females were not only warriors but also priestesses. In fact, Helen of Troy and the chief female warrior(s) of the Amazons were both priestesses; they were all priestesses of the sun-worshipping cult with considerable power. The depiction of Helen on clay potteries, for example, clearly shows that her forehead, cheeks and chin were painted with the red image of a radiating sun. One of the important ritual instruments for the priestesses in performance of various rites was the mirror. And, along with the tall and pointed hat and jewelry of semi-precious stones or sea-shells, attaching of small metal bells to the sleeves and skirts of their priestly gowns is a prominent feature. These indications also imply that, while the male more often than not held military power (with perhaps the only exception of the Amazons), the female often possessed near-equal power with males but in religious and cultic domains.

In the period of late antiquity and the early Greek era, there was a tremendous amount of conflicts between various ethnic tribes in the region we now refer to as the Near East and Middle East (Central Asia), and for those who had lost military, cultural and cultic advantages to the more powerful tribes had but one direction to escape for survival: east or northeast. The high and rugged regions surrounding Mount Ararat, as well as the even higher and more rugged terrains of the Himalayan mountain ranges served well as safe havens for many exiled tribes from the enemy's harms way. Hence a number of wandering and nomadic tribes took their migratory routes eastward, including the descendants of the female warrior tribe of the Amazons who have now been found to be still living in the western Mongolian steppes, giving powerful tangible proof to the favored migration route for many Near- and Middle-Eastern tribes in the direction of the Far East, even the Central Kingdom—China.

Even to this day, there is a Jewish community in the city of *Kaifen*, in north *Henan* Province (China), on the southern shore of the northern bend of *Huang*

He (the Yellow River). This community had been reported to have practiced until the relatively recent past the "ritual of *knife*" (in reference to the rite of *circumcision*) and, hence, the religion of this community is known to the native Chinese as the *dau-jin-jiao* (religion of knife [to extract] tendon). Michael Pollak in *The Torah Scrolls of the Chinese Jews* gives a fascinating and informative account of Jewish descendants and remnants of Judaism in the Kaifen area. In it, however, Pollak interprets the Chinese word *jin* to mean tendon. This is a slightly cryptic Chinese manner in refering to the foreskin (of the penis). More correctly, then, the "*knife's cult*" should be read as in reference to ritualistic *circumcision*. This ritual act was particularly important to the exiled Jewish (and Semitic) *diaspora*, even entering into a newly conquered land (*cf.* Joshua 5:2 *ff.*). In recognizing the history and proof of a widespread Semitic *diaspora*, it is only reasonable to believe the possible scenario of a few other Semitic tribes who had pressed on further eastward, to the farthest eastern shores of the Eurasian Continent, entering and going through (the north-central plains region of) China, to Korea, southward through the peninsula, and finally arriving on the Japan archipelago.

There is no denying that, in the millennia immediately preceding and through the age of *kami*, a great flux and commingling of different ethnic groups had taken place in all parts of the Eurasian Continent and had left its impression as far as the farthest corner of the continent—the Japan archipelago. Particularly, the (Asian-)Mongolians, Chinese and Koreans, as well as people from the South China Sea islands, had entered the Japanese archipelago in ever greater numbers since about the early Heian period (5th century). Hence the isolation and identification of any "pure" Japanese race must be seen as a virtual anthropological impossibility.

Many genetic studies in recent decades reveal a fairly accurate sequence mapping of early human migrations "out of Africa." Particularly noteworthy are those studies of the discovery of Y-chromosomal DNA to be the most stable (least subjective to mutation) and therefore the more reliable clues in identifying and mapping the complex lineage trees and branches of human (*i.e.*, ethnic) migration. The majority of these studies focus on human migratory routes of the prehistoric period, as far back to about 130 thousand years ago (to a few studies on more recent periods). The findings are highly complex especially to non-specialists such as this writer. Still, these findings, though they may not be immediately applicable to the present study, provide additional support to the perspective of the uniqueness of Japanese ethnic lineage and its 'lost' origin. The graphics (pp. 45, 47) and maps (pp. 47-48) in the study by P. A. Underhill and colleagues (*cf.* Bibliography, **C.** Genetic Study, *etc.*) are particularly informative and revealing even to non-specialists. Together with narratives in the study, these genetic scientists have clearly identified the modern Japanese as from a 'lost' ethnic ancestral origin, still containing a genetic signature that is entirely different from its immediate and far more dominant neighbor—the Chinese or Mongolians.

More specifically, genetic scientists have shown that as much as ten percent of modern Japanese belong to the genetic lineages that originated in Near- and Middle-Eastern (Central Asian) and even European stocks, and that Japanese are not only a mixed race but in fact are *"related more to Middle Eastern* (and European) *than to Chinese."* Archaeologists add another support to this opinion of the early Japanese's most likely offshoot from the Middle Eastern lineage in observing the fact that the earliest settlers had brought with them iron tools and weapons, along with others made of bronze. For iron tools from these early periods (*i.e.*, pre-third to fourth century B.C.E.) were associated with cultures in the Middle Eastern—rather than the Far Eastern—region of the Eurasian Continent. For, until then, China was still in the bronze age, and the Chinese did not possess iron tools or weapons.

Besides scientific and genetic evidences, the linguistic study also lends a considerable support to the perspective that a few culturally—and militarily—dominant stocks of early Japanese are of the Middle-Eastern and Central Asian lineage. The consensus among the majority of linguists (as, for instance, indicated or inferred in various encyclopedias, including *Encyclopedia Britannica*) is that the original Japanese tongue (*i.e.*, before the shaping forces of the Chinese language began to leave a more lasting impact on the old Japanese tongue) belonged to the [early] Altaic-Turk language, and that Japanese is related to old Finnish and Turkish in terms of the linguistic lineage. Linguists also take note of the fact that this similarity is most noticeable in grammatical structure of these languages— the language group which is classified as "synthetic" rather than "analytic" (to the latter belong Chinese, Mongolian and Korean languages). Thus Morton and Olenik, in their *Japan: Its History and Culture*, would state that

> "Japanese in its syllabary (consonant followed by vowel) and
> in certain roots shows some similarities to Hungarian Magyar
> and to Finnish. All three probably stem from a common central
> Asian source."[30]

A more learned opinion is expressed by Gary Jennings in his *Personalities of Language*—a delightful and most informative book written for general readership rather than for specialists. The following is a citation from Jennings' book:

"Turkish is the European representative of a language group which includes Tataric, Kirghizic and numerous other tongues in use across wide belts of central and northern Asia.

The Semitic group once supplied the world with its widest used languages of commerce and diplomacy: Babylonian-Assyrian, Phoenician, Aramaic. Today its chief representatives are the Arabic of the Near East and Mediterranean Africa, the Amharic of Ethiopia, Maltese and Hebrew ...

The Sinitic languages of Asia ... [This] language family now includes the myriad spoken dialects of China, plus Tibetan, Burmese, Thai and various other languages of Indo-China.

The Japanese and Korean languages may or may not be related to one another—linguists differ on this—*but neither of them is related to Chinese or another of the Sinitic tongues* ...

... Korean and Japanese may be [linguistic] orphans, too, unless further linguistic research somehow links them together. Others include a number of hermit languages in Kamchatka and far northeast Siberia, the tongue of the Andaman Islands in the Bay of Bengal, and *that of the hairy Ainu of northern Japan.*[31]

The Japanese archipelago, Kamchatka, and far northeastern Siberia, *etc.*, are all geographic extremities of the Eurasian Continent, where migratory journeys of nomadic tribes would have to halt their wandering, where any linguistic twigs will not be further morphed. As ripples on a pond spreading from the point where a stone entered the water, these languages of people living in the extreme regions of the continent would likely still possess remnants of their original and much earlier language elements. If indeed a few stocks of proto Japanese (and proto Korean) had come from Central Asia or even the Near Eastern regions of the Continent, then perhaps such linguistic fragments—though morphed time and again during the course of its migration of perhaps as much as several centuries before the Common Era, commingling with different people of alien cultures and cults—may still be detectable.

(It may be noted here that, ethnographically, Koreans are more complex than Japanese. In the early first millennium B.C.E., bronze age warriors of the Turgusic lineage had invaded Manchuria and entered the Korean peninsula. There the Central Asian tribe mixed with earlier inhabitants of Sinitic lineage. Hence while in facial and other physical features Koreans may resemble more northern Chinese, their language and mythology strongly suggest an important cultural linkage with a non-Sinitic source from a much earlier time. Similarly, Tibetan mythology tends to show non-Sinitic features, while Japanese *kami* legends in *Kojiki* and *Hihon Shoki* contain threads from both the Korean and Tibetan mythological tales, implying thereby that, during their long migratory journey, the proto-Japanese had passed through and perhaps even sojourned for a while in both Tibet and Korea before entering the Japanese archipelago. It should be mentioned that Tibetan and Japanese are *linguistic cousins*. Additionally, anyone who has observed performance of *gagaku* (imperial court music), and especially its *kagura* dances (*i.e.* divine, shamanistic dances) would notice immediately that those grotesque devil masks that the dancers wear while moving to the rhythmic pulsation of the flat single-sided drums are all identical with masks and instruments found in Tibetan rituals.)

On the eastern shore of Honshu (the main Japanese island) directly east of the tip of the Korean Peninsula across the Korean Strait is an ancient city called Izumo. It is the home of the Great *Izumo* Shrine. It is not the point of shortest distance from Korea, but, if a boat sails from Korea, it will eventually come ashore on the shores near Izumo on western Japan, carried by the powerful west-to-eastward flowing ocean current known as *Kuro-shiwo* (the *black current* of the Pacific Ocean, warmer in temperature and hence appearing "black" when viewed from afar). The *Izumo* Shrine, with a great rope a few feet thick in diameter hanging on its main entrance, is the oldest *shinto* shrine in Japan, and the site is believed to be the location where *Amaterasu* had descended from *Takama ga Hara* (the name *Izumo* means "[descending] out of the cloud"). The air of reverence permeating throughout the hushed courtyard evokes in the mind of visitors a sense of being in the presence of *kami*. Even without being knowledgeable of ancient history of Japan, there is an unmistakable air of great antiquity. And in reflecting on the phonetic sound of the name *Izumo*, one could not help but wonder whether this name *Izumo* has a phonetic connection to *Ishmael*, the first son of Abraham born to the maid-servant of Sarai his wife. Or, perhaps there is another possible connection, to *Edom*, the homeland of the Edomites whose ancestor was *Esau*, the hapless son of Isaac who had lost his birthright (as the first born) to his more cunning younger brother Jacob (*cf.* Gen. 27-28). Adding to this, one may also learn that the Ainu people called themselves—and also were called (by the other Japanese) as—*Ebisu* or *Ezo*. Could *Ezo* be connected to *Esau*, or *Jebusite* to *Ebisu* and, hence, to *Izumo*?

The Semitic names all end with a syllable 'hite' or 'ite' (with a silent 'e' in English spelling; in Hebrew pronunciation it is more like a strong exhaling sound similar to "hit"), such as Israel*ites*, Hitt*ites*, Jebus*ites*, Amor*ites*, and Edom*ites* (the 's' is added at word end to signify plural, as in modern European languages). Israel*ites* means literally "*people* of Israel" and Edom*ites* the "*people* of Edom," *etc.* In Japanese, the word for people or person is 'hito' and, to express plural or emphasis, the same word is repeated (as also often in Semitic languages) to become 'hito-bito'. The self-name of a people is one of the words which tends to resist change, no doubt due to a sense of self identity and self-preservation. This universal egocentricism is observable also in the fact that a people or tribe is prone to regard only themselves as "people" or "man," while others as non-equal. Jennings points to this fact by mentioning that Eskimos call themselves *Innuit* which means "the people" and, likewise, Illeni Indians (*illeni* "the men" from which the name of Illinois), the African *Bantu* (lit. "the men") and Hottentots calling themselves *Khoi-khoin* (lit. "men among men").

Regarding 'hito-bito' to refer to many men, Japanese and Semitic languages also do not possess different *superlative* words such as to express a degree of quality, *e.g.,* good, better, and best in English. Superlative is more often than not expressed by word repetition. Hence, to express the state of the *most holy*, the word is repeated, (translated) as "*holy, holy, holy*" to describe the *holiest* God (*cf.* Isaiah 6:3). This form of superlative is also true in the Japanese spoken language.

There are other isolated Japanese words which have (near) identical meaning with similar phonetic sounds with their counterparts in the Semitic (Hebrew) language. For example, "*mori*" for forrest in Japanese is to *Moreh* in the Bible (a place of forrest, *cf.* Gen 12; also 22) is a case in point. In the next chapter, we shall examine a selection of Japanese names, words and customs which may further support the possibility of ethnic, cultural and cultic connection between the Japanese and Semitic peoples.

CHAPTER SIXTEEN

WHAT'S IN THE NAME: ASPECTS OF JAPANESE NAMES, WORDS, AND CUSTOMS

Any attempt to establish the evidence or simply to identify credible elements of a linguistic connection between the spoken languages of the early (proto-) Japanese stocks and the Semitic people would seem to be a wholly improbable if not an outright impossible task. For one thing, language by its very nature will undergo complex and profound mutation and alteration during the course of history. It would be reasonable to assume that such changes would be greater during the migratory journey in the Middle East and particularly on the vast and complex geographic terrains of Central Asia. For example, the language which the ancient Israelites spoke was not 'Hebrew' (which actually was referred to as the "*lip* [*i.e.*, the language] *of Canaan* (*cf.* Isaiah 19:18) or *Judaic* (*cf.* Isaiah 36: 11*f.*) but, rather, Aramaic. The reference to the latter is worth quoting, in order to notice the different names by which the common language (Aramaic or Syrian) and peculiar 'dialect' (Judaic or Jewish) were referred to :

"Then Eliakim, Shebna, and Joan said to the Rebshakeh,
'Pray, speak to your servants in *Aramaic*, for we understand it;
[but] do not speak to us in the language of *Judah* [*i.e.*, the 'Hebrew or Canaanite language] within the hearing of the people ..." (RSV)

"Then said Eliakim and Shebna and Joah unto Rabshakeh,
'Speak, I pray thee, unto thy servants in the Syrian language;
for we understand it; and speak not to us in the Jews' language,
in the ears of the people ...'" (King James)

And it was this *Aramaic* a.k.a. *Syrian* script—the diplomatic and the commercial language in the Semitic world from the late eighth century B.C.E.—that the above quotations refer to. Later, Aramaic became the official language of the Persian Empire, as well as the language of the Old Testament. This should not be regarded as strange, since Aramaic and Judaic (or Hebrew) are close cognate languages, and not one a derivative of the other.

Ancient Japanese, too, has gone through numerous stages of morphosis of varying degrees and extent. Notable are the effects of the Heian period, under the regency of Shotoku Taishi (Prince Shotoku), in importing Buddhism through China and Korea, and in Japan's all-out effort, with the sending of *kento-shi*—the emissary to *To* or Tang, *i.e.*, China—to adopt and emulate the entire cultural institution of China. The changes were fundamental, forever affecting arts, language and writing in Japan, as well as the philosophical and religious perspectives of Japanese people. This period is referred to by the historians as *Taika*—the "Great Change"—the first of the two greatest national reformation movements (the second was the "Restoration" under Emperor Meiji in the last decades of the nineteenth century, referring specifically to restoration of power of the imperial throne). In comparison, all the changes during the long feudal period lasting several centuries until the Meiji restoration were political in nature, more subtle, intricate, internal, even cosmetic, and harshly cruel.

But even through stages of the most extensive—some fundamental—changes, linguists generally believe that some part of the language, especially nouns and icons—both general and particularly significant proper names associated with legends and beliefs—have a greater tenacity to weather the forces of change and remain relatively unaffected. It is the accepted view (born out of scholarly research) that the majority of names of Japan's cities, towns, fields, mountains and rivers are the original or a corrupt version of the original names given by the *Ezo* (or, variously, *Iso, Eso, Ebisu*) people, the earlier inhabitants of the Japanese archipelago whose greatly reduced number of descendants still live in the northern islands of Hokkaido and Sakhalin, now an "endangered" ethnic tribe known as the "hairy" *Ainu*.

A more dramatic and poignant case for the enduring image of icons can be made with *menorah*, an important ritual symbol which for millennia has existed in both Semitic religions (Judaism and others). However, this all-too-familiar *menorah* figure, familiar to many as the candle stands in synagogues but also depicted as iconographic representations on drapes and paintings and numerous other religious art works, was discovered as a cave drawing in Japan, in Fukuoka *Ken* (Prefecture), in Kurate *Gun* (County), dated to be of pre-fifth century work (*cf.* **Fig. 15**). Why and how was this *menorah* figure in a cave in Japan? Or, is the *menorah* figure an universal icon, or Pan-Asiatic, or unique to Middle Eastern cultic heritage?

The one prevailing perspective regarding cave art is that such figures were created in remembrance of articles, both animate and inanimate, of cultic prominence that were no more. Additionally, an accepted perspective regarding cave art of earlier people is that these paintings were not intended as an aesthetic drawing but, rather, a means of non-verbal communication with the spirit—*e.g.*, *kami*—as was believed to be the case with Europe's stone-age cave arts of wild beasts (most famously in Spain and France, *e.g.* the incredible Altamira and Lascaux Caves) and also in several southwestern states in the United States, in South Africa, and elsewhere. To put it simply, these were never meant to be *object d'art* but icons of ritual signification. Also, in more recent studies, scholars seem to agree that these cave arts are not merely for ritual purposes but likely the products of ritualistic phenomena (see below).

For a long time, scientists were unable to explain or come to a concensus, as to *why* early man painted—or had the need to paint—those fantastic animal figures deep inside caves, often in areas far from the location of communal habitations. The earlier—and what seemed the most logical—explanation was that these figures represented animals which these primitive painters hunted, or they represented an incantation—a wishful prayer, so to speak—for good hunting. Scientists soon began to suspect that this explanation was too pat; bones found in the vicinity were not at all of the same animals these cave paintings depicted. In other words, cave paintings did not (mean to) represent diet. Consider also the fact that these paintings are always found in the deepest and narrowest parts of the cave, where little or no light could penetrate. Apparently, the purpose of these paintings was not for admiration by the populace.

As the result of notable studies by Profs. David Lewis Williams in South Africa, David Whitley in California, and Wilhelm Blake of Germany (his extensive documentary archives on South Africa's San Indians and the cave arts of their ancestors), the concensus among modern archaeologists regarding the cave arts is that these paintings were *works of shamans in trance*. These were images seen by the shamans in their 'altered state of consciousness' (or hallucinating images), and in their spirit world, they would record images that had "haunted" them, had left an imprint in the very depth of their psychological conscious. Things that were imposing, significant, fearsome, and awe-inspiring.

If this is indeed the shared signification of all cave paintings found in all continents and all regions of the world, then this Japanese cave painting with two *menorah* figures framing human and animal figures may be regarded as a most vivid portrayal of proto-*shinto* priests/priestesses-shamans attempting to summon and communicate with the spirit of their ancestors whose image lingers still, though now appearing faintly, in the *kami* legends of *Kojiki* and

Shoki. This cave painting was created long before the same legends were cast into writing, of *Kojiki (and Nihon Shoki).* Still, this Japanese *menorah* figure may very well be the singular, most powerful representation of the true image of *shinto* faith, more than can be imagined from reading the entire *Kojiki* and *Nihon Shoki* narratives and all the later supplementary chronicles combined. For, in its raw and primitive way, this cave image, mysterious and unimaginably eloquent even in its total silence, is a powerful testimony to the mind of an early or proto-*shinto* priest who, in his—or her—altered state of consciousness, had uttered its prayer to the spirit of their ancestors of the *kami* legends. Like all *menorahs* throughout history of the ancient fertile crescent region and indeed in all synagogues everywhere today, this Japanese *menorah,* too, was an image of the instrument summoning the spirit, and in transporting the prayers of the faithful to the spirit world of their ancestors. In its unique way, this *menorah* stands for the same hidden—or lost—legends of, and the faith in, *MiFune-Shiro.* There seems no denying that this Japanese *menorah* is another stylized figuration of the Middle-Eastern *tree of life,* symbolized also by Aaron's rod that budded, which was then placed inside the ark of the Covenant, to be a witness.

Less dramatic, the link between the original people on the western shores of the Eurasian Continent, and the original people whose descendants now are believed to be living on the island archipelago off the far eastern shore of the continent, may also be suggested—if not substantiated—in linguistic and verbal elements, particularly in general and proper nouns. The following are but a handful of examples of phonetic parallels. This may be regarded as decidedly unscientific (*i.e.,* meager sampling). Nonetheless, they provide an added dimension in support of the thesis proposed in this study.

> **Shilloh**: a fortified city of biblical times (*cf.* Judges 21) where the ark of the Covenant was once kept, *versus*
> '*shilo*' in Japanese which means a fortified city or a (military) castle;
> **Hara(n)**: a city on the plain on the main road (in otherwise a mountainous region, *cf.* Gen.9, 12 and elsewhere), *versus*
> '*hara*' in Japanese which means a plain or field;
> **moreh**: originally refers to an oak tree or simply a tree (*cf.* Gen. 12, Dt. 11, Jdg. 9, and elsewhere), *versus*
> '*mori*' in Japanese which means woods or forest;
> **hite**: man or people (e.g. Israel*ite,* Jebus*ite,* Hitt*ite,* and Hebr*ite*), *versus*
> '*hito*' in Japanese which means a man or people
>   (in the plural case the word is often repeated, *e.g.* to become *hito-bito,* when the second consonant '*h*' is changed to '*b*');

horites or *horim*: originally refers to "cave-dwelling people"
(*cf.* Gen. 14, 36, Dt. 2, and elsewhere), *versus*
'*hora*' in Japanese which means a cave; also, '*hori*' in Japanese which
means 'ditch' or 'dug pit' *i.e.*, man-made pond, canal, or even cave;
and
œsia or *œsha*, and *nisha*: both words from the Indo-European root
word/sound for "east" (direction of rising sun, whence came
the word Asia) and "west" (direction of setting sun),
respectively, *versus*
'*asa*' in Japanese for morning, or '*ashita*' for "the next morning"
(*i.e.*, tomorrow), and
'*nishi*' for "west" or "evening" (the latter often used in a poetic idiom).

More significantly curious examples of coincidence in phonetic similarities or parallels than the above are the nouns associated with cultic and ethnic names:

During the early century of the Common Era when Japan began to send tributes to the Chinese court (perhaps during the earliest presence of *kento-shi* at the Tang court), Japanese 'ambassadors' were asked by the Chinese emperor what was the 'official' name of his country. For, until then, all Chinese chronicles referred to Japan simply as "country of 'dwarfs'" (*wei-guo*) or *wei-ren-guo* (*lit.* country of dwarf people), and never as *Jih-ben* (*i.e.* Japan) or *Jih-pen Guo* (*i.e.*, *Cipango* as known to the sixteenth century European sailors arriving on the Far-Eastern shores). The legend has it that the answer from the emissary from the 'country of dwarfs' to the royal inquiry was that

"Our land is called [*by their own people as*] '*Jip-pon*.'

Thereupon the Tang court proclaimed that henceforth *Wei-ren Guo* shall be called *Jih-ben* (or *Jip-pun*).

The modern Chinese ideograms for Japan are the two characters "sun" (*jih* in Mandarin or *jit* in northern dialect) and "origin" (*ben* in Mandarin or *bun* in northern dialect). It has been taken to mean that this Chinese 'given' name referred to Japan as the country "in the direction of the rising sun." And it was from this historical point, during the Era of *Taika* (the 'Great Reformation' of the *Nara* Period) that the modern name *Jih-ben* (*Nihon* or *Nippon* in the Japanese pronunciation) was entered in the Japanese chronicles. Hence, Japan has been referred to by Western writers as the "country of the Rising Sun."

However, the name—that is, the phonetic sound of the name—did not originate from Chinese ideograms bestowed by the Chinese court (as in the case of *ateji*), but *was uttered by the Japanese officials before the Chinese name was conferred*. We must recognize, therefore, that the newly *bestowed* signification of this given name of *Jip-pon* was correct only in respect to China, as Japan indeed lies to the east of China. However, this directional reference would be entirely improper with respect to the people living on the Japanese island. For, to the Japanese, the sun rises yet further east of the eastern shores of their islands, and it sets on their western shores. It is therefore implausible—indeed, incredulous—that the people of the island of *Jip-pon* would have referred to their own country as the "land of the rising sun."

Why, then, did the people on this most far-eastern island call the name of their land as '*Jip-pon*'? Could the name or its phonetic sound be in reference to the country whence their ancestors had come but by then its historical and geographical significance had long been lost and forgotten?

In the Book of Numbers (Chapter 26) is an extensive narrative enumerating all the lineages of all the Hebrew tribes, among them the "sons of Gad." The tribe of Gad was one of the twelve tribes from Israel (Israel was the new personal name given to Jacob after his wrestling encounter with the angel of the Lord), and the first family of the tribe of Gad was Zephon, this people called Zephonites. However, the '*ph*' in Ze*ph*one belies its proper pronunciation which is '*p*' rather than '*f*.' Hence, a more accurate pronunciation of Zephone is *zepon*. Also, a more proper pronunciation of Gad is *gado* with an unaccented (nearly neutral) '*o*.'

The term of reverence in referring to the Japanese imperial house and specifically the ancestral lineage is *Mi-Kado*. This is the only term which has been used throughout history—and most probably had been a part of the oral tradition for countless centuries before Chinese literacy entered Japan—in referring to Japan's imperial house. The two Chinese ideograms for *Mi-Kado* are "reverend" (*mi* as in *MiFune*, referring to an article or person of divine character), and "gate" or "door." However, it is most curious that the ideogram for gate is rarely, if ever, pronounced as *kado* in Japanese except in the case of referring to the imperial ancestral lineage.

The name *Gad(o)* in Hebrew (*i.e.*, Aramaic) language means "good fortune," and the tribe of Gad had occupied a plain area in Canaan west of the River Jordan, adjoining the land of the tribe of Reuben in the south, Manasseh (of Israel) in the north, and the people of Gilead (the former inhabitants of Canaan) in the east. Later, the people of Gad expanded their territory into the land of Gilead, causing the two peoples to be interchangeably identified or regarded as one tribe. The (former) people of Gilead were believed to be a people of short stature, heavily haired or bearded, with light brown or yellowish skin complexion, and had migrated farther eastward. This people was also known as having become habitual cave dwellers (but the "poorer" among them simply dwelt in open-air plots) during the course of its eastward migration from their ancestral homeland in Canaan.

The *Zep*(h)*on* are the children of *Gad*(*o*) of the ancient Hebrites *versus* the land—and the people—of *Jip-pon* who are of the "gate" (the lineage of "the house") of *Mi-Kado*. It is curious still that the ideograms "revered gate" is more often pronounced by elder *kannushi*—*shinto* priests—as *Mi-Gado*, rather than *Mi-Kado* (*cf.* Oyabe, p. 367).

To this, an anthropological footnote may be added:

A people known as *Gilliak*—variously spelled—dwelled in the area from the eastern tip of Russia near the mouth of the river Songhua Jiang—previously known as Heilung Jiang—to Karafuto, *a.k.a.* Sakhalin Island of the Japanese archipelago. The "orphan" people of Ainu who live on Sakhalin and Hokkaido islands are related to this Gilliak people. And the Ainu people were also called variously by other Japanese names as *Esso* or *Ezo (Esau?)*, Ebisu (Jebusite?) or *Jigumo*. The last of which, a spiteful and derogatory term, is written with *ateji* ideograms that denote "earth-dwelling spiders" or cave dwelling insects, *i.e.*, small creatures).

As to the similarity in the sound of personal names between the Japanese and Semitic people, the coincidence is far too numerous to give even a near-complete listing. Listed below are a selected few of the most common Japanese personal names (only given names are shown here). Often "O" (meaning male, signifying 'son of') is added at the end of male names, and "Ko" (meaning female, signifying "child of") of female names. These suffixes are omitted from the name spellings below.

> male name: Eisaku, Isaku, Masa, Uri, Yuri, Taka, Katsu, Shige, Toshi, *etc.*
> female names: Misa, Isa, Tama, Hana, Eri, Uri, Yuri, Emi, Esa, Masa,
> Kiku, Aki, Haru, *etc.*

But the most significant are the curious parallels between certain folk, cultic or semi-religious customs among the Japanese and Semitic people. While the parallels are indeed numerous, the following three may be regarded as particularly significant:

1. The summer *matsuri* (festival) of *Gion* (July 14-17), culminating with the parade of *o-mikoshi* (during the Gion *matsuri*), which is a square ritual chest with ornate roof topped with a bird figure.
During the wild procession the onlookers would splash water on the divine chest and, at the end of the procession, the pole bearers will carry the divine chest into waterways before returning the chest to the shrine. This may be regarded (and in fact has been likend to)
as a ritual reenactment of
the ark of the Covenant crossing the Red Sea and River Jordan during the exodus, the ark that featured prominently the two figures of winged cherubins with spread wings atop the ark;
2. The *sumo* wrestling (which was not conceived as a sport but) as a ritual, with presiding *kannushi* (*shinto priest*) and *shime-nawa* (ropes or *kami*-paper string to mark off the sacred bounds of the mound) to ward off evil spirits, and the act of scattering salt by the wrestlers to consecrate the ground,
as a ritual reenactment of
(the legend behind it but since long forgotten) a wrestling match between Jacob and the Lord at Bethel, and Jacob consecrating the spot as a holy ground;
3. The eating of bitter herbs and unleavened rice cakes and other customs as part of the new year's eve ritual in Japanese families (the custom had been preserved until about the time of World War II)
as a ritual reenactment of
the eating of bitter herbs and unleavened bread as the Passover Feast, on the eve of the Israelite exodus from Egypt
(the custom which survives as the *seder* dinner among Christians in commemoration of the Passover and the exodus).

But, far more mysterious than the *menorah* figure in the Kurate cave, far more puzzling than all the parallel sounding names and customs, and even far more enigmatic than these *reenactments* of ancient cultic legends, is the wooden chest reposed in the depth of the Grand *Ise* Shrine, the chest that contains three sacred relics, the relics with names that are baffling, their shapes still unverified and their historical and archaeological ramification beyond belief. These are the *Sanpo* in *MiFune-Shiro*, the articles and the chest bearing an uncanny parallel with the articles and the chest of the Ark of the Covenant of the ancient Israelis. And these three sacred relics, together regarded as *the* imperial and cultic regalia, are mentioned not only in *Kojiki* and *Nihon Shoki* but also in the historical writings such as *Heike Monogatari*, the latter being one of the most important and fact-based tales from the early feudal era of Japan. And while eye-witness accounts of these articles of great mystery are but a few, they are credible beyond a doubt.

CHAPTER SEVENTEEN

THE STORY OF *SANPO* IN *KOJIKI*, *NIHON SHOKI*, *KUJI HONKI*, AND *HEIKE MONOGATARI*

The mention of *sanpo* appears early in the sequence of narratives in all three chronicles. For example, it is given in Part III in *Kuji Honki* (pp.74-5 in the most recent edition by S. Ono), and similarly in *Nihon Shoki*. The earliest mention of *sanpo* is in the narrative related to *Ninigi no Mikoto* when he was commissioned to depart from *Takama ga Hara*, the celestial plains, to descend to earth. The story tells that it was on this occasion that *Amaterasu Omikami*, the supreme goddess of the sun, conferred the three treasures on *Ninigi no Mikoto*, her grandson. This same narrative, found in all three ancient chronicles and told in essentially the same terms, enumerates the three treasure items. Here, we should take note of the meaning of the name *Ninigi*, literally "*rice-ear-ruddy-[a]plenty.*" The important inference, in this writer's view, is in the immediate and earliest of ritualistic associations between rice—here, represented in human form—and the items of sacred relics of *sanpo*.

The three treasures (called by various names) as identified and described in Japan's ancient writings are the following:
1) the precious, crescent-shaped **stones** (*maga-tama*) from the eight-forked hilly road (*yasakani*) of *Takama ga Hara*, along with white crystal balls;
2) a divine **sword** that has six sprouted branches, three on each side of the blade and, together with the top end of the blade, forming a seven-branched sword; and
3) the star-mirror, called *yata no* **kagami** (eight-feet mirror).

This set of three divine articles forming the imperial regalia, or *sanpo*, was eventually passed on to Emperor *Jimmu* who was the great grandson of *Ninigi* in (the legend of) the imperial lineage, and the grandson of *Hoori* and the princess *Toyotama*, a sea dragon. This same *sanpo* is believed to still exist in

Japan, in the *Grand Ise Shrine,* and *replicas* of the set or of certain item(s) of the *sanpo* are said also to be housed in different shrines in Japan, specifically the Imperial Shrine within the present imperial palace grounds in the center of Tokyo. The imperial palace grounds, now open to the public, are landscaped with hundreds of immaculately manicured and graciously contoured ancient *kuromatsu* (Japanese black-pine), and a wide moat surrounding the entire palace compound.

It was from Emperor *Jimmu* that *sanpo* was believed to have become the official regal emblem for the succession of the *earthly* imperial scepter. That is, unlike all his *kami* ancestors, including his father and grandfather immediately before him, *Jimmu* is regarded by present-day historians as the historically verifiable first true—that is, *human*—emperor of Japan. For historians are even able to name his human surname—*Monobe*, pointing to the fact that many generations of emperors after *Jimmu* were all from the house of *Monobe.* At the same time, it is well to remember that *Jimmu* was a warrior leader and not of the priestly caste, and that *sanpo* was most likely the ritual articles brought by the earlier clan who had occupied the area of *Izumo.* When the Izumo clan submitted themselves to *Jimmu,* he accepted the *sanpo* as the symbol of unification of the two earlier opposing clans. In other words, this political marriage was the first joining of celestial (*Izumo shinto* clan) and terrestrial (*Jimmu* warrior clan) powers.

There are many colorful tales and descriptions about these items of sacred treasure. For example, the mirror was the one which *Amaterasu Omikami* had looked into with curiosity when she hid herself in the cave (in protest of humiliation by utterly disgusting deeds which her brother *Susa-no O* had committed against her), the mirror which would show the reflection of her countenance. And it was for this very reason, so the legend goes, that *Amaterasu* had given the mirror to *Ninigi no Mikoto,* when he was "commissioned" to leave the celestial realm to descend to claim the earthly dominion, so that, even on earth, he could continue to see her radiant countenance in the mirror. The above account is narrated in *Kojiki* and other chronicles, but the same account can also be found in other historical writings. For example, a section is devoted to the narrative of the sword in *Heike Monogatari,* as follows:

> "… Now, the *naisho-dokoro* was the mirror cast by *Amaterasu Omikami* of ancient days when she hid herself in the *Ama no Iwato* [the heavenly gate of stone]; she desired to have her own image reflected so that her descendants may still see [her]. [The mirror that was first made] did not meet her approval and hence

[she] recast [another mirror]. The first divine mirror is now kept
in *Kokuken Shrine* in *Nichizen* in the country of *Ki*; the second
divine mirror was given to her divine son *Ihomi no Mikoto* [the name
meaning "concealed rice-ears," the child who was born of the crescent
stones when she and her brother pledged an oath at the River of
Celestial Peace]."[32]

The narrative continues and describes how the mirror was taken away from
an emperor and from one location to another, how it had escaped the terrible
fate of burning by a lady in waiting (*naisho*) when she bravely leaped into the
burning flame and *wrapped the sacred treasure in her sleeve* and, after one hundred and sixty years, is now safely housed in *Unmei Palace*" (vol. IV, pp. 238–40;
italics mine). Here, a question must be posed: How could an eight-foot mirror
be wrapped in the sleeve of a lady's gown, which is no more than two to three
feet long, is a curious point that begs for an explanation.

Similar fantastic tales are told about the sword. The most famous story tells
how this sword had enabled *Ninigi no Mikoto* to escape a sure death by mowing
down the grass when his enemy had set it on fire around him. Hence the sword
is also called *kusa-nagi no tsurugi*—the grass-cleaving sword. Perhaps equally
interesting is the story that tells how this sword had come about: it was taken
out from the belly of a giant serpent which *Susa-no O*, the riotous brother
of *Amaterasu*, had slain. When the sword was shown to *Amaterasu*, she con-
fided that it had belonged to her but she had "lost" it. Again, *Heike Monogatari*
devotes a section in narrating the history of the divine sword, as follows:

"… There are three divine [*i.e.*, spiritual] swords that have been
bequeathed from ancient days: the *totsuka* sword, the "heavenly
swift cutting sword" [which was used in slaying the giant serpent],
and the "grass-cleaving sword," these three.
The *totsuka* sword is housed in *Furu* Shrine for [worship of] *Iso no
Kami* in the country of *Yamato*; the serpent slaying sword is said
to be housed in a shrine in *Atsuta*; the grass-cleaving sword is kept
in the holy of holies [of *Ise* Shrine?].
On the origin of this [particular] sword, it was on the occasion in
ancient days when *Susa-no O no Mikoto* was building [his] palace
in the village of *Soga* in *Izumo*, that he gazed on eight-color clouds
rising, and recited the following [thirty-one syllable] poem … "[33]

The narrative then gives a rather elaborate account of how *Susa-no-O* slew the giant eight-headed and eight-tailed serpent to save the beautiful Princess *Inada*. It was in the body of the slain serpent, so the story continues, that *Suna-no O* found the sword and submitted it to *Amaterasu*, his divine sister, who immediately identified it to be her own lost sword, and hence renamed it as *Mura-kumo* [village-cloud], and designated it a divine sword. *Amaterasu* then conferred both the sword and the mirror to her grandson, on his departure from the celestial plains to descend to earth, so that her descendants would forever continue the lineage of divine sovereignty over the earthly dominion with these treasures as the emblem. This belief in divine sovereignty gave rise to the name *Shin-koku*, meaning the "Country of [or, ruled by] God['s descendants]" or "Divine[-ly ordained] Nation." The following is a literal translation of the farewell remarks of *Amaterasu* in conferring the three treasures to her departing grandson (the same—though not *verbatim*—narrative is contained in every chronicle of ancient Japan, such as *Kojiki*, *Nihon Shoki*, and *Sendai Kuji Honki*; the present translation is based on the passage in *Sendai Kuji Hongi*, Vol. 3, pp. 74; *cf.* Bibliography):

> "*Amaterasu Omikami*, conferring [to her grandson] the divine
> mirror which was in her hand, blessed [him] saying:
> > 'My child, your gazing upon this treasured mirror will be like
> > gazing on my face; keep [it with you] in bed and in the hall,
> > and regard it a mirror of witness, and its inheritance [from
> > one generation to the next] shall continue forever as long as
> > heaven and earth shall last.'"

It should be pointed out that, here in this particular narrative, the string of precious stones was not mentioned as one of the articles of the imperial regalia. The narrative also delineates several times that the sword was transferred from one emperor to another. In narrating these events during the transition, the names of the shrines where the sword had been kept are also mentioned (*cf. Heike Monogatari*, Vol. IV, pp. 222-227). The generally accepted early account of how the articles of *sanpo* were distributed is that, during the reign of Emperor *Suishin*: (1) the mirror was stored at *Ise* Shrine; (2) the sword was dedicated as divine (*corpus sacrae*) to *Atsuta* Shrine, and (3) the emperor himself took possession of *magatama* (crescent-shaped stones). The *replica* of the mirror and sword were then made for the dedication of the imperial insignia at coronation rituals. It is also accepted as historical fact that the sword was lost during the last battle between the Heike (Taira) and Genji (Minamoto) clans (see below), that there were actually only two surviving original divine articles in the set of three treasures, the *sanpo*.

However, there is a particularly noteworthy eyewitness account of the *sanpo* and the sword. In the appended commentary to *Gyokusen Shu* (loosely translated here as *Anthology of Jewel Notes*) is the following narrative:

> "About eighty years ago, the administrative priest-officers of *Atsuta* Shrine [in Kyoto] made a pact of agreement in quest of the "divine body" [*i.e., corpus sacrae*, the true identity of the divine articles]. Entering the central [chamber] of *koyoden*, nothing was visible for thickness of misty fog, and the fans and small torch had to be used to clear the vision. The *Chest of Witness* is a wooden box about five feet in length, and inside the Chest was stone box[es], with layers of red clay packed between [the boxes].
>
> The box on the right was like a round cedar piece but with inside carved out as a box [or urn], and inlaid with gold and a divine seat on top of it and … each of the boxes had a lock which was to be opened with a key …
>
> The divine body [*corpus sacrae*] is approximately two feet and seven to eight inches in length, with the blade point in the shape of '*shobu no ha-giri*' with slightly elevated [ridge] running the length of the body, with ribs on about every six inches, and the entire [blade] shaped like the spine rib of a fish bone, whit[-ish] in its coloration." [34]

This sword was also witnessed much later by a present-day scholar-author of Japanese history, Yamamura Masao, who posed the question in the title of his article "Was *Amaterasu* a Sun-God[dess]?"[35] From the description, there is little doubt that this object is an ancient sword with a distinctively unique shape of fish bone. In other words, the sword features several ribs branched out on both sides of the blade, essentially in the familiar figure—however elongated—of the *Menorah* (*cf. Fig.* 14).

In contrast to the sword and the mirror, there are preciously few tales surrounding the (string of precious or semi-precious) stones. Perhaps stones were too common, especially in light of the fact that it was one of the most ordinary personal ornaments in ancient ages, worn not only by people of position and wealth, male and female, but also by any commoners who could afford one. Throughout the entire ancient world, such jewelry items were found in abundance in virtually all archaeological digs. Hence, stones may not have had a near-equal ritual significance with the other two items—the mirror and the sword—that were always mentioned together in the chronicles as symbolizing the succession of imperial power, or in connection with the move of the imperial seat or shrine where *sanpo* was kept.

Still, it begs the question as to why the trouble of mentioning two particular items and not all three, if the reference is indeed for the *three* treasure items and, hence, would not merely the mention of *sanpo* have sufficed? While mentioning the *sanpo* (variously pronounced and differently ideogrammed) in the transition of royal authority from one emperor to the next, it is to be noted that in several narratives, often only two items are specifically mentioned: *tsurugi* (the sword) and *kagami* (the mirror).

Sendai Kuji Honki is the chronicle among the three which more recent scholarship recognizes as the most credible in terms of genealogical succession of *kami*. It was also written much later than *Kojiki* (712) and *Nihon Shoki* (720). By the author's own words, it can be ascertained that *Kuji Honki* was written during the Heian Period (781-1167). The original was lost, however, and only a copy of the original (written in 1521-22) has survived. The narratives in this particular chronicle, therefore, are believed by modern scholars of ancient Japanese history to be more reliably accurate particularly in regards to historical events and sequence. Hence the following citation is of significance: In the Fifth Book of *Sendai Kuji Honki,* it is mentioned that

> "… *Ameno Tomi no Mikoto*, the son of [Emperor] *Takami-Musubi no Mikoto*, led all the priests in dedicating *the mirror and the sword of the Amatsu-Shirushi* [*i.e.*, the chest of *Divine Testimony*] for worship by placing [them] in the Right Hall [of the shrine]."[36]

Another "two-items only" reference is found in *Heike Monogatari* (*The Tales of Heike*). In Book IV, on the event of an imperial visit to *Itsuku Shima* (*Itsuku* Island), is the following passage:

> "As it is determined that an opportune time has arrived. *Naishi-dokoro, shinshi* and the *treasure sword* were submitted....
> … in accordance with the established ritual, the *naishi* of *Ben* [lady in waiting] steps forward holding the *sword*....
> [Then] the *naishi* of *Hichu* [lady in waiting] takes out the *Chest of Witness* …"[37]

Here, two points of reference require additional comment:

First, the name *naishi-dokoro* is not one of the traditional names of the three sacred treasures. Although the editor's note (No. 11) states that *naishi-dokoro* is *the* "eight-foot mirror," and that the chest of witness refers to *magatama* (the crescent-shaped stones), the fact also is that the term *naishi dokoro* is used in various passages in *Heike Monogatari* as the name of the office or chamber where the sacred treasures are kept (and hence the ladies administering the handling of the treasures are called *naishi*). (The word *tokoro* or *-dokoro* literally means place or room.) (This same citation of the three "items" of the sacred treasures, with the same editorial note, can be found elsewhere in *Heike Monogatari*; for example, in Vol. III, pp. 81-82, and p. 276.)

Second, in spite of the mention of the three items, the fact of the event as narrated is that there were only two articles which were actually brought forth in the ritual presentation: the sword and the "chest of witness." This pattern of giving "eyewitness" to only two treasure items can be seen elsewhere, clearly suggesting that there were actually only two items in what is claimed to be the *"three* treasures"—the *sanpo* or *sanho*. In later writings, *sanpo* is more often referred to as "*san-ju no shingi*," meaning three kinds of divine vessel. (*Ju* or *shu* means kinds or types, and *shin-gi* means divine vessels. For mention of *sanju no shingi*, *cf. Heiki Monogatari*, Vol. III, p. 276, and Vol. IV, p. 33, 40, 138 and 216, and elsewhere. To be noted also is that, in Japanese, there are no plural forms of nouns.)

Does this and other similar mention of "the two sacred articles only" in reference to *sanpo* (three treasures) infer that there were actually only two articles in the *regalia*, and that "three" was the number in referring to the original number of ritual items in the set that was (believed to have been) placed in the chest of the *Amatsu-Shirushi* or the Divine *Testimony* (a.k.a., the ark of *the Covenant*)?

In contrast to the sword and mirror, the divine chest is absent with any definitive description, and is seldom given historical or even mythological accounts such as those accorded the sword and mirror. There are, in fact, only less than a handful of "historical" accounts on this elusive *Mi-Koshi*, the Divine Chest. In a number of places, the editor of *Heike Monogatari* identifies the *Shin-shi* (i.e., another pronunciation of the same ideograms *Mi-koshi*, the divine chest) as the receptacle of *both* the *kagami* and *magatama* (mirror and string of stones), while in others simply as the receptacle or identical with mirror. Indeed, from time to time, the reference to *sanpo* is simply stated as "the sword and *other* sacred vessels" or "the sword and the *divine chest*." Even in such non-uniformed nomenclature in referring to *sanpo*, any actual description of the divine chest or its content(s) is nearly totally absent, except on three particular occasions.

These are without doubt the preciously few and thus greatly significant references to understand and unveil the mystery of *sanpo*.

There are four accounts, of which two give account to opening of the "lid" of the receptacle. One is in *National History* (*Koku-shi*) which contains the following narrative:

> "Emperor Yuriaku thought that, as the emperor, there is nothing under the heavens that he could not open and examine. Hence he opened the lid of the golden urn. Immediately there arose a puff of white smoke which caused fear to come over the emperor, and [he] quickly replaced the lid tightly."
> (translation mine)

The second is in *Heike Monogatari* which also tells of opening of the lid:

> "The so-called *Divine Box* [or receptacle] is [an article which has been] transmitted since the age of *kami* and kept by generations of emperors, and is kept in the *Chest of Testimony*. [As] no one has ever opened this chest, [Emperor] *Go-lei-sei* became curious, and [he] attempted to remove the lid. But immediately a white cloud arose [from the receptacle] … Thereby the *naishi* [lady in waiting] of [the house of] *Kii* quickly replaced the lid and tightly bound it."
> (translation mine)

There are two other references, perhaps more intriguing than the above, that may be regarded as "eyewitnesses" where the (approximate) measurement of the size and the form of this sacred vessel are given. One is an entry in *Kodai Jingu Gishiki Cho* (*Registry of the Rituals of the Kodai Shrine*), where the chest is described as:

> "the height one foot four inches, depth eight-point-three inches, inner circumference one foot six-point-three inches, and the outer circumference two feet. The shape is like a long tube and hence called *mito-yu-shiro* [replica of divine tube], and its table [or container] is called *MiFune-Shiro* [the replica of the divine boat]."
> (translation mine)

The other description of this sacred vessel is found in an editorial note in *Nihon Shoki Tsu-Yaku*, by Handa (surname) who had published papers perhaps a decade or so into Emperor Meiji's "Reign of Restoration" ("restoration" is in reference to Meiji's reclaiming of the imperial right and authority from the hands of the shogunates who were the virtual rulers of Japan for over eight centuries). The following is the description in the author's editorial note:

> "In the innermost part of *kangami* is a golden urn, its height being one foot three inches, diameter nine inches; the urn has a lid, and the hinge [plate around the urn] is of golden chain, and both the urn and the lid are decorated with 'roof' [-like] figurations ..."
> (translation mine)

To this information, the author of the edition adds a commentary note in verifying the referred fact, to the effect that the sacred vessel was "examined by the emperor himself, in the imperial palace [where there is an imperial shrine], in the "month of April of the sixth year of [Meiji's] reign." (The month of April is the first month of the year in Japan's traditional calendar, which also marks the beginning of a school year as well as the official calendar.)

There is a historical account that seems to provide credence to the above references on the *MiFune Shiro* and its contents. In *Heike Monogatari* we would read one of the most poignant stories, on the death of *Antoku Tenno*, an emperor of a tender age (six or seven). The event took place in the last great sea battle between the armies of the house of *Tahira* (or *Taira*, *i.e.* the *Heike* clan) and *Minamoto* (the *Genji* clan). *Tahira*, by virtue of its claim of imperial lineage, had yielded an uncontested and unbridled power over Japan, becoming its virtual ruler. As such, the house and lords of the *Tahira* clan also became—or had self-appointed—the guardian of the imperial regalia, the *sanpo*. Such high-handed and, worse, often brutal reign of *Tahira* clan on every level of government was such that a deep resentment and widespread hatred for the house of *Taira* was fermented over the years, leading ultimately to one of the greatest contests of the warlords's military might in the entire history of Japan. *Heike Monogatari* was written (during the Kamakura Period, 1185-1392) as an eyewitness account (by a leading Buddhist priest) of the "rise and fall"—the greater details given to the latter—of the house of *Tahira*. As one of the only handful of great historical literary masterpieces of Japan, *Heike Monogatari* contains literally hundreds of passionate tales great and small, of gallant chivalry, cunning intrigue and tender passion, concluding with the great sea battle at *Dan no Ura*, in which nearly all the warriors, along with thousands of ships, of the *Tahira* clan were decimated by the clever maneuver of young *Yoshitsune* (and his constant companion *Benkei*) as the leader of their chief adversary, the

Genji clan. It was in one of the last scenes of the great sea battle that the drowning death of the young Emperor *Antoku* was narrated. Below is this particular passage; the second half of the citation is quoted from Hadland's *Myths and Legends of Japan* (the English translation by W. G. Aston):

"Warriors of Genji had already boarded the Heiki ship, where the bodies of its sailors and pilots were all scattered, shot dead by the arrows …

When *Nii-dono* [the wife of *Taira Kiyomori*] [realized that there was no hope left], … she held the Divine Chest to her side and put the Treasure Sword to her waist [belt], then holding up the Emperor, shouted,

'Even a female, I shall not yield to the enemy. [Rather,] I shall follow the Master. Those who hold loyalty [to the emperor], make haste and follow [me],' and

she walked out to the side of the ship. Although a mere lad of eight [by traditional reckoning of age; factual age was either six or seven], the emperor appeared more mature, with adorable countenance which radiated on all surrounding [him]. With a lock of long black hair on his back, he inquired

'Maid, where are you taking me?'

Holding back her tears, she replied,

'Master, have you not yet perceived? While by the grace of the perfect good deeds of your ancestors you have now become the lord over all, you [now] have been pulled by the [force of] *karma* of the evil deeds [of *Kiyomori*, your maternal grandfather].

Now, your fate has reached its very end. Now, then, face the east and bid farewell to Grand *Ise* Shrine, then … face the west to recite the *sutra* of Buddha [that he may] welcome you to the Land of Purity in the West.[38]

[For …]

"… 'This world is the region of sorrow, a remote spot small as a grain of millet. But beneath the waves there is a fair city called the Pure Land of Perfect Happiness. Thither it is that I am taking you.' With such words she soothed him. The child then tied his top-knot to the Imperial robe of the color of a mountain-dove, and tearfully [cupped] together his tender little hands in propitiation. First he turned to the East … then to the West …

When he had done so, *Niidono* [embraced] him in her arms and,

while leaping [herself with the emperor] down into the [ocean] bottom
one thousand fathoms deep, cried out her final words [of comfort to
the infant emperor],
'There is [yet] a [capital] city way below the ocean waves!'"[39]

With regard to the *sanpo*, however, the story actually does not end here. While
the narrative above indicates that at least two of the sacred articles (the chest and
the sword) went down to the bottom of the ocean with the infant emperor and
his lady in waiting, in the ensuring narrative is found the following passage:

> "[… amidst the riotous turmoil abroad the Heike ship]
> *Dainagon no Suke* attempted to take the *Mi-Karauto* [chest
> containing *kagami*, the sacred mirror] and enter the water. However,
> an arrow pinned his skirt to the side of a ship board …
> **Several warriors tried to wrestle the chest [from Dainagon] and
> to open the lid. However, [in doing so] their eyes immediately
> became blurred, and [some] started to bleed from their nose.**
> Thereupon *Dainagon* rebuked them, saying:
> 'That is the item of the *naishisho*, and not to be seen by ordinary men.'
> Hearing this, the warriors stepped back. Afterward, the officer-judge
> of the [bureau of] rites discussed the matter with *Dainagon*, and
> they had agreed to rewrap [the chest] to its previous condition."[40]

There is yet another narrative—more like an epilogue—closely following the
"eyewitness" account of the fate of *sanpo* cited above:

> "On the third of April of the same year … when *Yoshitsune* …
> was being inquired in the hall of the rites, [he submitted that]
> 'On the twenty-fourth of March last, [the army of] *Heike* was
> being defeated at *Akama ga Seki*, and that all three divine articles
> have been returned safely to the sacred halls.'
> Immediately this saying caused a great disturbance among the
> people present in the hall [of rites] …
> … [Thereafter, several named officers were dispatched to investigate
> the truthfulness of *Yoshitsune*'s claim.]
> "On the twenty-fifth [of April] … deep into the midnight hour,
> *naishisho*, the Chest of Witness, was brought into the hall of the
> Great Executive Palace. [However, it was determined that indeed]
> the sword had been lost.

It is told that *Shinji* [the *Divine Chest of Testimony*, or the
Chest of Covenant] *was found afloat in the ocean*, and was picked
up by [a man called] *Kataoka no Taro Tsuneharu*."[41]

From these and other documentary evidences, there is no denying that the
sanpo did exist, and there was a divine chest of *mi-fune-shiro* which housed
the *sanpo*. Certain details such as the measurement of the article differ slightly
from one account to the other, and this may be due to the fact that the unit of
measurement was never constant throughout history (the case which was more
detailedly accounted for in Chinese chronicles, since measurement and number were closely related to the ritual system of the imperial court of China). It
is an awesome archaeological subject, awe-inspiring for anyone in realizing that
these very same artifacts have survived until now, for as long as two millennia,
still strictly guarded in the innermost sanctum of the Grand Ise Shrine, as the
undeniable emblem of Japan's imperial throne and the imperial house as the
direct descendant of the sun goddess *A-Materasu*.

One puzzling question may be posed: in all the eyewitness accounts, the urn
is described as containing a white powdery substance that caused a foul smell
and irritation to the senses. In the Old Testament, the urn is said to contain a
portion (omer) of *manna*, the "bread from heaven." The study on *manna* (*cf.* the
summary article in *Encyclopædia Britannica*) indicates that it was a plant substance found in the desert land (*e.g.*, in the Sinai). Several candidates have been
identified, such as lichens (*Lecanora esculenta*), resins (*Alhagi maurorum*), tamarisk (*Tamarix gallica*), and others. Specifically, tamarisk, common in the Sinai,
is called even by the Bedouin Arabs living in the area '*Mann es-Sama*'—literally
"*manna from heaven*." The substance is exudation from the stem of the plant
(*e.g.*, *Alhagi*) when scale insects puncture the stem. The secretion soon hardens
to become small droplets, whitish in color and sweet in taste like honey. Left in
the sun, the substance would soon turn yellowish, and insects, including ants,
would devour them. Or, under hot desert sun, the substance would soon rot
and breed worms and emit a foul smell. All such descriptions appear to agree
with the biblical description of *manna* (Exodus 16: 14-22; 31-36).

If the substance in the urn was indeed such plant secretion which is known
to easily breed worms and emit a foul smell, it would not be difficult to imagine how such a substance, in the amount as much as half a gallon, left tightly
sealed in an urn for many centuries and perhaps as long as over two millennia,
would have become *fungi* infested, *porous and poisonous, capable of causing a
most immediate irritation to human senses*.

CHAPTER EIGHTEEN

THE HEART OF THE MYSTERY: *KANGAMI* OR *KANGAME*?

One of the most elaborate religious ceremonies in the modern world—and arguably the most costly—is *Shingu Shunen Sengu*. It is the moving of the entire shrine and the entire sacred regalia from one site to another a short distance away, from the old shrine structures to the *identically* constructed new buildings, the inner and outer sanctuaries of the Grand *Ise* Shrine. The solemn event—in fact a series of events over the period of several years—was started in the late seventh century, during the reign of Emperor *Temmu* (670, in the *Nara* Period) and, except for the warring years, has been repeated every twenty years. Even spreading over twenty years, the entire cost of the event is nothing short of astonishing. Today the expenditure for each move is estimated to be equivalent of over three hundred million US dollars, about two-thirds of which comes from the Shrine budget, with the remainder from public donations.

The move actually consists of a series of several events over a period of nearly a decade. These ceremonies are called by different names in identifying the nature of each event, from the "cutting of the tree" to "transporting of timbre," to the final installation of sacred relics and the offering of *mi-Kagura*, the "divine music" (which is a portion in the *gagaku* repertoire). The elaborate and most meticulous preparation for the move is unlike anything in the world; the preparation of the *next Sengu* has already begun, with the concluding ceremony for the installation of the next new shrine scheduled in 2013.

The entire *Sengu* rites consist of thirty-three separate events. The following is a partial listing of the events, noted with their proper names* (in *italics*) with their English translation by this writer. The dates, the year and month of each event, are of the most recent, that is, the sixty-first *sengu* ritual, which took place from the sixtieth year of *Showa* (1985) to the fifth year of *Heisei* (1993). The next sengu is expected to be exactly twenty years from 1993, that is, in the year 2013.

May 1985	*Yamaguchi Sai* (Ceremony** at the foot of the mountain)
May 1985	*Konomoto Sai* (Ceremony at the foot of the tree)
September 1985	*Mi-Funa Shiro Sai* (Ceremony of **Replica of the Divine Boat**)
April 1986	*MiKi Hiki Hajime Sai* (Ceremony of Commencing the Tree Move)
April 1988	*Chin-Chi Sai* (Ceremony of Ground Consecration)
November 1989	*Uji-Bashi Watari-Hajime Shiki* (Ceremony of Commencing the Passing Over the Bridge *Uji*)
March 1992	*Ritschu Sai* (Ceremony of Erecting [the main] Post)
March 1992	*Jo-To Sai* (Ceremony of [installing] the Cross [the roof] Beam)
July 1992	*Iuka Sai* (Ceremony of [installing] the Thatch [roof])
September 1993	*Mi-To Sai* (Ceremony of [installing] the Door)
September 1993	*Mi-Funa-Shiro Hou-Nou Sai* (Ceremony of Installation of the **Replica of the Divine Boat**)
September 1993	**Arai-Kiyomi** (Purification of Washing)
September 1993	*Shin no Mi-Hashira Hou-Ken* (Offering of the Core Post)
October 1993	*Go-Chin Sai* (Ceremony of Post (*i.e.*, after the) Consecration)
October 1993	*O-Sho-Zoku Shin-Po Toku-Go* (Inventory Reading of Regalia and of Sacred Treasures)
October 1993	*Sen-gu* (the Move)
October 1993	*Oo-Mi-ke* (the Great Offering)
October 1993	*Hou-Hei* (the Offering of Curtains [or Bills])
October 1993	*Ko-Motsu Watashi* (Transfer of Ancient Articles)
October 1993	*Mi-Kagura Mi-ke* (the offering of Divine Music)
October 1993	*Mi-Kagura* ([the performance of Divine Music)

[*Note*: The event names in English are the present author's own translation.
** "*Sai*" has the same ideogram as "*matsuri*." The word may mean either ordinary festival or ritual ceremony. For a more formal regard of the nature and solemnity of these events, "Ceremony" is opted here.]

Unfortunately, the attendance to this most elaborate, mysterious, and pro-hibitively exorbitant religious event is restricted only to a small exclusive audi-ence—the immediate family members of the imperial household and a few high-ranking government ministers and officers by special invitation only. It is furthermore curious that the climactic events in these rituals—the last dozen or so—are always conducted in the evening hours, and, with the exception of *kagura* (divine music) performance, all other processions are nearly always exe-cuted in utter silence; the only sound is from the shuffling of the priests' stiffly starched regalia, and from their wooden shoes against the pebbled ground. There is occasional chirping of insects and cries of night fowls. In the twilight, the whole atmosphere—indeed the whole sacred compound—is filled with an erie spirit, out-of-this worldly, one of profound enigma, an endless conun-drum. And, in viewing the video documentary shown on national television newscast (NHK), one could not help but wonder how it is possible that such a cloaked mystery still exists in this modern world of science and enlightenment where, elsewhere in the world, nothing remains *sacrosanct*, nothing escapes the probing eyes of investigative reporters, nothing is beyond the reach of the scalpel of unrelenting prying curiosity of the masses and the media reporters. And one could not help but wonder also why it is that not only the common people of Japan but particularly the scholars of Japanese history and anthro-pology remain disassociated, never vocal in expressing their desire or the "right to know" the mystery of *their own cultural* ancestry.

As mentioned, the *Sengu* rituals are repeated every twenty years, and this length of period is officially designated as *Shiki-nen* which literally means "year(s) of the rites." The ideogram for *shiki* (rites) shares the same etymologi-cal root with *ni* and *ni-ju* (twenty) and, in fact, the archaic Chinese character for number two or twenty (in a simplified script) is nearly identical with the ideogram for *shiki*. This may be a case of calligraphic coincidence. However, there is an aspect of their cultural signification associated with the number *twenty*, an aspect of their number system which may suggest another possible element of connection in cultural heritages.

Even before the invention of pictograms and ideograms, China had already developed one of the earliest—and complete—number systems in the history of civilized man. From the earliest written records (*e.g.*, the pre-Qin dynasty court chronicles), it can be attested that the Chinese number system has always been ten-based (*decimal* system), as was with the areas of "Oriental high cul-ture" such as India and Arabia.

In contrast, the number system in the Near-Eastern world (the earliest fer-tile-crescent cultures such as Sumer and Chaldea) had developed along the line of number system that was "multi-decimal based" of twenty and sixty—the latter being the famous *hexagesimal* system of the Sumerians. The residue of this multi-decimal based numerical system can still be detected even after so many millennia. Consider, for example, the use of the word *score* [meaning twenty, as in "Four *score* and seven years ago …" of the Gettysburg address, or "… and his number is 'six hundred three *score* and six" [*cf. Revelation* 13: 18b], or the division of time (as in number of minutes in an hour, number of seconds in a minute, *etc.*) and of angle (circle of three hundred and sixty degrees, which is multiplying of six and sixty). In other words, instead of numbers 40, 50, 60, 70, 80, and 90 (as discrete multiples of ten), the ancient Middle-Eastern (*e.g.*, Sumerian and Semitic) people would number these same figures as: two-twenties; ten-plus-two-twenties (or ten-plus-forty); three-twenties; ten-plus-three-twenties (or ten-plus-sixty); four-twenties; and ten-plus-four-twenties. It is indeed curious to note that the same manner of counting was used by the ancient Japanese people (as also survived among the Ainu people), but not among people of the Sinitic culture.

Turning to the Bible, we find that there are a number of times when "twenty years" was referred to in the experience of religious life of the Israelites, for example, in the moving of the Israelite camp and the ark during the years in the dessert, and the ark being in the hands of enemies and of custodians before it was finally returned to David's camp. This "twenty" year period may therefore be regarded as having ritual signification rather than the coincidence of actual events' chronological time lapse. It may be argued that there is no reference to the "years of the rites" in any ancient chronicles of Japan. However, the fact that ancient Japanese had possessed this particular system of numerical accounting provides support to the perspective that this number system was a part of the ancient heritage of Japan's oraclers, and the lack of other extant reference to *sengu* was due perhaps to its low(er) ritual priority (than, say, mythological legends) and hence, along with countless other information, was being extricated from being transcribed into *Kojiki* and *Nihon Shoki*.

Another number with cultural significance is twelve, the number of Hebrew tribes, after the twelve sons of Jacob the son of Abraham. In Exodus 24 is the following narrative:

"… And [Moses] rose early in the morning, and built an altar
at the foot of the mountain, and twelve pillars, according to the
twelve tribes of Israel." (v. 4)

It is of interest that we too find this "twelve pillars" as a distinct feature of a holy ground in many ancient *shinto* shrines in Japan, explicitly or implicitly in reference to worship of twelve *kami*. Examples are too numerous to list, but the following three better known shrine names would suffice to substantiate this perspective:

> *Juni-So Jinja* (The Shrine of *Twelve* Ancestries), in Musashi,
>   outskirts of Tokyo Prefecture;
> *Juni-Dokoro Jinja* (The Shrine of *Twelve* Places/Persons),
>   in Izumo Zaki, Echigo Prefecture; and
> *Aso Jinja* (Aso Shrine), of Aso-Gun Miya Chi,
>   in Hyogo Prefecture (which is dedicated toworship of
>   twelve deities).

Indeed, the entire mystery of not only the *Sengu* but the whole *Shinto* cult still so tenaciously surrounds the imperial regalia which have been kept for countless generations in the Grand Ise Shrine. This is the legendary regalia of the imperial lineage, consisting of the *sanpo* which are kept in wooden chest called *MiFune-Shiro*, literally the "Replica of the *Divine Boat*" or the Divine *ark*. One would further notice that, while this same sacred receptacle ia also called by several various names, all of the names possess the same connotation, as the Israelites ark of the Covenant was also variously called: the "ark (or Chest) of *Witness*," the "ark of the *Testimony*" and the "ark of *Promise*."

The contents of the *MiFune-Shiro* are presumably "known": (a) a sword (*tsurugi*), a replica of the original sword which was lost in the last sea battle of the Genji-Heike conflict; (b) a string of crescent-shaped semi-precious stones (*maga-tama*); and (c) an item called *kan-gami* which, as signified by Chinese ideograms, has been *traditionally* accepted as a mirror.

However, it is this third item that is at the core of the deepest mystery of all mysteries of imperial lineage, where the accepted view does not seem to agree with the recorded (and documentably substantiable) eyewitness descriptions. The *tsurugi* sword has been eyewitnessed by many and on various occasions throughout history. It has been described in various passages in *Kojiki* and *Nihon Shoki* as well as in other historical works such as *Heike Monogatari*. The *magatama* also, but appearing to be the least revered of the *sanpo* treasure, was only occasionally mentioned but often was left out in referring to *sanpo* in not only *Kojiki* and *Nihon Shoki* but also in other historical chronicles. In fact, the overabundance of *magatama* stones unearthed in *kofun* (ancient tombs) throughout central Japan's archaeological sites may perhaps suggest that *magatama* was not even an item of the original *sanpo* but a mere symbolic substitute for the missing stone tablets with cursive marks, perhaps in some way signifying the (lost) stone tablets of the *Decalogue*. The lesser importance of the stones, whether they are crescent stone pieces or stone tablets, may be attributed also to the (assumed) fact that the invaders of the ark sometime between the days of King David and King Solomon took only two items, the sword (Aaron's rod with seven branches), and the pot of manna, the two items of the three sacred regalia, the sanpo. In other words, the people of the proto-*shinto* cult carried with them on their migratory journey only two items of the original three.

In contrast, there has never been any clear information on the third item, now known as *kangami*. The only descriptions come from the handful of eye-witnesses who all seem to refer to it as an article (1) more like a container, being carefully wrapped with many layers of heavy brocade, since (2) it is in eminent danger of falling apart, and (3) when *the lid of the container is opened*, it instantly emits a puff of smoke (powdery substance?) or an odor such as to cause suffocation or sickness to those nearby, (4) that the "effect" of the article has been described in (at least three) sources, the last of which was from the early decades of the nineteenth century (during the Meiji period). And, as to the size of this article (or box), (5) it was small enough to be carried under the arm (*e.g.*, of an imperial maid-in-waiting).

If *Kangami*—or should it be pronounced *Kan-Kagami*, in order to correctly identify it as a *"Holy mirror"*—and there are literally hundreds of such holy mirrors—is indeed a mirror, it should be a flat, round metal (bronze) plate, polished on one side to reflect images and with ornate relief on the other (*cf. FIG. 9*). Such bronze mirrors, more often than not made as ritual items, are found also in abundant number elsewhere, throughout the Eurasian Continent and in Far-Eastern Asia (*e.g.*, China and Korea). If *Kangami* is indeed one such bronze mirror, then it would never be in danger of falling apart. It would never require a container or protective wrapping, or emit powdery smoke or faul smell.

Hence, *kangami*, in most likelihood, is not a mirror. The name *kangami* was in the most likehood a mis-appropriation of ideograms—a case of incorrect *ateji*—for what should have been *kan-game*, a divine *urn*, a *jar*. A wooden or metalic jar with a lid. From extant descriptions, there apparently was an amount of foreign substance inside this jar which, when the lid was opened and fresh air gushed in, gave rise to a puff of air, smoke, a pungent odor, that caused eye irritation and stench, causing nausea and even nose bleeding to the people close by. It is also recorded at least in one instance that this jar, the container, had golden inlaid plates or hinges. If so, then it may be conjectured that such metal fixtures would have become frail and indeed would be in danger of falling apart.

This is precisely what is described in Davis' narratives in *From the Age of the Gods* …, that (to repeat the quote cited earlier, *cf. Note* 12),

> "The Divine Mirror [called *kangami*] … is kept in a box of
> chamacyparis in the *Naiku* [or *Naigu*] (the *Inner Ise Shrine*) …
> wrapped in brocade, and when it *begins to fall to pieces* it is …
> covered with a fresh [layer of] wrapping, so that the precious
> relic is now protected with many layers of silk [brocade] …
> The *box* and its coverings are placed in a cage (chest?) elaborately
> *ornamented in gold*, and this again is covered with a silk cloth."[42]

And this description of *kangami*—or shall we *now* more *correctly* refer to it as *kan-game*—is virtually identical with the description of the *urn of manna* that was placed in the ark of the Covenant of the ancient Israelites (*cf.* Hebrews, Chapter 9). For *kan-game* is not a mirror but an *urn*, made of wood but covered with "ornamental" golden plates, possibly with golden hinges, and that the wooden box, with plates and hinges, would be in frail condition due to its extreme ancient age of possibly more than two millennia.

One may dismiss this as nothing but another curious coincidence. But to regard it as such would be tantamount to ignoring the odds against the presence of so numerous other coincidences, all occurring in one place, in one legend, in one general historical period, all on a handful of items the source of which has never been satisfactorily explained by anyone or could be dismissed otherwise. As all these aspects have been mentioned previously, I should like to briefly mention twelve more notable items, in a somewhat outlined format:

1) First, the curious coincidence that the words ark (English or Aramaic) and *fune* (Japanese) connote both boat and receptacle (box, chest). Though rarely used, in Japanese *fune* (boat) may also mean receptacle or box, with or without the lid, even a hewn timbre such as manger (which was most probably what the original urn containing the *manna* was). The case in point is a Japanese Christmas carol quoted below, where *ma-bune*, literally meaning a 'horse boat,' is used to refer to a manger—a receptacle. (The English translation of the hymn stanza mine).

MABUNE

Seigi Abe (1930)

MA - BU - ME NO   NA - KA NI   U - BU GO - E   A - GE,

TA - KU - MI NO   I - HE NI   HI - TO TO— NA - RI - TE,

MA - ZU - SHI - KI   U - RE - I   I - KU - RU NA - YA - MI,

TSU - BU - SA NI   NA - ME SHI   KO - NO HI - TO   WO   MI-YO.

> "[Born] in the *horse-boat* (manger), to utter an infant's first cry,
> In the house of a carpenter, He became a man;
> Anxiety of poverty, and burdens of living,
> [He has] tasted them all;
> Behold, this Man!"

2) the period of the disappearance of the two articles from the ark of the Covenant and the period of the *diaspora* segue to the period of time when the *shinto* relics arrived on the Japanese archipelago;

3) the direction of *diaspora*, and the general geographical region where the proto-Japanese could (only) have come from;

4) the political and cultic environment and political map during the *diaspora* and the post-*diaspora* periods, in the entire "central" region of the Eurasian Continent, especially Central Asia to the Far East (*cf.* 6 below);

5) the names in the *Shinto* legends (*A-Materasu*) as well as its beliefs that parallel the names (in phonetic sounds) of the location and the religious beliefs (*e.g.*, *Mithras, Mezzullash*) in the western part of the Eurasian Continent;

6) the record in official chronicles (The *Western Han* portion of *Shi-Ji*, third century, B.C.E.) giving reference to the migration of the tribe of "knife's cult" passing through northern China in the period of c. 2nd to 3rd centuries, B.C.E.;

7) the genetic factors—blood lineage of a lost tribe, and also

8) the linguistic elements—a language of the "lost" tribe (a.k.a. an "orphan" language);

9) the names and the folk and ritual customs, and more specifically the major festivals of Japan, such as Feast of Gion—Zion?—and the procession of *O-Mikoshi*, the parade of the *Chest of Witness*, all belonging to *shinto* rituals;

10) the description of the lost items in the Bible, *vesus* the description of the *sanpo* items, with similar size and parallel details;

11) the name and signification of *MiFune-Shiro* (the *Replica of the Divine Ark*, *i.e.*, the *Sacred Boat*) and *kan-game* (the divine urn); and

12) the several eyewitness accounts and descriptions of this *kan-game*.

EPILOGUE

WHERE ARE
THE *LOST* TREASURES OF
THE ARK OF THE COVENANT?

[I]

On a particularly hot and humid August morning in 1980 I boarded a bus from Shibuya station (a suburb of Tokyo) to Haneda Airport to begin my journey back to the United States. I had been in Japan for about six weeks studying ancient Japanese music (specifically the *gagaku*, the ritual music of the Japanese imperial court). *En route*, the bus made a stopover at a hotel in *Shinjiku* (or *Shinjuku*) to pick up additional passengers. As I watched the people getting on board, my eyes were inexplicably drawn to an elderly Japanese lady, perhaps in her seventies, cheerfully chatting with her travel companion as she gingerly climbed up the steps. She was very "Japanese" in her exquisitely graceful way of speech and mannerism. But what had drawn my gaze (she would have felt uncomfortable had she noticed my scrutinizing stare) was her countenance and, for the next few minutes, I was unable to take my eyes off her. She must be from an aristocratic or at least a wealthy family. But my eyes were drawn to "analyzing" her facial features. For had it not been for her *kimono* (traditional Japanese dress) and her manner of speech in a most graceful and refined Japanese (*Tokyo-ben*, or the Tokyo *tongue*, regarded as the classic of Japanese dialects), I would have mistaken her for a twin sister of Mrs. Snider, who was the next-door Jewish neighbor of ours of two years (1967-69) in Detroit.

I was teaching at the Music Department of Detroit Bible College, then on Meyers Road, and our apartment building (owned by the college) was on the busy thoroughfare directly across from the college. Since we moved into the apartment, Mr. and Mrs. Snider had extended to us a warm friendship, and Mrs. Snider was particularly fond of our daughter, showing and showering on her a genuine grandmother-like affection. Besides gifts to our daughter, she also had invited us on several occasions to her home for tea and snacks, and we were introduced to many traditional Jewish dishes and sweets. As I looked at this Japanese lady, I not only recalled so much of the impression Mrs. Snider had left on me, but also pondered the probability that there might indeed be a genetic tie between Mrs. Snider and this Japanese lady sitting immediately across the less than two feet wide isle from me on the bus. And I thought of Oyabe's book which featured the Star of David on its cover, and remembered another book, titled *The Japanese and the Jews* (by Isaiah Ben-Dashan, in Japanese; English translation by Richard Gage), given to me by Rev. Nambu of Northshore Japanese Church in Chicago. Ben-Dashan's book also had the same *Star of David* figured prominently on its cover. I then recalled reading in this book about this Star of the symbol of Israel also being a family crest of Japanese people of bygone eras, called *kagome* (meaning "basket weaving"). And I could not make myself believe that there is not a shred of ethnic and cultural tie between this Japanese lady and Mrs. Snider. Indeed, both of them may very possibly be daughters of Abraham. Had not God blessed Abraham that his children and children's children would be as great in number as the stars in heaven and the sands in the ocean?

This was not the first time I had noticed certain resemblances of facial features between Jewish—or, rather, Semitic—and Japanese people, more evident in women than men. And one of the more particularly notable features is the shape of the nose. At the same time, I also noticed that many Japanese men have facial features—the "Greek nose," thick eyebrows and heavy beard—that are characteristic of their Middle Eastern and Central Asian counterparts, particularly the Turks and Greeks. In my study of ethnic music, I also noticed certain similar features between the traditional music of Japan and the Mediterranean and Middle Eastern regions (*e.g.*, *hemitonic pentatonic* pattern, such as MI-FA-LA-TI-DO-MI or MI-FA-LA-TI-RE-MI, or *hemitonic hexatonic* pattern of MI-FA-SI-LA-TI-DO/RE-MI, as in *solmization* syllable sequence).

Linguists would point out parallels in the grammar of (ancient) Japanese and Turkish languages, that they, along with over half (or as much as two-thirds) of the languages spoken in the world today, are offshoots—the limbs—from what linguists called the Indo-European language. Still, curiously, Japanese is regarded as one of the 'orphan languages,' in that its exact linguistic lineage origin is all but impossible to be credibly identified (*cf.* map of language distribution, *Fig.* 16). Meanwhile, linguists would unequivocally state that (old) Japanese did not belong to, and was not derived from, the Sinitic (Chinese) tongue but instead came from the same linguistic origin of Turkish and Finnish languages, that they are related to the Altaic linguistic branch, a limb of Indo-European proto-language (see below).

The existence of any possible kinship between the two peoples—one on the islands off the farthest eastern shores, and the other on the farthest western coastal regions, of the Eurasian Continent—finds support not from any direct primary documents but, rather, from other sister disciplines of archaeology and anthropology, and in genetic study also, that at least some stocks of the early (*i.e.*, proto-) Japanese are more closely related to Semitic and "European" stocks (the latter in a generalized term) than to Sinitic (Chinese and Mongolian) stocks.

[II]

Japanese mythological tales contain features that parallel those in ancient Middle Eastern regions, and the archaeological finds such as iron weapons, jewelry, and ritual articles which have been unearthed from the tombs in many parts of the two larger Japanese islands also suggest that these artifacts are of Middle Eastern and Central Asian origin. Certain ritual concepts, particularly the curiously unique ones, also parallel those in the religious beliefs of Middle Eastern people. And certain archaic names in mythology, such as *Amaterasu*, *Izumo*, as well as favored personal names such as *Yisaku*, *Eisaku* and *Yuri* (for male), and *Kazu*, *Tama*, *Hana*, and *Kemi* (for female) are all but identical with common Semitic names (*e.g.*, *Issak*, *Izak*, *Yuri*, *Hanna*, *Tama*, etc.).

But the most curious of all is the revered sacred regalia called **MiFune-Shiro**, which literally means **Replica of the Divine 'Boat'** (or '**Ark**'), and its contents called *sanpo*, the "three treasure" articles. In fact this chest or receptacle is also called the **Shirushi no Mi-Koshi** or **Shirushi no Mi-Hako** (the meaning of *shirushi* being the same as **Testimony** or **Witness**). It is a historically verifiable fact also that the treasures and the chest have been handed down as *the* quintessential imperial regalia for some two millennia.

Sacred chest as a seat of god and a receptacle for safekeeping and transporting sacred articles was a common cultic practice in the ancient Near- and Middle East, including Egypt, where, scholars believe, the practice had originated and, from there, had spread to other regions in the Middle East. An important aspect of this practice is the fact that such sacred chests were made in fairly large quantities, in order to resolve the problem inherent in their theological concept, that god's potency was territorial and, hence, a need to make multiple copies of the seat of god to be available to the faithful in various locations. This practice of making replicas of holy relics can still be observed in Ethiopia, where every church claims to possess an ark of the covenant, even if it is as simple as a stone or wooden slab.

Hence, the fact that the Japanese claim of possessing a *"shiro"* (replica) of the Divine Chest must be regarded as an unequivocal evidence that *the people of the shinto cult had come from the Middle Eastern region and had arrived at Japan's archipelago, carrying with them a replica of the ark.* For the practice of carrying the "chest of testimony" or the "chest of promise" was common especially among the nomadic people of the Middle East. At the same time, this practice is distinctly different from the carrying of idols such as was practiced by the Buddhist faithful. The former carried a *representation* of their invisible deity, the latter the *image*—the very likeness—of their deities. This distinction is to be recognized also between the Shinto *shrines* and the Buddhist *temples*—the former hold *no image of god*, the latter possess the *graven image of deities.*

What, then, is *shintoism*, and where is its likely source of origin?

First, *shintoism* is not a religion. Rather, it is a belief, a state of mind, an attitude. The original *tenet* of *shintoism*—if the word is even appropriate here—did not possess a *theistic* doctrine or even behold the imperial house as *divine* lineage. Nowhere in *Kojiki* or *Nihon Shoki* could one find a clearly articulated catechism on *shintoism. Kami* does not refer to any particular deity, and there was—and still is—no established dogma. All things visible and invisible, all things that are worthy of reverence, are *kami.* This includes ancestors, animals with any effectuating power, and natural things with forces that impact human lives. There is *kami* in mountains and rivers, rocks and trees, fires and clouds. And above all is the mighty sun, which is personified in the goddess of *Amaterasu* who is believed to rule the celestial domain of *Takama ga Hara,* which was in *Ame*—heaven. And it was believed that she was the one who had not only given life to all all the emperors in the lineage of *Ninigi, Amaterasu's* own grandson, but also form to all things, including islands, mountains and rivers. Hence, *shintoism* is also—and particularly more importantly in the historical-political perspectives—the belief that all people and all things are under and within the dominion of the supreme *kami,* represented on earth by the imperial throne.

Hence *shintoism* is often categorized by Western scholars as belonging to polytheism or animism. Neither is appropriate. If a label is necessary, perhaps *pantheism* may be more proper, but it still needs a qualifier. For *shintoism* does not possess any formal theological dogma or connote moral-ethical posture. It may be described as a belief in the sacredness of all manifestation of life and spirit, and an attitude of reverence for all that transcends our understanding. It is a belief in the purity of life and mind, where life and death have no boundary. This was articulated in the opening of the creation story of *Kojiki.* It is, in essence, a belief in all things intangible as well as a belief in nothing tangible. In short, it is a true faith in the philosophy of Zen. Thus *shintoism* appeals to both the people of profound sophistication and those of little learning. Hence, there is no distinction of social or intellectual castes. As water and fire which cover all things and consume all things, *shintoism* accepts and accommodates all things and all people. Here, the words of Ernest Wright may help to illuminate the 'universal' concept of god:

> "In polytheism, the gods were actually the elements and
> powers in the world, personalized and given names. The
> primary setting of divine life was thus nature, and the
> life of nature was the life of the gods."[43]
> (Biblical Archaeology)

To be sure, there are many historical documents, and countless studies of *shinto* "theology" based on these documents. These theological—if such a term is even appropriate—arguments are of considerable interest particularly toward understanding the social climates and intellectual changes since the introduction of Buddhism into Japan in the fifth to sixth centuries. It must be said, however, that all these documents are produced long after the writing of *Nihon Shoki* and *Kojiki*. One should also note that one of the central topics of these historical documents and remarks is over the contradicting interpretation on the *hierarchical positions* of the two deities represented by the two shrines of *Ise*, the *Inner* and the *Outer* Shrines (the latter became known as *watarai shinto* or *Ise shinto*).[44]

The divergence of *shintoism* into these two schools that had lasted for several centuries, however, should be viewed as a latter-day sectarian schism (begun after the thirteenth century), each claiming an orthodoxy that was founded on the "original" shinto belief, in spite of the fact that there is little factual basis for such a claim. It is more accurate to say that the *shinto* schism was due primarily to the political power struggle—both feudal and royal—of the time, all vying for control of the imperial authority that was represented by Ise Shrine. Are we not familiar with the fact, as history bears witness, that every major religion of the world had its share of un-reversible schism: division of Buddhism in India, Christianity in Europe and Asia Minor, and Islam in Arabia.

Shintoism or, rather, the belief, was based on the legends embraced by the migrant tribes, but the name *shinto* came into being much later, after Buddhism entered Japan. *Shintoism*, essentially a belief founded on folk legends, had at its core a concept of veneration of the "ways of the *ancestors (kami)*" which dwell in nature, and in the "sanctity of all *spirits* that permeates nature (also *kami*)."

Perhaps such a concept—not a theology but a belief—was a tie that had bound the people of different backgrounds and social castes together, and had made them into one people who otherwise had little else in common, except the shared fate of facing the difficulty of survival, to seek escape from harms way of neighboring warring tribes, and the harsh elements of the great mother nature. This can be gauged from the mythological tales in *Kojiki* and *Nihon Shoki*; they are tales of adventure and struggle, tales that are anything but peaceful and harmonious, where bloodshed was a normal course in the lives of the *kami*.

[III]

There were many people with such a fate in the ancient Near East to Central Asia plains. Of the Semitic people, there were the Edomites, Jebusites and Hittites, who were dealt with most mercilessly by a fast rising powerful people of Israel who, though of the same ethnic lineage, had now become their sworn enemy and unforgiving task master (see below). During the period from Moses to Joshua and finally to David and Solomon, Yahweh led the Israel to conquer nearly the entire Sinai region. This was also the height of the *Nation* of Israel, when the ark of the Covenant was created, exalted and honored, and marched in front of the Israeli armies in their military conquest of neighboring tribes. As a result, a deep hatred was fermented in these tribes toward the Israelis.

It was during the time of great and successive military victories and conquests (particularly under David) that the ark was stolen. The sacred chest was eventually returned to the Israeli camp. But sometime afterward or before, we could never be certain, the ark was clandestinely invaded, and it was not until the dedication festivities of "Solomon's" Temple that the loss of the sacred articles from the ark was discovered, now with *only* the stone tablets still remaining inside the ark. Thereafter, the ark was left to repose in the Temple, and soon neglected, virtually forgotten by the Israeli people and their king. Subsequently, the Israelis also lost their City of Zion to new and even mightier powers, who carried away all the sacred relics of the Temple, including the ark, the chest, and all the golden vessels in the Holy of Holies.

There are several likely candidates who would want to steal from the ark the sacred regalia, those articles that were relatively easy to carry and conceal. Edomites (less likely), or Jebusites and Hittites (these two tribes are related), or Zephanites, all lived alongside the Israelis in one form or another, and all have suffered greatly under David's armies, and thus harbored a hatred for the Israelites. For many of these people either died in the battle or were massacred afterward, or enslaved by the Israelis. It is true that some from these defeated tribes found their niches among the Israelites, and some even rose to positions of authority. Uriah the Hittite, for example, was a trusted general in David's army, and was royal to the point of choosing rather to stay outside the King's court with his soldiers and be near (to guard) the ark of the Covenant, than to return to his own house for a well-deserved night's rest (II Samuel 11:8-11). Yet it would not be difficult to imagine that bands of the brave and rebellious few of these subjugated people would scheme a plot to steal the sacred regalia from their enemy, if only to repay the shame by the self-claimed *chosen* people of God, before escaping from Jerusalem. After committing such an act, these bands of strong-willed braves would steal away as quickly as possible, to a land as far away and as safely as possible. And the direction of this escape could only have been to an eastern land, for there was already a well established "royal highway" eastward, from Haran in Armenia, leading all the way through much of the land of ancient Hittite Empire, now the territory of the Persian Empire. This route of escape from oppression to safety may be surmised as follows:

> First, northward to *Haran* of *Armenia*, in the general district of *Togarmah*; then eastward, beyond the upper Mesopotamia and beyond the Euphrates (the present Iraq and Iran), through the mountainous region of the Ararat (present Turkey); then along the "royal highway" to continue moving east; then northward (due to the impassable Himalayan mountain ranges) and then further eastward through the only passable plateau (of present Tibet); then continuing further in the direction of the rising sun, until the far-eastern end (of the Eurasian Continent).

We could only conjecture these events and could never be sure when the (second) exile took place. We do know, however, that articles from the ark were stolen, and that, later, Assyrians had taken captive ten of the northern tribes of Israel and marched them off into the Sinai Desert. Still later, the two southern tribes of Judah were also sent to captivity in Babylon, but a kindlier Persian, King Cyrus, had allowed the two tribes to return to Jerusalem. However, the ten northern tribes vanished into history and, hence, referred to as the "lost tribes," and the world would never hear of them again. But we may also conjecture that not all these "lost tribes" were lost or disappeared from the cultural map. For, certainly, some may or would have survived the "death march" and amalgamated with the local tribes along the way. That is, some—or many— might have self-exiled further only to distance themselves from the cruel rules of the Assyrians. And we may conjecture—we may even dare to be virtually certain—that people from these lost tribes may have carried with them the sacred article(s) stolen from the ark—not the not-so-useful stone tablets, but the more easily concealable items such as the urn and the rod.

[IV]

Why did they not self-exile back to or near their original homeland? Perhaps it was fear of military force of the conquerors. Or perhaps it was a psychology of these conquered people. For we know it to be a historical fact that, even long before the Assyrian invasion and Babylonian conquest, the Hebrew nation was already on the road to self-destruction. King David had shown himself to be arrogant, greedy and cruel. For he not only massacred the earlier inhabitants—who were of his ethnic siblings—of Jerusalem, but also gathered around him hundreds of foreign wives and, still unsatisfied, took away the wife of his own general and sent him to die. His hands were bloodied by all the slaughter he had committed, and his own house was also tainted with blood. Jerusalem was no longer the City of Salem—the city of Peace. The land of Canaan and even Jerusalem seemed to have been abandoned by God. It was no longer the land of milk and honey. The throne of David seemed no longer blessed or secured by the Lord of the ark of the Covenant. The people of "second-class" status—or worse—among the dominant tribes, ethnic siblings or foreign, would not have much incentive to return to the same land where their lives for centuries were ones of sustained suffering.

So it was also that the transferring of the throne of David was not without conflict and without bloodletting among the royal siblings. And so was with the throne of Solomon to his heir. And it was the abhorrent reign of King Rehoboam, Solomon's son, that the Hebrew nation had split into the two irreconcilably hostile kingdoms: the Northern Kingdom (with the ten tribes which later became "lost"); and the Southern Kingdom (the tribes of Judah and Benjamin). The two kingdoms squabbled and fought each other, creating a situation and opportunity for the Assyrian king Tiglath-Pileser III to conquer Damascus (732 B.C.E.) and, a mere decade later (722 to 721), Assyrian kings Shalmaneser and Sargon II to completely sack the Northern Kingdom. Thus began the exile of the ten lost tribes of Israel, vanishing into history without a trace. For a while, the Southern Kingdom seemed to have fared better. But Jerusalem fell to the Babylonians in 586, and the people were exiled in 539. Later, the kindlier Cyrus—the Persian king who defeated Nebucadnezzar of Babylon—allowed the Israelis to return to Jerusalem, to allow them to rebuild the temple and restore the worship of God Yahweh. However, *there was no ark of the Covenant in the Second Temple.* Indeed, the glory of God had forever left *His* people.

There is no established extra-biblical account of the fate or the where-abouts of the ten "lost tribes" of Israel. The first hint of the whereabouts of these people is found in the Bible, in II Kings 17:6

> "In the ninth year of Hoshea, the king of Assyria captured Samaria, and he carried the Israelites away to Assyria, and placed them in Halah, and on the Habor, the river of Gozan, and in the cities of the Medes."

These places are located in upper Mesopotamia. The Hebrew historian Josephus believed the lost tribes were dispersed even *further to the east*, "beyond the Euphrates." An interesting account is found in another Greek historian's account, that these tribes "set off for a place called *Azareth.*" However, no historical geographer was able to identify the location of this Azareth; some scholars speculate that this name may have been formed by corrupting a Hebrew descriptive clause "*erez aharet*" which simply meant "another place."

The mystery of the Ten Lost Tribes of Israel has fascinated historians and speculating amateurs alike, and legends abound. Early missionaries to South America had reported witnessing Peruvian indians practicing "Jewish rituals"; William Penn—the founder of Pennsylvania—is said to have declared, upon observing Indians in that area, that "I imagine myself in *the* Quarter of London" (in reference to London's Jewish Quarter). Joseph Smith—the founder of the Mormons—in the *Book of Mormon*, claimed the early (native) Americans to be the direct descendants of the lost tribes. And travellers and anthropologists would point to the similarities in cultural, religious and ethnic features between the (modern) Jews and Falashas (Ethiopia), or Tartars (western Mongolian-Turkish area), or even the Britons (!). Finally, Eldad ha-Dani, a ninth-century Jewish traveler, claimed to have seen the lost tribes beyond the River of *Sambatyon* (the legendary "Sabbath River" which no Jewish person could ever cross, due to the fact—or the legend—that the terrible torrent would only subside on the sabbath day, when no self-respecting Jew would ever attempt to cross and thereby break the law). No one is certain of the exact location of this river; historian Josephus claimed it to be in Syria, while another Greek historian Pliny asserted that it was in Judea, and still others claimed it to be in India, in Spain, in China, or even in Japan.

The fate of these lost tribes may never be correctly discovered. But it is more than likely that the story was rather ordinary, and the process of their becoming "lost" may be more mundane. More likely, these "lost" tribes (here, lost in the sense of having lost the war, their families and their homeland), comprising more than two-thirds of the population of the once entire Hebrew nation, now gathered to form one or several self-exiled and semi-nomadic peoples, traveling first with a sense of urgency but gradually slowing down and even tarrying for some time amidst the locals, perhaps in the safer mountainous region near the Ararat or in other locations, or continuing still in their eastward journey. The leading entourage of the second exodus might have been carrying a *replica* of the original chest containing one or two (original?) items of ritual significance, which enabled the disheartened itinerant people to unify their spirit and uplift their hope. To them, the story of the exodus of their forefathers must have been retold with a new and far greater meaning, and a new sense of self-identity with the ark of the Covenant, even if it was only a *replica*.

In due course, they became mingled with the farming and sheep-herding people (who had gradually descended from the western Altaic mountain region), and it was there that the exiled people found a solace among the people who worshipped a sun-god administered by a priestess-sorceress. There, this "lost" tribe had the occasion to not only enjoy relative peace and safety but also began to adopt and subscribe to beliefs and rituals of the host culture of the land—the most powerful cult of sun-god(dess) *Mithras* who, in more than a probability, was of the lineage of an earlier Hittite (and possibly related) to sun-god(dess) **Mezzullash**. This, they would do, to juxtapose the local cult of sun-god(dess) **Mithras** and/or **Mezzullash** on the chest they still held sacred, and fathoming thereby a cult of *A-Materasu*.

[V]

But how could the people who were known for their zealousness, who had been indoctrinated by Moses and Joshua throughout their national history on a firm belief in the monotheistic god Yahweh, be so willing to accommodate alien gods and strange beliefs? The answer may lie in the fact that it is the nature of human thought pattern, where no belief ever remains unchanging. We know, too, that, before Moses, the Israelis did not know God. Even when God made himself known to them, he did not tell them his personal name and, instead, called himself "I AM." In fact, Elohim, which is the personal name of God, is etymologically related to (or a derivative of) El-, Al-, or Allah, which means "one on high," a descriptive term rather than a proper name. And throughout the history of the Hebrites, there are many indications that the idea of accommodating other gods had crept into the collective belief of the people, and the exotic practices being incorporated into the rituals and icons. The depiction of Egyptian and Phoenician religious art motifs found in Solomon's temple, and King Solomon's taking part in worship rituals of many gods of his exotic wives are well documented in archaeological studies and in the Bible. One may be attemped to read into the following passage a broader theological inference that, as in the opening sentence of the Book of Hebrews,

> "In *many and various ways God [had made himself known]* to our fathers by the prophets but in these last days [he had further made himself known to us] by a Son [... then by the holy spirit].

If, indeed, man is created by God, how could the created ever be able to completely and accurately know the *persona* of the Creator? Can the clay pots comprehend the mind of the Potter?

Religious belief is but a human conception of a higher, all-wise and incomprehensible Mind. And as man lives through changing stages of life in ever shifting historical settings, his perception of himself and his understanding of his surroundings also change, including his understanding of his Creator. In this regard, the advice of Dr. Ernest Wright comes to mind: that

> "The Bible is a 'historical' literature in which God is proclaimed as the chief actor in history who alone gives history its meaning." and that
> "There is nothing so vitiating to interesting and productive Bible study as the continual focusing on individual verses or passages without relating them to their context ... and ... to the movement of the whole [history]."

Hence, juxtaposing newer religious perspectives to give rise to yet another new belief was never a unique phenomenon. In fact, it is a product of the natural process of acculturation and an expected occurrence whenever different peoples with different cultural backgrounds merge. Just as hundreds and thousands of different languages exist today (the French school of linguists lists some three hundred, without any consensus on what constitutes language as opposed to dialect), linguists believe they could all be systematized into a much fewer proto-language lineages (*e.g.*, the Indo-European language being regarded as the oldest and most influential). Likewise, acculturation or process of cultural merging and commingling has been taking place since the dawn of human history, and is still polymorphosing today.

It must be remembered that there were no canonic writings about God Yahweh until the time of the *diaspora*, and there were no written laws and codes of conduct until the time of the exile. (On this topic, Wright gives perhaps the best and a most concise narrative on "How the Bible Came to Be Written" in Chapter III, *The Book of the Acts of God*.) Even in the presence of the Ten Words on the Stone Tablets, the Laws were never read or seen even by priests. In essence, the Israeli people did not really know who their God was, except by their shared fear of God beside whom no other god was allowed.

It was this vaguely conceived belief in the God of Abraham that had served the soil which gave rise to different theological interpretations. It produced Judaism (through Moses's perception of God), Eastern Orthodox and the Western, *i.e.*, the Catholic churches, the latter two based on a flimsy excuse of disagreement over the dating of Easter (along with other 'doctrinal' issues). It also produced Islam (through Mohammed's perception of the same God El, or Allah). Meanwhile, Judaism gave rise to still other strains, such as the *Coptics* in Egypt, as well as a brand of Christianity in Ethiopia (alleged to have received teaching from early disciples), each taking on a distinctive 'local' interpretive outlook about God and salvation, and rituals. The Christian church became further divided and gave rise to 'reformed' Christianity (through Martin Luther's perception of the very same God) and, since the sixteenth century, it further splintered into more denominations and sects than one could—or cares to—enumerate. In each claiming to have the most correct understanding of biblical truth, John Calvin (a fierce Presbyterian; *cf.* the *predestination* belief of salvation) would regard those not fully subscribing to his views as sinners beyond redemption, and in fact had succeeded in conspiring to have Miquel Serveto (Servetus, a Spanish theologian-physician) burned on stake as a heathen and heretic. While the killings of the Catholics by the Presbyterians in Ireland have ended, the leadership of Southern Baptists would continue to regard the people of Judaic faith as beyond the salvation of God. On this, may we dare pose the question, "Whose God?"

If all this religious conflict is seen as caused by reading the same Bible or Koran but with diferent eyes and minds, then the difference, the conflict and strife, must be regarded not as caused by the written Word or certainly not by the very *persona* of God but, rather, in the all-too-human and subjective—even self-serving and self-righteous—interpretation of the meaning of and the message in the written Word. Or, worse, it is due to man's inherent inability to comprehend the truth behind the written Word. But what and which is the true written Word of God? Besides the two Testaments, we are today faced also with the implication in the discovery of not only the *Dead Sea Scrolls* and the *Nag*

Hammadi documents, but also the more recently discovered gospels *According to Judas, According to Mary*, and others. And when we realize that there are many other writings that are regarded as sacred writ in one time or another, in one location and another, one must sadly acknowledge that the extent of potential diversion is all but uncontrollable, that the human mind will never comprehend the whole truth.

Indeed, as the puzzled Pontius Pilate had asked at the trial of Jesus, "What is the Truth?" To which Jesus gave no reply.

History bears witness to the fact that, wherever Christianity was propagated, the 'orthodox' belief began to take on a new posture. When the Jesuit priests brought Christianity to Indian tribes in South and North America, the converted natives quickly incorporated local beliefs and superstitions, while in China Christianity took on a decidedly Asian temperament when Jesuit missionaries (notably Father Matteo Ricci, arguably the most famous of Jesuit priests ever to work in the Far East) brought the Gospel there in the late sixteenth century. To make his faith more acceptable to the locals, Father Ricci not only permitted Chinese converts to continue their custom of ancestor veneration (not worship in the true sense of the word) but also took the ingenious initiative in adopting the Chinese term *Shang-Di* (meaning the Emperor of Heaven) to refer to the God of Abraham, of Jacob and, by implication, of Mohammed, of Luther, and of all professed and non-professed Christians living in all corners of the earth. For this "accommodation" philosophy of Christian evangelism, Matteo Ricci and his later brethren had incurred the wrath and censor of the Mother Church.

We must know, too, that, even during the lifetime of Christ's apostles (and especially during Paul's missionary work), religious difference and strife among the early Christians were a rather common occurrence. Could we not ask, then, were the authors of the *Gospel According to Mary* (*Magdalene*) and the *Gospel According to Judas* (*Iscariot*), or the followers of Coptics or Gnostic beliefs, not also faithful followers of the same Jesus Christ and seekers of His truth?

[VI]

It should not to be regarded as strange, therefore, if the people of the "knife's cult" and the followers of the ark had shifted their belief from a fearful and vengeful (but now defeated) god Yahweh, to a more lenient, accommodating and kindlier god who permeated throughout all the natural forces, the sun and moon, fire and water, and wind (air) and earth, the spirit which is in and above all four earthly elements (thus the concept of god of quintessence). And it would not be strange, too, if this people had decided not to join with others to return to Jerusalem and Judea but, instead, chose rather to take up their journey eastward, toward the direction of the rising sun. It was a sensible thing to do, for survival and preservation of the people and their changed perspective in their heritage and their god. After all, the territorial concept of God had made the people believe that God Yahweh could not live in the strange land far from Jerusalem. They had been abandoned by their God, they were left destitute, and "by the waters of Babylon, [they] sat and wept" (*cf.* Psalm 137:1), because "there is [no] sorrow like the sorrow that was brought upon them which the Lord inflicted on the day of his fierce anger" (*cf.* Lamentation 1:12).

This destitute and forsaken people had tarried in Central Asia and within the Persian Empire territory for a considerable period of time, twenty years, or twice twenty years, perhaps even finding a measure of comfort, free from further warfare. Still, they soon realized that this was not their land, that they must either return to the land where their God dwelled, or seek another land not dominated by people of a strange culture. So when King Cyrus gave permission for the Jews to return westward toward Jerusalem, the people of a different mindset lifted up their chest of witness and began their self-imposed exile eastward.

It was a treacherous journey, climbing up the rugged plateau reaching up to cloud-level heights, perhaps as high as the Ararat ranges they had come from. Then, from the cold highland and arid rugged mountainous area (of Afghanistan and Tibet), they entered the fertile, plain *zhong-yuan* ("central plains") region of China. They pitched tents by the banks of the Huang River (the Yellow River), and received permission from the officials to tarry outside the city gates. For the Chinese were not at all threatened by this roaming band of migrants with peculiar ritual customs. Indeed, the Chinese had lived side by side with their northern and northwestern alien neighbor tribes for many centuries, and even had grown accustomed to seeing steady flow of travelers and traders from the "*regions of west*"—the *Xi-yü.*

In the "*Xi Han*" (the Western Han dynasty) portion of *Shi-Shu* (*Chronicle of History*), there is indeed a brief passage which mentions a tribe (of several hundred or perhaps thousands) migrating eastward, that this people distinguished themselves with the practice of a curious religious ritual which the Chinese had coined "*dao-jin jiao*"—the religion of *circumcision*. (*Jin* literally means tendon; however, it is a 'polite' word in referring to the foreskin.) This passage in the official chronicles in referring to migratory movements a few centuries before the Common Era of "the people of *knife's cult migrating from the west and traveling* [continually] *eastward* [through China]" is, in most probability, not the first wave of migration of Semitic people. The hairy Ainu of the northern Japanese island were likely of the stock of earlier migrants from the Middle East, and there still live a few descendants of the later migrants of the people of *"knife's cult"* in the City of Kaifeng, on the bank of the Huang River.

While some of these Semitic migrants had opted to remain in villages along the Huang River, the main body of this semi-nomadic tribe had chosen not to tarry in China's plains region. Perhaps the culture of China was too rigidly complex for their way of life, with a language and customs far too strangely different, and the military might and social codes awfully suppressive. Also, perhaps the host people were too self-appointed and arrogant to pay more than casual and curious—if not outwardly spiteful—gaze to this band of migrant vagabond. So this transient tribe moved on, leaving behind some who preferred to tarry and settle, and eventually entered the Korean Peninsula.

From archaeological finds, it was apparent that this transient tribe had found a more accommodating host in the Koreans, with a kindred spirit and of similar "ethnic temperament," even sharing some common linguistic features. For it is well to point out that Japanese and Korean (as well as Tibetan) belong to the Altaic linguistic lineage. Hence, more than a cordial relationship was formed between the migrating people and the Korean hosts. For there are a considerable number of acculturation imprints, important among them is the commonality in mythological tales and certain geographic names. Apparently, this relationship had lasted for a considerable length of time even after the migrating tribe left the Korean Peninsula, and crossed the narrow ocean strait to come ashore on their new "land of Canaan" on the Japanese archipelago. Also, it was through Korea, a few centuries later, that Buddhism entered Japan, that much of Chinese culture was introduced to Japan (especially during the period of the fifth through tenth centuries), and the cultural and political relationship between Japan and Korea was to accelerate continually throughout history even if not always harmoniously. For the Japanese-Korean relationship had become a "love-and-hate" sort, especially after Japan had become sufficiently powerful militant nation to expand its territorial claim (the sentiment which has not completely diminished even to this day). For Japanese and Koreans, like the two sons of Abraham and Jacob, were cultural and ethnic siblings in more complex ways than can be delineated. As in the case of so many ethnic and cultural siblings, the two people have been, for nearly two millennia, constantly dealing, exchanging, squabbling and fighting with each other.

[VII]

It was during the period of about two to three centuries before the Common Era that this migrating tribe finally left the soil of the Eurasian Continent behind, and entered Japan. (This dating is also in agreement with the opinion of the more recent Japanese archaeologists and anthropologists.) This, their own version of "crossing the Jordan into Canaan" occurred in at least two—perhaps more—waves. Perhaps by this time the original tribe had enlarged and, after so much acculturation, had splintered into at least two major theo-political parties.

One of the earliest sizable groups to enter the Japanese islands arrived in the *Izumo* area. This people was the *cultic*-orthodox branch, carrying the *chest of witness* and held the belief that was fathomed during the course of their sojourn in Central Asia. This was the peaceable *Yayoi* tribe which established (what was to become) the *shinto* faith. Upon arriving on the island (northwest coast of Honshu), this tribe also found the even earlier settlers (the *Ezo*—Esau?—people, more commonly known today as the Ainus). By all account, these two people had managed to coexist without hurtful enmity toward or harmful injury to the other.

The next large wave of new arrivals came ashore on the "lower" (southeastern) shores of Kyushu island. This was the militant branch, bent on claiming the new land by forceful conquest. After initial conflicts, this militant branch enjoined with the cultic branch, with the former securing military leadership in exchange for accommodating the rituals of (the proto-) *shinto* cult. And it was the leader of this militant branch who was subsequently given the pseudo-historical name *Jimmu Tenno* (Emperor *Jimmu*, a posthumous name) in replacing his original (long, multi-syllabic and Altaic-sounding) name. Thus, his political and military role was woven into the mythological tales of *Amaterasu*, as of the direct lineage of the *kami* from *Ame no Takama ga Hara*, the "Celestial High Plains" (or, the land of *Haran* in the district of *Togarmah* in the country of *Armenia*), to be recognized as the first emperor of Japan. Thus the mythological legends regarding the origin and founding of Japan was fathomed, and was orally transmitted for several centuries, perhaps almost a millennium, before they were finally written down as *Kojiki* and *Nihon Shoki* in the early decades of the eighth century. The writing of these two chronicles was commissioned by the imperial household, for the sole purpose of solidifying its inheritance, in providing a believable documentation for claiming the legitimacy of the military leader as the heir apparent to the imperial throne.

While much of the earlier legends of the imperial lineage are mythological or of later fabrication, where elements of Sumerian, Semitic, Persian and even Korean mythological tales are still identifiable, credency of Japan as a nation

and as a people rests to a considerable extent on the existence of the historical ritual items of great antiquity. The sacred chest and its divine articles have
served, and will continue to serve, as the inviolable witness to the mythological
origin of their ancestors. In a sense these sacred regalia are the tangible and
indomitable proof of their *shinto* faith, more true and powerful than the stories
of god in the *Torah* or the *Koran*. For during the long and arduous migratory
journey lasting perhaps as long as a century or two (with later waves of like
migration continuing until as late as the seventh century C.E. or even later),
traversing the entire width of the Eurasian Continent while assimilating the
languages and cultic practices of a number of host countries along the way,
this tribe had tenaciously preserved that mysterious wooden chest which, upon
arriving at the farthest eastern shores, named it **MiFune-Shiro**—the **Replica
of Divine Chest**. We are unable to ascertain when this name was given, or
when the chest was created. But we know for certain that in this chest were
three sacred treasures, one of which was inside another container called the
"*Shirushi no Mihako*"—the "Chest of Witness," also called *Kangami* or, possibly,
Kangame.

In the narratives early in the chronicles of *Kojiki, Nihon Shoki* and *Kuji
Honki, Ame no Takama ga Hara* was given as the name of the "original" land
of celestial plains ruled by the goddess *Amaterasu*. She then conferred the three
sacred articles on her earthly heir, and these sacred articles have been identified
and described as: (a string of) crescent-shaped stones; a seven-branched sword;
and a *kagami* or *kangami*—a mirror.

In nearly every *shinto* shrine in Japan, there is a replica of the divine chest
and, in it, a set of replicas of *sanpo*. However, these sacred articles were seldom
seen by prying eyes of commoners, and those who were their appointed guardians—the *shinto* priests—would never describe or even admit to having seen
them. Mr. Omura, who was an elementary classmate of mine, had told me a
few years ago when we had met for the first time since we parted ways at the
end of the World War II (when all the Japanese living in Taiwan were ordered
to return to Japan), that his father who was a *kan-nushi* (a *shinto* priest), on
the evening of learing of the defeat of the Japanese empire and the broadcast
speech of Emperor Hirohito over the radio, went to a secluded spot in the back
of the shrine, and buried the *sanpo* which had been kept in his shrine. However,
my friend Omura was unable—or unwilling—to tell me what those *sanpo* articles were. Apparently he, too, had not been permitted to look at those replicas
of the sacred relics or, if he had, was forbidden or unwilling to confide to anyone else.

Regarding the stones, there have been many similar artifacts from archaeological finds. There are also many replicas, as they were, in comparison to other sacred articles, the easiest to duplicate. These crescent-shaped stones were always of natural semi-precious stones or meteorites (rightfully believed to have fallen from heaven and thus also believed to possess mysterious power), and were always a ritual item worn by a priestess or sorceress in the entire Central Asian region, including Da-Hae to Daxia, on the western border of China. (However, crescent-shaped stones as ear-rings were never worn by priests in China. Also, there were no priestesses in China.) Symbolically, such stones may be regarded as representing the stone tablets of the Israelites' *Decalogue*, on which were imprints of curious shape (which, in turn, may have been *replicated* as the crescent-shape stone, the *magatama*?).

[VIII]

In *Heike Monogatari* narrative, it is said that the original sword with "sprouted" branches (as in fish ribs) had been lost, in the final and great sea battle between the armies of the houses of Tahira and Minamoto (the Genji clan). Still, there were—and are—many other swords, all associated with mythological tales of notable encounters of *kami*. The most auspicious sword is the one which is in the shape of six branches (and, together with the sword point, seven branches) which is not only so much reminiscent of the rod of Aaron that had sprouted, but also symbolized the potency of Aaron's rod. A well-told story about Aaron's rod was when it was entwined with a bronze snake on its stem raised high, when the Israelis had angered God and his servant Moses, and caused a plague to fall on the rebellious people of Israel, that they might gaze on it and be cleansed of their sins and healed of their diseases. This rod with an entwined snake, today more familiar as the universal symbol of medical profession, was used as the ritual instrument, as was the *Suna-no O* sword, to cleanse the soul, to cure disease, and to rid men of harms and evil spirits. (See below.)

The more important point of this seven-branched sword of Japanese imperial regalia is the fact that it has essentially the identical shape—if not in proportional details—of the well-known *menorah*, the candlestand that is ever present in every Jewish synagogue. While the shape of the candlestand is explicitly described in the Bible (*e.g.*, Exodus 37:17), it must be noted that this six (actually seven) branched *menorah* is believed by archaeologists to be from the (Sumerian) legend of the tree of life, mentioned also in the Book of Genesis, and symbolized in many artifacts all across the Near East, of different faiths, with variously designed but still uniquely recognizable images that may appear on the faces of coinage or on the pages in sacred script.

While the sacred sword is mentioned early in the sequence of events in *Kojiki* legends, the actual sword with six branches ((*cf. Fig.* 10), once kept in the shrine of the imperial household or other shrines but subsequently reposited in *Ishigami* Shrine in Kyushu, is recorded (in *Nihon Shoki*) as a gift from a Korean envoy. It seemed that the sword was forged by a renowned Korean swordsmith in the mid-fourth century (precise dating of the sword cannot be determined due to lack of an unified calendar in China which was then under different regional rulers). It is also during the same period that a considerable number of bronze mirrors had come into Japan from both Korea and China, most likely as diplomatic gifts to tribal chieftains in Japan. Many metal mirrors (*cf. Fig.* 9) excavated from numerous *kofun* (ancient tombs) bear inscriptions (Chinese ideographs) and relief figurations of ritual and calendrical signification and, hence, a fairly accurate dating of these *kagami* (mirrors) has been a relatively easy archaeological task.

In contrast to *magatama* (stone) and *tsurugi* (sword), however, there is precious little information on the third sacred article. It is called *kangami*, a divine mirror specifically mentioned in the farewell speech of goddess *Amaterasu* when she commissioned her grandson to descend to the terrestrial domain. It was to be *the memorial of the very presence of Amaterasu herself* and therefore has been regarded as the most sacred of all imperial regalia.

However, the most difficult problem associated with this *kangami* is that no archaeological study had ever been done on this alleged mirror, and there has never been any mention of eyewitness accounts, except those mentioned here and elsewhere in this study. To be sure, there were several accounts, three "close encounters" of which two were by different emperors, and one by a court officer and warriors during the final sea battle between the Genji and Heike armies. There is a fourth account, mentioned by a historian in reference to his *own* eyewitness of the sacred treasures in the last two decades of the nineteenth century (in the early years of Emperor Meiji).

All these virtual and real eyewitness accounts—three in historical chronicles and one in more recent print from the early days of Emperor Meiji as just mentioned—are what may be regarded as the only historically credible documentations. The details of these sightings can be restated as follows:

> 1) that, on two occasions, no sooner than the lid [of the receptacle] was removed then white puffs immediately rose up from the receptacle, causing a sense of fear in the emperors, thereby the frightened servants

in-waiting immediately replaced the lid and tightly resealed the vessel;
2) that the vessel is frail and in danger of "falling into pieces,"
thus requiring a multiple layer of wrappings to protect the vessel;
3) in the confusion of battle, several warriors attempted to open the
lid of the vessel, but immediately they became sickened in their eyes
and noses, so that they began bleeding from their noses, hence the lid
was immediately replaced and the vessel was quickly resealed;
and finally,
4) the most recent eyewitness account (from the late nineteenth century)
provides a description and general measurements of this vessel, that
from the description and measurements, there is little doubt that
the article is not a flat shaped item (like a bronze or iron mirror) but
more like a tube, an urn, perhaps made of wood, but was covered with
gold plates which in turn were joined with golden chains at the hinges.

From these reliable accounts, it is more than a fair assumption that this
article which has been called *kan-gami* is in fact not a *kagami* (mirror) but
was most likely intended to be a *kan-game*, a *sacred urn*. This error, along with
countless like errors, was caused during the process of transcribing the oral narratives into ideographic writing of the *Kojiki*. However, the scribes had but one
kind of script available—that of *kanji* (Chinese ideograph) and, in the process,
there was much use of *ateji* ('false' ideogram), engaging Chinese ideograms in
erroneous or false ways as if they were phonetic symbols or *alphabet* letters. It
was in this process that the error of (mis)appropriating ideograms to represent
phonetic sound had occurred. In other words, it was more than likely that the
original pronunciation of the name *kan-game* was mistaken by the scribe and
was written as *ka(n)gami,* understanding the article as a mirror (notice that the
first word is hyphenated but the second is not).

Earlier, it was noted that this form of *ateji* had caused a considerable literary (and literacy) problem in Chinese-Japanese transliteration which, in turn,
became a critical issue for modern scholars in deciphering the original signification in the *Kojiki* narratives. This problem is of a lesser issue in reading *Shoki*
since, there, the Chinese ideograms were used as characters and words—with
specific meanings—and not as phonetic symbols which were devoid of meaning. However, regarding *kagami* for *kan-game,* the mistake was never realized,
and this possible error was left uncorrected in *Nihon Shoki*. Or it could also
have been intentional, since this mistaken reading as mirror had fit rather conveniently in the mythology and with the purpose of the chronicle writing. In
contrast, an urn would have been a curious oddity and not able to fit in the

scheme of the *kami* legend (for example, in the story of Amaterasu emerging from the cave to investigate her likeness reflected in a *mirror*).

However, if indeed *kagami* is a *kan-game*, an urn, what substance was inside the urn which had caused puffs of white smoke to rise and caused irritation to the eyes and noses of those nearby?

We read in the Old Testament that one of the three sacred articles in the ark of the Covenant is a golden urn of *manna,* and that the Lord had commanded that a portion of this white grain-like substance which the people had called *manna* (meaning "What is it?") to be kept inside it as the testimony to the wondrous act of God. This receptacle, an urn, was eventually put into the ark of the Covenant, along with the *Decalogue,* and Aaron's rod. We also read in the Old Testament that, when King Solomon opened the ark of the Covenant at the dedication of the Temple, both Aaron's rod and the urn of *manna* were found missing, that "there was *nothing* in the ark *except* the stone tablets."

The stones were not ordinary rocks, but meteorites fallen from heaven and thus was believed to possess mysterious power. The rod that had branched ("budded") was believed to symbolize the tree of life (in the even earlier legends, *e.g.,* of the Sumerians). These two articles and even the ritual chests were all a part of religious regalia in the ancient Near Eastern world. And all these sacred vessels were made in quantities to meet the religious needs of the people in different locations. In this perspective, therefore, nothing about the ark of the Covenant or the individual sacred articles of the Israelis can be regarded as uniquely Hebraic.

Except the urn of *manna.* For from all the legends and historical information on the ark as the receptacle of significant religious articles and hence the ark represented the presence of a deity such as practiced in ancient Egypt and many of the Semitic tribes, there was no other mention of any urn containing food stuff as worthy of being placed in the sacred chest. Except that of the urn of *manna* prepared by Aaron and kept by Moses as a witness, the urn that was placed inside the ark of the Covenant, according to God's command.

[IX]

Far from the land of the early Semitic people, there is a sacred regalia called *kangami* kept in a chest called *MiFune-Shiro* deep inside the holy of holies in the *Grand Ise Shrine* in Ise, Japan. This item, from all eyewitness accounts, could not be a bronze or iron mirror but, rather, a *kan-game,* a "divine urn" made of wood and inlaid (or overlaid) with gold. This urn, on a number of occasions when the lid was opened, gave rise to puffs of fume which instantly caused irritation to the eyes and noses of those nearby. Such a phenomenon of physical reaction could only be most logically explained as an effect from coming into contact with a poisonous substance, perhaps fungal, micro-grain poisonous powder. For indeed if any food stuff such as *manna* had been kept in an urn for many, many centuries or as much as three millennia or more, with the urn being sealed tightly most of that time, the only possible natural consequence would be a growth of fungi from decayed substance.

It is without doubt a most incredulous notion that the original urn that was put inside the ark of the Covenant, along with an unknown substance and hence called by the ancient Israelis as *manna* ("what is it?") might have not only survived but was transported across the full width of the Eurasian Continent to Japan more than two millennia ago, and still exists in the Grand *Ise* Shrine in Japan. And for historians and lay people alike, it is even more frustrating that this mysterious article is beyond the bounds of archaeological inquiry. For there is little possibility that this urn with its mysterious contents would ever be permitted to be the subject of chemical analysis or otherwise scientific examination such as carbon-14 dating. The inquiry into unveiling the mystery of *MiFune-Shiro* and the *kan-game*, to determine the age and to identify the substance inside the urn, or the origin of the urn itself, the golden plates inside the urn, or the wood of the chest, will likely remain an enigma so long as the imperial throne of Japan remains the symbol of the nation and its people.

This sacred *kangame* is inside the "Chest of Witness," in the innermost chamber of *Ise* Shrine, and is taken out of the Shrine only once every twenty years, during the *sengu* ritual (*cf.* **Fig.** 21), always in the evening hours when light is dim and the Chest hidden from view of even the immediate members of the imperial household and invited high-ranking ministers, being draped under several layers of heavy brocade. We only know that this *kangami* or *kan-game*—we may never be certain whether it is a round metal mirror or an urn—was the most revered and the most mystic of the three imperial treasures which holds the key to the mystery of the origin of *shinto* and the cult of *Amaterasu*.

The importance of this set of imperial regalia can testify to the fact that Emperor Hirohito had acted so anxiously in attempting to take possession of it during the final days of World War II. His intention was singular: to safeguard at all costs the mystery of the sacred *shinto* relics in order to defend the legitimacy of the imperial throne. The very irony of the culture of Japan is that, even today, when few Japanese still subscribe to the belief that their emperor is divine, no Japanese would ever desire that the mystery of *shinto* and of the imperial lineage from the sun-goddess *Amaterasu* would be subjected to scientific scrutiny. For this belief is inseparable from the spirit of Japan and the

Yamato-tamashii (or *Yamato-damashii*)—the *Yamato* spirit—the collective psyche of the Japanese people. It is this spirit that has made them a nation of the most unique people, even out of mixed ethnic lineages and unknown anthropological origin.

Hence it is understandable that, while both the sword and the crescent stones have been seen and described on many occasions, in official chronicles and narratives in historical literary works, the *kangami* or *kan-game* alone remains veiled and cryptic, with no additional eyewitness description in any publication. Even the few modern scholars who were once given the privilege of observing the sacred relics from a relative close proximity had never written any description of this most sacred of the three treasures, except in expressing a sense of awe-inspired reverence.

I can still remember visiting Meiji Shrine some years ago with my wife, and we approached an outer office of *kan-nushi* (priests) for a respite from the heat of the noonday sun. No sooner than we were about to sit down in the shade of the office awning to catch a breath when a bespekled *kannushi* shuffled up from inside, and harshly reprimanded us for being so *insolently* close, and nearly chased us out of the shrine premises.

The impossibility of obtaining any sort of scientific data on *kangami* or *kan-game* is due to the fundamentally esoteric personality manifest in a collective posture of the followers of *shintoism,* from the imperial house to the common folk. For the mysticism of the *Shinto* faith, like the spirit of Mount Fuji, would never allow any act of profanity in defiling and undermining its divinity. This was so with the ark of the Covenant of the Israelites of old, and it remains so still with the *MiFune-Shiro* of *Shinto*. For to do so would be tantamount to exposing in total nakedness the body of *Amaterasu* and its mysterious and impenetrable spirit. Unlike the academic efforts of more recent Western theologians, any effort at *demythologizing* the *Shinto kami* would be wholly and utterly inconceivable.

[X]

This desire to preserve the mystique of our veiled past may be a universal phenomenon. It is perhaps because life itself is a mystery, and the wonder of life needs an element of faith to undergird our sense of security and to sustain the cause of its sustenance. Even while the people of the West would boast their collective empirical objectivity and scientific posture to all things, they still cling to a healthy share of historical mystique. For example, scholars and theologians still are not certain of the verifiable historical Moses, or his leadership in the formative years of the nation of Israel, or of the historical Jesus, and legends surrounding his birth, death and resurrection. Similarly, scholars are not altogether sure of a historical Queen of Sheba, in spite of the fact that she was mentioned in both the Bible and Koran (where she is mentioned as the Queen of the South), as well as and in much greater detail in another ancient historical work *Kebla Nagast* (on the history of Ethiopia mentioned earlier). Scholars question the person of the Queen of Sheba, the story of her visit to Solomon's court, or even the land which she was said to have ruled, and to which she had returned after visiting Jerusalem and given birth to Menelik (the name means "Son of the Wise Man" in an obvious reference to the Solomonian lineage), the future King of Ethiopia. Or we may consider the case of another famous historical figure, King Arthur of England. He is regarded as an inseparable part of the history of Great Britain, so much so that his portrait is prominently displayed in the House of Parliament in London. Yet, in actuality, Arthur was only a *persona* born of a wild figment of imagination, a product of a fanciful—or wishful—poetic dream of a young monk who was not even a Brit. Or, consider the case of the Shroud of Turin: the mysterious linen cloth which is seen to show the image of the deceased Christ. The linen was shown to the public for the first time in 1355, escaped a fire in 1532, and finally reached the monastery in Turin and reposed there ever since. Since its first being photographed in 1998, various teams of scientists have conducted carbon-14 dating experiments on the material cut from the linen, in order to ascertain the age of the cloth and the DNA of the stain believed to be from the wounded body of Christ. Contradictory claims and heated debates ensued, with credible scientific camps offering totally different perspective on the relic, one supporting its *authenticity and verifiability of the miracle* (a contradiction in terms?), while the other claiming it as a hoax. After years of debate, the matter is still unresolved, and its mystique would likely remain "shrouded" so long as mankind has a choice of—and in—faith.

Perhaps historical credence is not a necessary cornerstone for faith to be founded. Or, the two are essentially antithetic.

Perhaps it matters little, therefore, if the ark of the Covenant was Egyptian or Hebrew, if the stone tablets actually contained the writings of the fingers of God, or the natural markings on meteorites. It may matter little, too, if the lineage of *MiFune-Shiro* came from the Semitic land, or the chest was created during the journey of a transient tribe, or fathomed in Japan, or if the sun goddess *Amaterasu* was the same sun god(dess) *Mythra* of the Persian folk religion or sun god(dess) *Mezzullash* of the earlier Hittites, or if *kangami* is a bronze mirror or an urn—a *kan-game*—holding an amount (or residue) of *manna*. Still, from all the evidences examined in this study, both documentary and factual, there is reason for an opinion and even a belief that a transient people had carried with them a replica of the sacred relics, much like the ancient Israelis, on their long migratory journey, always moving toward the direction of the rising sun. A verse from a familiar hymn (a traditional *spiritual*) comes to mind:

> "Let us break bread together on our knees,
>> Let us break bread together on our knees;
> When I fall on my knees,
>> *with my* FACE TO THE RISING SUN,
> O, Lord, have mercy on me."

This chest and the articles of regalia which, together, had served to unite the people and sustain their hope and spirit throughout the journey, have become the undeniable *testimony* to the founding faith of their ancestors. For these very same regalia still exist, reposed for over two millennia, in their very bodily form.

If faith (and hope) is everything for a transient people, then that people would do anything to preserve the tangible evidence on which their faith is founded. This evidence is the *MiFune Shiro* and the still mysterious *kan-game*. It is the same tenacious faith which is still clung to by Ethiopian Christians. In each of their churches is a *replica of the ark* of Moses; the original is *believed* to be housed in Church of Mary in Axum.

Hence, the question of the origin of Japan's imperial regalia, or any thought or need to conduct an objective inquiry to ascertain their true identity, would also raise the question of whether the Japanese would be happier in knowing if *MiFune-Shiro* and *kan-game* are the lost relics of Judaism, or even the question of whether the Japanese of today still carry the same blood lineage with Mr. and Mrs. Snider. For history bears witness over and over again that being a kindred, or sharing a common ethnic lineage or same cultural and religious heritage, has never served any useful function toward fostering a peaceable kingdom. Are we not today the living witness to the *family feud* that has persisted for over millennia, as the descendants of Esau and Jacob, or of Isaac and Ishmael, continued to commit senseless bloodletting, all the while declaring such atrocities in the name of the same god *Elohim* or *Allah*, and their father Abraham, that the reality is quite the opposite.

Yet, *MiFune-Shiro* is singularly unique. Unlike Moses, the Queen of Sheba, or King Arthur, or any relics of ancient legends and myths, there, in the inner sanctum of the Grand *Ise* Shrine, is that *Mi-koshi*, the *Chest of Witness*, which contains the real, factual, bodily evidence of history. And, in contrast to the claim of the existence of the alleged original ark of the Covenant in Axum, Ethiopia, or any other place with similar claim that has never been objectively verified, we have both eyewitness accounts and substantiating documentation to provide credence to the existence of a *Replica of the Divine Ark* in Japan. The only part of the mystery yet to be unveiled is whether the most revered item contained in the divine chest is a *kangami*, a bronze mirror, or *kan-game*, the urn inlaid with gold plates that might still contain some residue of *manna*.

Perhaps there may come a day when the imperial house would show a gesture of openness, to permit a handful of most eminent scholars of historical archaeology of Japan to gaze upon—if not conduct a scientific examination on—the most sacred relic, thereby to finally lift the veil of mystery.

Perchance, thereupon, the sacred relic was found to be a bronze mirror, after all. If so, would this make *MiFune-Shiro* less of an incredible insignia of *shinto* faith? Perhaps it is worth reconsidering the words in *Amaterasu Omikami's* farewell speech to her departing grandson:

'My child, your gazing upon this treasured mirror will be like gazing on my face; keep [it with you] in bed and in the hall, and regard it a mirror of witness, and its inheritance [from one generation to the next] shall continue forever as long as heaven and earth shall last.'"

Would this not be closely paralleling the words of Yahweh regarding His tabernacle and the ark of the Covenant in the midst of the Israelites? For the ark of the *Covenant*, as has been mentioned, is also called the ark of *Witness*, the ark of *Testimony* and even of "*Remembrance*." And two of the three articles—Aaron's rod and the pot of *manna*—were put inside the ark for the specific purpose of *bringing to remembrance what the Lord has done for the people of Israel*. Thus, included in the Lord's commandments regarding these articles of witness and the tablets of law are the following words:

"… and I will meet with you, to speak there to you … and
I will dwell among the people of Israel, and will be their God …
… [and] it shall be a statute for ever to them, even to him and
to his descendants throughout their generations.
(Exodus 29:42-30:21)

This, in fact, is also the very same message and significance in the Christian faithful's observation of the Lord's Supper or the Mass: the breaking of the bread and drinking of the cup *in remembrance* of the Lord's sacrifice.

From this, one may come to a realization that, in terms of the significance of the sacred relics of the Japanese and ancient Israelites, both the pot of *manna* and the mirror represent ways in which the faithful may contemplate and "see" in their heart the divine images and bring to remembrance the divine deeds which their god had performed on their behalf. In examining both the Semitic (Hebrew and Aramaic) and Japanese words used to refer to these sacred regalia, we find that the connoted signification is identical: they refer not to the "*act*" (the deed) of testimony such as to demonstrate in a court of law, or the *article of evidence*, or the proof, with a physical, tangible evidence." Rather, it is in essence in referring to the presence of an article that will "serve as a *reminder* of past deeds," such as an oath, contract or promise, or the spirit of the relationship that was therewith established.

It was in this sense that the ark of the *Covenant* was also called the ark of the *Testimony*, the tent was called the Tabernacle of *Testimony*, and the veil that separated the Holy of Holies from other quarters of the Temple as the veil of *Testimony*. And when we consider the meaning of the various Japanese words (such as *shirushi*) used to refer to *MiFune Shiro* and every sacred relic especially the *kangami* or *kan-game*—and realize that these relics were regarded as the treasure of *testimony*, treasure of *witness*, and *the* treasure of *remembrance* and *reflection* (*i.e., contemplation*)—we come to a deeper realization that all these Japanese words do in fact connote exactly the same signification as the Hebrew words of *Covenant*, *Testimony*, and *Witness* that were used in referring to the ark.

As to the word *Fune* which literally means a 'boat,' it has been noted previously the double-meaning of 'ark' to refer to both chest (*e.g.* the ark of the Covenant) and boat (*e.g.,* Noah's boat, and the small reed basket to hide the infant Moses). We have examined, too, the tradition of the ark as a sacred chest (or even a divination box) in ancient Egypt, the land where Moses received all his wisdom. And we are familiar with the funeral rites of ancient Egypt where the dead Pharaoh was "set sail" into the world beyond, in a boat, to be reunited with his spiritual father, the sun god RA. Hence, after Joseph, who had risen from the rank of a slave to become a grand minister under Pharaoh, died, his bones (ashes) were put into an ark which Moses and the Israelis brought out with them during the Exodus. In the cultural context, this ark was also a funeral boat as that of a dead Pharaoh. Thus we come to a realization that, in etymology and in practice, ark the *chest* was also ark the *boat*. Likewise, the sacred ark of Japan—the *MiFune*—is both the divine chest and the divine boat, the chest that had led the itinerant people from their old world, as well as the boat that carried them into a new world. This boat set sail toward the sun, as in ancient Egypt, carrying the people to join with the sun god **RA**, or the goddess aMat-eRAsu, or the sun god MithRAs or MezzuLLAsh.

Perhaps it is of lesser importance, therefore, whether *kangami*—mirror—is actually a *kan-game*—urn or pot. Greater importance may lie in the fact that there *is* an article of *witness*, to give *testimony* and cause remembrance, for they have been associated with the legend and, together, have been transmitted through countless generations. This *is* an article which has no other purpose except to serve as an object of *reflection* for the people of Japan (of the image of *Amaterasu* and thus functioning as a mirror). Likewise, there is an article of *remembrance* for an act of God in feeding the Israelis with *manna* preserved with a pot containing a portion of the food stuff, or the tablets of stone with God's writings, for the Christians in Ethiopia and all the faithful in the entire Christendom. Whether it is in Axum church, or in Ise Shrine, these articles of witness and reflection are "for ever as long as heaven and earth shall last."

[XI]

Still there remains the mystery of the *Replica of the ark* of Japan's imperial house, and in the Japanese people's collective reverence for this mystery. Perhaps what distinguishes the Japanese from all peoples of the world, including the people of other Asian nations, is their genuine and unchanging attitude of reverence for all nature's spirits, which are symbolized in *Amaterasu* and the imperial regalia. This attitude of reverence for nature is cultivated in every aspect of Japanese people's lives, in daily cleaning of their body, of their houses and shrubs in their yards, in the art of *ikebana* (flower arrangement but, literally, "living flower" or "making flowers alive"), or manicuring the *bonsai*, all for the preservation of their natural spirit.

In this respect, perhaps I may be allocated a space for my own personal *reflection* and *remembrance*:

For some time I have wondered why the Japanese people possess such a singular belief in reverence for all things in nature, animate and inanimate. I have known since my childhood days that the majority of Japanese family names is after things of the natural world. Note how many Japanese surnames contain one of the following words: Kawa or -Gawa (river), Yama (mountain), Oka (hill), Ki (tree), Ishi (stone), Ta (field), Mura (village), Zaki (land point in the sea), Saki (village area), Matsu (pine), Mizu (water), Mori (forrest), Hayashi (woods), *etc., etc.* (These common surnames were created/bestowed during the late feudal period, somewhat paralleing the trade-signifying surnames given to commoners in England—Taylor, Smith, Fisher, Baker, Miller, Farmer, *etc.* only in the relative recent historical past). As a music educator, I have come to realize also that this may very well be the result—or a formative effect—from an educational component throughout their entire public schooling years. That is, this national posture of reverence for nature may be due to educational nurturing, specifically by way of countless *songs* taught to all Japanese school children. And children's songs are one of the most effective but unrecognized or underrated instruments for nurturing a person's character.

Consider the fact that, for countless generations, songs of religious lessons are taught in synagogues, and Bible verses set to music are taught in Sunday schools. While no *shinto* priest gives lessons in singing (perhaps because there are no theological doctrines in *shintoism*), students in Japanese schools are taught by way of songs to revere their emperors (until the end of World War II) and all things in nature.

This perspective is particularly meaningful to me as a musician. Even after six decades, I can still sing many of the songs I had learned in Japanese primary school, and many of them are innocent songs about nature or things in nature. There are, for example, songs of rain (*"Ame, Ame, Fure, Fure."* and *"Furu Tomo Miezu Haru No Ame"*), song of long, evening road (*"Doko made itte mo nagai michi"*), song of sunset (*"Yu-yake, Ko-yake"*), song of spring (*"Haru ga kita"*) and of spring brook (*"Haru no Ogawa"*), song of sea (*"Yumi wa hiroi na, okii na"*), song of horse family (*"O-uma no Oyako"*), song of dragon fly (*"Aka Tombo"*), song of flower (*"Hana"*) which actually is about the River *Sumida* (*"Haru no Urara no Sumida-Gawa"*) and, familiar to many American GIs stationed in Japan right after World War II, the song of cherry blossom (*"Sakura, Sakura"*). Indeed the list of Japanese songs of nature is very long. In contrast and to the best of my knowledge, no Western country has any comparable extent of *songs of nature* both in kind and number to those Japanese songs.[45] And we wonder why Western industrial societies seem to have less regard for ecological issues.

Visit a Japanese garden—better still, a *zen* garden—then compare it to a Western-style garden, and realize the difference not only in aesthetics but also in the *spiritual attitude* toward nature: the Japanese way is to coexist and harmonize with nature, to experience the eternal beauty in and peace with the way of nature. This is the quintessence of the *"Way of Kami"* which is *Shinto*. In contrast, the Western way, it seems, is to discipline, conquer, alter and tame nature to conform to the ways and whims of man.

This may also explain why Japanese people's collective posture of reverence for all things in nature cannot be fully appreciated apart from their "other" *ethnic* personality—secrecy and mystery. (Ever wonder why Japanese houses have high wooden fences?) As Mount *Fuji* is eternal (*fu-shi*, never dying), incomparable (*fu-ji*, no second other), and forever pure, its spiritual hold on Japanese people is also a mystery. And as every blade of grass, every tree and brook, every rock and waterfall, is *kami*, all enjoined as an eloquent *testimony* and *reflection*—the remembrance—of eternal beauty and tranquility that can also be equally manifested in miniature, in a *zen* garden, still worthy of all reverence, so is the all-penetrating radiance of mysterious *Amaterasu Omikami*, and *MiFune-Shiro*. The insignia of this goddess worthy of reverence, will forever remain veiled in mystery, never to be prodded, dissected and analyzed, as if she is a lifeless cadaver. And, like the bright radiant Sun which would not allow itself to be gazed upon by the eye of mortals, and like the mysterious Moon which eternally hides one of its hemispheres from the probing eye of earthbound men, so shall, in most likelihood, *MiFune-Shiro* forever remain the enigmatic *witness* and *testimony* to Goddess *Amaterasu*, and continue to cloak the incomprehensible mystery of *KAN-GAME*.

Likewise, all people who are on this planet are together sailing on this earthly *fune* over a fathomlessly deep space and history toward an unknown future. And we pause to reflect on our past, our origin, whence we came from, and long for knowledge—for a sign—which may help us in reflecting on who we are, in the hope of gaining a better sense of our own being. We are created in God's image, so the Bible tells us. Yet we are neither god nor will we ever be. Then we discover the existence of this mysterious box called *MiFune-Shiro*, the *Replica of Divine Ark of Testimony*, for *Remembrance* and *Reflection* ...

[XII]

As I reflect on the significance of a possible connection between the ark of the Covenant of the ancient Israelites and *Mi-Fune Shiro* of the Japanese, I felt a need to find an answer to the question:

> "Why would the Israelis, a Semitic tribe beholden to the Ark
> of Witness to God Yahweh, abandon their worship of God
> Yahweh and, instead, opt to resurrect antiquated Mezzullash
> and to embrace Mithras of the Persian common folk?"

The author of the Letter to the Hebrews opens his messsage with a statement of profound insight:

> "In many and *various* ways God [had] spoke to our fathers
> and ... [now] to us."

The implication here, without being too theological, is that God's revelation is pending on the extent of our understanding. In other words, the ability of man to comprehend the infinite wisdom of God is conditioned and limited only by the scope of man's finite mind, just as a cup could never contain all the waters of the ocean. Before Moses, the people did not know the name of God; when asked, God would only say "I am I AM." Monotheism was not always the belief of the people of Israel. Even conditioned during the years of sojourning in the land of Egypt, the Israelis and even their priest Aaron would not hesitate to ask for another deity and was given a golden calf. Perhaps the first commandment

"Thou Shall Not Have Any Other God Before Me ..."

"I am Who I AM, a jealous God ..."

must have come as a complete surprise, and the people could only perceive God of Abraham as angry, vengeful and a law-giving God. However, Jesus came and revealed God as a Father, a merciful and long-suffering God who would want his people to obey but one law: the law of love.

As man lived in different historical periods, through different encounters and experienced ever shifting and evolving cultural environments, God's message to them also must have seemed to change. Is this what Paul had meant when he said,

> "For our knowledge is imperfect and our prophecy is imperfect ...
> When I was a child, I spoke like a child, I thought like a chiild,
> I reasoned like a child;
> [but] when I became a man, I gave up childish ways ...
> For now we see in a mirror dimly ...
> Now I [*only*] know in part ..."
> (RSV. I Corinthians 13: 9-12)

In this sense, perhaps the people of the *Replica of the ark* did not substantially *change their concept of God*. Rather, perhaps it was that they saw a *changed God*, because the priests had from time to time *falsely represented the true persona of God*. This sentiment is reflected in several passages in the post-exilic writing:

"Your prophets have seen for you false and deceptive visions
[and] ... have seen for you false and misleading [oracles]."
                    (Lamentations 2:14)

"You false prophets! You who lead his people astray!
You who cry 'Peace' to those who give you food,
and threaten those who will not pay!"
                    (Micah 3:5)

"... for you are prophesying lies in the name of the Lord"
No one will be boasting then of his prophetic gift!
No one will wear a prophet's clothes to try to fool the people then.
                    (Zechariah 13:3b-4)

And, therefore,

"... My name will be honored by the Gentiles from morning to night.
All around the world they will offer sweet incense and pure offerings
in honor of my name ... and my name is to be mightily revered
among the Gentiles."
                    (Malachi 1:11. 14b)

*   *   *   *   *   *   *   *   *   *   *   *

The most precious gift of the All-Wise God, the Creator, to Man, his created,
is an inquisitive mind, an innate and insatiable desire to know why and how. The
words *scientia* (in Latin, from which are words such as *science*, omni*scient*, con-
science) and *gnosis* (in Greek, also to *know* and *know*ledge) characterize *why* man
has become what he is today. To put it in a nutshell, the picture of mankind's history is a continuum of searching to know what, how, and why about all the things
around him, and seeking the "truth" (*cf.* Daniel Boorstine's *The Discoverers*). In
discovering it, the new knowledge and realization will also cause a man to alter
not only his beliefs and actions but also the way he sees himself. It was through
this "knowing" that man will forever need to redefine a sense of himself and his
surroundings, and to come closer to understanding the "mind" of his Creator.

Hence, as all lives and minds are preconditioned by past knowledge but also
continually reconditioned by the new, no theological doctrine will ever remain
immutable, and no two theological perspectives would ever be identical. The
question to us the common man, then, is: is one correct and the other incorrect,

or is one *more* correct than the other? Are the Anglicans more righteous than the Catholics, the Congregationalists more Christian than the Baptists? Or, is Judaism or Islam the more rightful lineage of father Abraham's faith? And, are the faithful of *Shintoism* and Buddhism *equally* (?!) embraced by God?

The early wave(s) of migrants arriving on Japan were worshippers of a sun-goddess and nature. To them, god may not necessarily be of male gender. The later wave(s) of arrivals were militant and believed in the superiority of the male gender. Hence we have a synthesis of two cultic beliefs to become the foundation of *shintoism*: the female goddess *Amaterasu* to be worshipped as supreme above all other *kami*, and the male Emperor Jimmu to be revered as the first in line of an unbroken imperial throne. Did not the early church fathers also silence the voice of the gnostics and suppress the "lost gospels"[46] in order to elevate the authority of the male-dominated "Gate of Peter," the Bascilica?

But, while the ark of the Covenant has never been re(dis)covered and restored in Jerusalem or elsewhere, deep inside the Grand Ise Shrine in Japan there is a *Replica of the Ark of the Covenant*, paralleling the original in name, in general shape, in contents, and in its awesome signification. The people who had stolen the relics from the ark were, after a long period of hiding and wandering, able to call up a congregation to shoulder the Chest of Witness in search for a new Canaan. And, instead of returning to Jerusalem to worship the fearful and vengeful God (as even David and Solomon had feared Him *and* the ark, and continued to be so portrayed even by the post-exilic prophets such as Haggai, Zechariah and Malachi), this splinter tribe saw another god who dwelled in nature, in the like image of the deity of their earlier heritage (*Mezzullash*) and the deity of their hosts during their years of sojourning (*Mithras*).

As I contemplate the possible signification and ramification of *MiFune-Shiro* and *Kan-game* which, in its deeper meaning, is also *kangami*, so to reflect on all that is mysterious and wonderfully fascinating, I begin to recite the school *motto* of my *alma mater* (Northwestern University), a seemingly simple and elegant verse from the New Testament that, now, seems to possess for me a far greater meaning:

> "Finally, brethren,
> whatever is true, whatever is honorable, whatever is just,
> whatever is pure, whatever is lovely, and whatever is gracious,
> if there is any excellence, if there is anything worth *celebrating*,
> *contemplate* [*on the significance of*] *these things*."
>
> (RSV, Philippians 4: 8,
italics and [insert] mine)

Notes

1. Hancock, *The Sign and the Seal*, p. 292.
2. Knight and Lomas, *The Hiram Key*, p. 24.
3. *Ibid.*, p. 157.

With regard to Egyptian script commonly known as hieroglyphics, it is of some—or, perhaps, a considerable—interest to note also that the revelation Joseph Smith, the founding prophet of the Church of Latter Day Saints, had received was said to have been written in a form of ancient Egyptian script. The name "Mormon" is supposed to have derived from the name of an angel named *Moroni*, a prophet told by Smith to have lived in ancient America, and had appeared to Smith with the revelation. Among Smith's fantastic faith statements was his identification of Jackson County in Missouri, U.S.A., to be the biblical site of the original Garden of Eden which would rightfully become the land of the latter-day Zion. However, arguably the most intriguing of all the Mormon legends, concerned about the birth of the *Book of Mormon, the* bible for the Mormons: In its early narratives, the *Book* tells about the resurrected Jesus visiting the New Continent, and that a remnant of ancient Israel—supposedly the so-called "lost tribe"—had migrated to the Americas in about the sixth century, B.C.E. Smith had told his followers that this revelation contained in the Mormon Bible was revealed to him by way of golden plates containing the message written in "reformed *Egyptian*" script, and Mormon historians maintain that these revelation plates were buried near Smith's house, along with *Urim Thummim*—a set of stone tablets attached to a breastplate that contained the code that enabled Smith to decipher and translate the *reformed Egyptian* script into English. Hence, the term "Latter Day" refers to the Mormon Temple as Christ's latter-day Church, built on the "latter-day" land of promise, founded on the faith revealed to its founder as the "latter-day" inspiration, and that its believers are the "latter-day" Israelites transplanting the old Israelite stock that had sinned against God. It is highly intriguing also to read about the existence of parallel legends in Japan. According to the believers of this legend, Jesus himself had visited Japan after his resurrection and there was tangible proof. Scholars contribute this Japanese legend of Jesus to the remnants of the faithful proselytized by the early Jesuits before Shogun *Iyeyasu* closed the doors to all foreigners in the seventeenth century. This curious legend in Japan was reported by another Smith: John Justin Smith, a journalist, in a series of five articles titled "Exploring the Legend of Jesus in Japan" in *Chicago Daily News*, August 2-6, 1971. See Bibliography). A highly informative and fully objective article by Elise Soukup on the Mormons—their history and present (and changed) attitudes—appeared in *Newsweek*, October 17, 2005. Another equally fascinating story of how written words were believed by illiterate people to be of Divine origin: When in 1443 Emperor Se-jong of Korea invented the Korean alphabet (the *hangul*, which refers to both alphabets and Korean spoken language), he was hesitant to present it to the court for adoption, for fear that the officials who were also ardent Confucian scholars would not likely accept any script other than Chinese. Hence Emperor Se-jong devised a most cunning scheme in order to lead the court soothsayer and officials into believing that the new Korean alphabets were given by God. *Cf.* Jennings, *Word of Words: Personalities of Language,* p. 50.

4. Hancock, *op. cit.*, p. 30; also p. 126.

5. *Ibid.*, p. 63; *italics* mine.

6   *Ibid.*, pp. 67-9.

7. *Bible Dictionary* p. 999, under "Pillars," *b. Monumental)*

8. Hancock, *op. cit.*, pp. 290-94.

9. Ernest Satow, Esq. "The Shinto Temples of Ise" in *Transactions of The Asiatic Society of Japan*, Vol. II (1873-74), pp. 113-139. *Italics* mine.

10. Edkins, F. J. Rev., "The Nature of the Japanese language, and its possible improvements" in *Transactions of The Asiatic Society of Japan*, Vol. I (1872-73), pp. 96-110. Rev. Edkins begins this paper with an analysis of the Japanese language from phenological perspectives. However, his suggestion for "improvement" is nothing more than a wholly biased and irrational narrative, exhibiting not only his entrenched ethno-centric attitude but also a lack of understanding and appreciation of language —Japanese or any other—as a unique byproduct of the people of a given culture. This is most unfortunate particularly for a person devoted to the Christian evangelical mission. In particular, when he regards Japanese as an "inferior" language from which "no good literature would come forth from such an irrational language," he is treating language not as a means of communica-

tion of a people but, instead, as a sociological specimen that must be made to conform to a particular and preconceived structural pattern. Perhaps this was a common European attitude in the nineteenth century, of the stance of *vergleichende Wissenschaft*.

11. Inoue, *Ninon No Rekishi: (1) Shinwa kara Rekishi He* (*The History of Japan*, Vol. I: *From Mythology to History*); p. 188-89.

12 Davis, *Myths and Legends of Japan*, p. 18; note 1.

13. *Ibid.*, p. 14.

14. R. K. Reischauer, *Early Japanese History*, pp. 4-8.

15. *No* and *ga* are conjunctions, similarly used in sentences to connect two parts expressing the possessive case, identical in usage with the English word "of." However, in the two languages the word order is reversed. The Japanese word order would be more in the manner where the 'apostrophe-s' is used. For example, "chichi **no** musuko" meaning "father **no** son" can be translated into English as "son of the father" where the word order is reversed, or "father's son" where the same word order is retained.

16. Wright, *The Book of the Acts of God: Contemporary Scholarship Interprets the Bible*, p. 140; *italics* mine.

17. *The New Bible Dictionary*, p. 1285.

18. *Ibid.*, p. 971.

19. Judaism was not as exclusively monotheistic and strictly adhered to as is generally held. Graham Phillips presents a most fascinating documentation on the concurrence—if not slightly earlier—of the monotheistic faith *Atenism* in Egypt which worshipped god Aten and no other. Phillips's narrative, citing studies and findings to support the many parallel beliefs and practices between Atenism and Judaism (or, perhaps to be more accurately called *Yahwehism*) is most revealing. See Phillips's *The Templars and the Ark of the Covenant*, "Moses and Yahweh" (Chapter IV), pp. 56-61 in particular. Noteworthy also is another monotheistic religion which came into prominence among the 6th century, B.C.E. Persians, slightly after Atenism and Judaism: *Zoroastrianism* which worshipped one supreme deity named *Ahura Mazda*. This worship of *Ahura Mazda* is closely related to the worship of the sun god *Mithra* (of *Mithraism*).

20. Grant, *The Ancient Historians*, pp. 10-11.

21. *Cf.* B. H. Chamberlain, *The Language, Mythology, and Geographical Nomenclature of Japan* ... Chamberlain is also the English translator of *Kojiki*.

22. Davis, *op. cit.*, p. 131.

23. *Cf.* Lewis, ed., *Great Civilizations*.

24. Reischauer & Fairbank, *East Asia, the Great Tradition*, pp. 15-18.

25. Toyota Aritoshi, "Observing Ancient Japan from its Surroundings" in *Nazo no Nihon Tanjo* (*The Puzzle of the Birth of Japan*), p. 132.

26. *Cf. Sendai Kuji Honki*, pp. 74-75; Book III, and elsewhere.

27. *Cf.* the map of Western Han Dynasty, *Fig.* 17-b, showing the near-straight eastward passage from the "land of *Da-xia*" (Togar or Togarma) through *Tibet*, the famous gateway of *Shanhai Guan* and *Dunhuang* (famously known for huge rock carvings and cave paintings of Buddha images), to *Xi'an* (the ancient capital of China), to the northern banks of *Huang He* (Yellow River), the cradle of the Chinese culture (where, in the city of Kaifeng, the community of remnants of transplanted Jewish people still exists), and from there, straight eastward to Shandong Peninsula, then enter North Korea which also was under the rule of the Western Han court, and through the peninsula to Japan, arriving first on the shore of the present Izumo on the main island of Japan, directly across (*i.e.*, east of the tip of) the Korean Peninsula. The likelihood of this migratory route taken by the people of "knife's cult" may thereby be visually ascertained.

28. Morton and Olenik, *Japan: Its History and Culture*, p. 4.

29. *Ibid.*, p. 4.

30. Jennings, *World of Words: Personalities of Language*, pp. 8-11; **bold face** for emphasis *mine*.

31. *Ibid.*, p. 25.

32. *Heike Monogatari*, Vol. IV, pp. 237-38; English translation *mine*.

33. *Ibid.*, pp. 218-20; English translation *mine*.

34. Yamamura Yoshio, "Is *Amaterasu* a Sun-goddess?" in *Nazo no Nihon Tanjo* (*The Puzzle of the Birth of Japan*), pp. 101-02. Mr. Yamamura (b. 1931) is a permanent committee member of *Suili Sakka Kyokai* (*The Society of the Authors of Speculative History*).

35. *Sendai Kuji Honki*, p. 113; the English translation and *italics* for emphasis *mine*.

36. *Heike Monogatari*, Vol. II, pp. 121-13; English translation *mine*.

37. *Ibid.*, pp. 200-02; English translation *mine*.

38. Hadland, p. 300; the English translation cited here is by W. G. Aston.

39. *Heike Monogatari*, Vol. IV; pp. 204-06; English translation *mine*.

40. *Op.cit.*, pp. 216-18; English translation *mine*.

41. *Op.cit.*

42. Davis, *op. cit.*, p. 18, *note* 1.

43. Wright, *Biblical Archaeology*, p. 1.

44. *Cf.* Teeuwen, *Watarai Shinto*: In the Introduction and Ch. 1 "Early Watarai Shinto," Mark Teeuwen gives a comprehensive account of all the disputes between the two *shinto* "sects" on "theological" issues regarding the hierarchical priority of Inner *versus* Outer Shrines. Clearly, the issues were on the matter of authority and hierarchy of the lineage positions of various deities in the *Kojiki* and *Nihon Shoki* narratives, with all the remaining documents of doctrinal statements of much later date, none of which were an integral part of the narratives in the original *kami* legends.

45. It should be of interest to educators—and music educators in particular—that the *educational* (of citizenship) value of Japanese school children's songs has been duly noted (even belatedly) in many Asian countries—Taiwan and China in particular—who have adopted many of these Japanese songs in their music curriculum. In this regard, it would seem odd that, while Japanese "*kara-o-ke*" [pronounced KAH-RAH-OH-KEH, where KARA means "empty" and OKEH stands for "OH-KESUTORA"—*i.e.* orchestra—and, hence, by inference, "KARA-OKE" refers to music accompaniment with absence of orchestra, thus in referring to canned (pre-recorded) instrumental (*i.e.*, orchestral) music designed to provide accompaniment for any aspiring vocalist in frenzied and often comical imitation of pop singers, a mode of entertainment] had been imported into the US and elsewhere in the world and has become universally popular, it may be worth noting that music educators in Western countries have yet to recognize the lasting impact of Japanese children (*i.e.*, school) songs in effectuating and molding the attitude—and sense of citizenship—of their future life. It also is glaringly curious that there is not a single *unified* song book adopted in any public school system in the United States.

46. *Cf.* Krosney, *The Lost Gospel. Cf.* also *National Geographic* magazine article (2006) on the subject.

SELECTED BIBLIOGRAPHY

[English titles in brackets are the *present author's*
own translation of the original Japanese titles.
The romanized names of Chinese and Japanese authors of
non-English titles are shown with surname first followed
by given name, without comma after the surname.]

A. Books on Topics Relevant to the Present Study (in English, Japanese, Chinese, and Korean):

Alexander, Kelly D. Jr. *ark of the Covenant: Simplified Information for Lay-Persons*. New York and Oxford: University Press of America, Inc. 2002.

Aston, W. G. *Nihongi: Chronicles of Japan from the Earliest Times to A.D. 697* (translated from the original Chinese and Japanese). Rutland, VT: Charles E. Tuttle Company, 1972.

Ben-Dasan, Isaiah. English translation by Gage, Richard. *Japanese and the Jews*. New York: Weatherhill, 1972.

Brown, Michael H. *The Search for Eve: Have Scientists Found the Mother of Us All?* New York: Harper & Row Publishers, Inc., 1990.

Cummings, Lewis V. *Alexander the Great*. New York, NY: Grove Press (1940); 1968.

Dan Hi-Rin. *Nihon ni Nokoru Kodai Cho-Sen* [Remnants of Ancient Korea in Japan]. Osaka; Sogen Sha, 1976.

Davis, F. Hadland. *Japan: From the Age of the Gods to the Fall of Tsingtau*. New York: Frederick A. Stokes Co., 1916.

_____. *Myths and Legends of Japan*. New York: Dover Publications, Inc. 1992 (originally published in 1913 by George G. Harrap & Company, London).

Doresse, Jean. *The Secret Books of the Egyptian Gnostics* (including *The Gospel According to Thomaas*) [The first English translation edition]. New York: MJF Books (First Communications), Inner Traditions International, 1986.

Edwards, Mike, photograph by O. Louis Mazzatenta. "HAN: A Chinese Empire to Rival Rome" in *National Geographic* Magazine, February 2004 (pp. 2–29).

Egami Minao, *et al.*, Suzuki Takeju, *ed. Lonshu Kiba Minzoku Seifuku O-Cho Setsu* [*Essays on the Theory of the Dynastic Conquest of the Mounted Tribe*]. Tokyo: Yamato Shobo, 1975.

Fairbank, John K., Reischauer, Edwin O., and Craig, Albert M. *East Asia, Tradition and Transformation*. Boston: Houghton Mifflin, 1973.

Gabel, John B. and Wheeler, Charles B. *The Bible as Literature: An Introduction*. Oxford: Oxford University Press, 1986.

Gardner, Laurence. *Lost Secrets of the Sacred ark : Amazing Revelations of the Incredible Power of Gold*. New York: Barnes & Noble, 2005 (originally HarperCollins, 2003).

_____. *The Shadow of Solomon: The Lost Secret of the Freemasons Revealed*. New York: Barnes and Noble (originally HarperCollins), 2005.

Gilbert, Martin. *Atlas of Jewish History* (4e). London: Weidenfeld and Nicholson (1969), 1992 (4e). *Chinese edition*, Shanghai: Zhonghua Publishing, Ltd., 2000.

Grant, Michael. *The Ancient Historians*. Michael Grant Publications, Inc. 1970; New York: Barnes and Noble Books, 1994.

Grousset, René. Eng. translation by Naomi Walford. *The Empire of the Steppes: A History of Central Asia*. New Brunswick, NJ: Rutgers University Press, 1970.

Haagensen, Erling, and Lincoln, Henry. *The Templars' Secret Island: The Knights, the Priest and the Treasure*. New York: Barnes and Noble Books, 2004.

Hall, John Whitney. *Japan from Prehistory to Modern Times*. New York: Dell Publishing, 1970.

Hancock, Graham. The *Sign and The Seal*: ... *The Quest for the Lost Ark of the Covenant*. New York: Simon & Schuster, Inc., 1993.

Inouye Mitsusada. *Ninon No Rekishi: (1) Shinwa kara Rekishi He* [*The History of Japan (1): From Mythology to History*]. Tokyo: Chuwo Koron-Sha, 1973.

Jennings, Gary. *Personalities of Language*. New York: T. Crowell Co., 1959.

Kajihara Masaaki, and Yamashita Hiroaki, eds. *Heike Mono-Gatari* [*The Tales of Tahira Clan*] (in 4 vols., 5th printing). Tokyo: Iwanami Publisher, 2005.

Kawazoe Noboru. *Ise Jingu: Mori to Heiwa No Shinden* [*The Ise Jingu: The Shrine of Forrest and Peace*]. Tokyo: Chikuma Shobo, 2007.

Keene, Donald. *Anthology of Japanese Literature from the Earliest Era to the Mid-Nineteenth Century*. New York: Grove Press, 1955.

Kitagawa, Joseph M. *Religion in Japanese History*. New York: Columbia University Press, 1966.

Knight, Christopher, and Lomas, Robert. *The Hiram Key: Pharaohs, Freemasons and the Discovery of the Secret Scrolls of Jesus*. Century (England), 1996; New York: Barnes and Noble, Inc. 1998.

Kojima Noriyuki, Naoki Kojuro, Nishimiya Kazutami, Kuranaka Susumu, and Mo(o)ri Masamori, eds. *Nihon Shoki* (vol. II; *Nihon Shoki*, Bks. XI-XX). Tokyo: Shogakkan, 2004 (5th printing).

Krosney, Herbert. *The Lost Gospel: The Quest for the Gospel of Judas Iscariot.* Washington, D.C. National Geographic Society, 2006.

Kumi Nanuri. *Ise no Jingu* [*The Shrine of Ise*]. Tokyo: Sekai Bunka Sha, 2003.

LaHaye, Tim, and Phillips, Bob. *The Secret on Ararat.* New York: Bantam Dell, Random House, Inc. 2004.

Lamy, Matt. *100 Strangest Mysteries.* New York: Metrobooks, 2005 (originally Arcturus Publishing Ltd., 2003). [*cf.* selected articles: "The Great Flood"; "Noah's Ark "; "The Queen of Sheba"; "The Knights Templars"; and "The Ark of the Covenant"]

Lewis, Brenda Ralph, general editor. *Great Civilizations.* Bath, UK: Parrragon Publishing, 2002.

Morton, W. Scott, and Olenik, J. Kenneth. *Japan: Its History and Culture* (4e). New York: McGraw-Hill, 2005.

Nakamura Yukihiro, and Endo Kazuo; Aoki Kigen, ed. *"Ko-go Shu-i" wo Yomu* [Reading of *Remnant of Ancient Tales*]. Tokyo: Migibumi Shoin, 2005.

Nakayama Kaneyoshi. English translation by De Lapp, Richard. *Pictorial Encyclopedia of Japanese Culture: The Soul and Heritage of Japan.* Tokyo: Gakken Co., Ltd., 1987.

Nosaka Toshio. *Keitei Tenno no Nazo: Nihon Kai O-cho no Keifu* [The Puzzle of Imperial Succession: The Dynastic Lineage of the Sea of Japan]. Tokyo: Shin Jinbutsu Olai Sha, 1975.

Ono Shichizou, ed. *Sendai Kuji Honki* [*True Records of (Old) Events in Ancient Times*] (*kunchu*; with annotated commentary). Tokyo: Hihyo Sha (Hihiosia), 2004 (4th printing).

Oyabe Zenichiro. *Nihon Oyobi Ninon Kokumin No Kigen* [*The Origin of Japan and The Japanese People*]. Tokyo: Kosei Kaku, (1929-) 1932.

Phillips, Graham. *The Templars and the Ark of the Covenant: The Discovery of the Treasure of Solomon.* Rochester, VT: Bear & Company, 2004.

Pollak, Michael. *The Torah Scrolls of the Chinese Jews: The History, Significance and Present Whereabouts of the Sifrei Torah of the Defunct Jewish Community of Kaifeng.* Dallas, TX: Southern Methodist University, 1975.

Reischauer, Edwin O. *Japan: The Story of A Nation* (rev. ed.). New York: Alfred Knopf, 1974.

——————. *The Japanese.* Cambridge, MA: Belknap-Harvard University Press, 1978.

Reischauer, Edwin O. and Fairbank, John K. *East Asia, The Great Tradition* (*A History of East Asian Civilization*, Vol. 1). Boston: Houghton Mifflin Co., 1960.

Reischauer, Robert Karl. *Early Japanese History* (*c.40 B.C.—A.D.1167*). Princeton, NJ: Princeton University Press, 1937.

Saito Hisho, English translation by Elizabeth Lee. *A History of Japan*. London: Kegan Paul, Trench, Trubner & Co., Ltd., 1912.

Santon, Kate, and McKay, Liz, ed. *Atlas of World History*. Bath, UK: Parragon Publishing, 2006.

Scarpari, Maurizio. *Ancient China: Chinese Civilization From Its Origins to the Tang Dynasty*. New York, NY: Barnes and Noble Publishing Co., 2006 (originally by White S.P.A., 2000).

Scherer, James A.B. *The Romance of Japan Through the Ages* (rev. ed.). Tokyo: Hokusei Do Press, 1932.

Silverberg, Robert. *Lost Cities and Vanished Civilizations*. New York: Bantam Books, 1963.

Sui-Ri Shi Wa-Kai [The Society for Speculative History]. *Nazo No Nihon Tanjo: Ko-dai Shi He No Cho-Sen* [*The Puzzle of the Birth of Japan: A Challenge to Ancient History*] (essays by five authors). Tokyo: Shin Jinbutsu Worai Sha, 1969.

Suzuki Takeju. *Ko-Daishi no Miwaku to Kiken* [*The Allure and Danger of The Ancient History* (of Japan)]. Tokyo: Aki Shobo, 1977.

_____. *Nihon Kodai-shi 99 no Nazo: Yamadai Koku kara To-ichi O-cho Made.* [*Ninety-Nine Puzzles of the Ancient History of Japan: From Yamatai Nation to Dynastic Unification*). Tokyo: Sanpo Co., Inc., 1974.

Tan Hilin. *Nihon ni Nokoru Kodai Chosen* [*Remnants of Ancient Korea in Japan*]. Osaka, Japan: Sogen Sha, 1976.

Teeuwen, Mark . *Watarai Shintō: An Intellectual History of the Outer Shrine in Ise*. Leiden, The Netherlands: Research School CNMW, School of Asian, African, and Amerindian Studies (Thesis), 1996.

Tsugita Masaki, ed. *Kojiki* (3 vols.). Tokyo: Kodansha Inc., 2004 (42nd printing).

Tsunoda, Ryusaki, DeBary, William Theodore, and Keene, Donald. *Sources of the Japanese Tradition*. New York: Columbia University Press, 1958.

Ueda Masaaki, *et al. Kodai Nihon-Shi To Kami-Gami* [*History of Ancient Japan and The (Mythological) Deities*]. Ecole de Royale (in *Contemplating Ancient Japan Series*, Vol. 8). Tokyo: Gakusei Sha, 2000 (3 ed.).

Ueyama Haruhira, ed. *Symposium on Ise Jingu*. Tokyo: Jinbun Shoin, 1993 (1995).

Whitfield, Roderick (text) and Otsuka, Seigo (photo) (two vol.). *Dunhuang: Caves of the Singing Sands, Buddhist Art from the Silk Road*. Textile & Art Publications, 1996.

Wright, G. Ernest. *Biblical Archaeology (Abridged Edition)*. Philadelphia, PA: The Westminster Press, 1960.

Yarden, L. *The Tree of Light: A Study of the Menorah, the Seven-Branched Lampstand*. Ithaca, NY: Cornell University Press, 1971.

Yoshida Akira. *Shichi-shi To No Nazo O Toku—Yon Seiki Kohan No Kudara To Wa* [*Deciphering the Puzzle of the Seven-Branched Sword—Korea and Japan in the Second Half of the Fourth Century*]. Tokyo: Shin Nihon Publisher, 2001.

Zhang ZeYi. *Zhong Ya Gu Guo Shi* [*History of Ancient Central Asian Empires*]. Beijing; Zhonghua Sujü, 2002. (A Chinese translation of McGovern, Wm. Montgomery. *The Early Empires of Central Asia*. 1939.)

B. Primary [Ancient] Source Documents (*in* Japanese)

Heike Monogatari [*The Tales of Heike (i.e.,* the House of Tahira)].

Ise Dai-Jingu Zobi Zatsu-butsu [*The Great Ise Shrine: Records of Preparatory Miscellany*].

Ko-Dai-Jingu Gishiki Cho [*Registry on The Rituals at the Great Imperial Shrine*].

Kojiki [*Record of Ancient Affairs*] (variously translated into English).

Koku-Shi [*The History of the Nation*].

Kuji Honki (or *Kyuji Honki*) [*The True Record of Ancient Affairs*] (only Books V and VI were consulted).

Nihon Shoki [*The Chronicle of Japan*].

C. Genetic and Ethnic Study: Journal and Newspaper Articles

Brown, P. "The First East Asians?" In *Interdisciplinary Perspectives on the Origin of the Japanese* (ed. K. Omoto), pp.105–124. Kyoto: International Centre for Japanese Studies, 1999.

Cavalli-Storza, L., Menozzi, P. and Piazza, A. *The History and Geography of Human Genes*. Princeton, NJ: Princeton University Press, 1994.

Edkins, Rev. F. J. "The Nature of the Japanese Language, and Its Possible Improvements," in *Transactions of The Asiatic Society of Japan*, pp. 96–110, Vol. I (1872–73). Reprint by Yushodo Booksellers Ltd., Tokyo, 1964.

Hammer, M. and Horai, S. "Y Chromosomal DNA Variation and the Peopling of Japan." In: *American Journal of Human Genetics*, 56:951–962, 1995.

Klein, G. *The Human Career: Human Biological and Cultural Origins*. Chicago, IL: University of Chicago Press, 1999.

Murayama Shichiro. "The Origin of the Japanese Language." In: *Minzokugaku Kenkyu* [*Study in Anthropology*]: 35/4 (March 1971), pp. 249–61.

Satow, Ernest M., *Esq.* "The Shintô Temples of Isé." In: *Transactions of The Asiatic Society of Japan*, pp. 113–139, Vol. II (1873–74). Tokyo: Yushodo Booksellers Ltd. (reprint),1964.

Shinka, T. *et al.* "Genetic Variations on the Y Chromosome in the Japanese Population and Implications for Modern Human Y Lineage. In: *Journal of Human Genetics* 44: 240–245, 1999.

Smith, John Justin. "Exploring the Legend of Jesus in Japan." In: *Chicago Daily News*, August 2–6, 1971. (A series of five articles on curious stories and early 'evidences' of Jews and Christianity in Japan).

Su, Bing, *et al.* "Y-Chromosome Evidence for a Northward Migration of Modern Humans into Eastern Asia during the Last Ice Age." In: *American Journal of Human Genetics*, 65:1718–24, 1999.

Underhill, P.A., *et al.* "The Phylogeography of Y Chromosome Binary Haplotypes and the Origins of Modern Human Populations." In *Annual Human Genetics* (Great Britain), 65:43–62 (2001).

Zerjal, T. *et al.* "Genetic Relationships of Asians and Northern Europeans Revealed by Y-chromosomal DNA Analysis." In: *American Journal of Human Genetics.* 60, 1174–83 (1997).

D. REFERENCES

Armstrong, Karen. *A History of God: The 4000-Year Quest of Judaism, Christianity and Islam*. New York: Gramercy Books, 2004 (1993).

Bowker, John. *The Complete Bible Handbook*. New York: Barnes and Noble, 2005 (1998).

Dailey, Timothy J. *Mysteries of the Bible: Secrets, Symbols, and Codes*. Lincolnwood, IL: Publications International, Ltd. 2004.

Douglas, J. D., *et al.* *The New Bible Dictionary*. Grand Rapids, MI: Wm. B. Erdmans Publishing Co., 1962.

ENCYCLOPÆDIA BRITANNICA. Chicago, Aukland, London, Paris, Tokyo: Encyclopedia Britannica, Inc., 1984 (15th edition; also other editions).

Green, Peter. *Alexander of Macedon, 356–323 B.C.: A Historical Biography*. Berkeley, CA: University of California Press, 1992.

Li Nuhao. *Zhongguo Lishi Shi-shi Xi Biao Jieh* (*Chronological Lineage and Map of China's History*). Taichung, Taiwan: Jih-Yung Commercial Company, Ltd., 1972.

Moore, Hyatt, ed. *The Alphabet Makers*. Huntington Beach, CA: Summer Institute of Linguistics. 1991 (2e).

Needham, Joseph. *Science and Civilization in China* (6 vols). Cambridge: Cambridge University Press, (1954-).

Rogers, Lester R., Fay Adams, and Walker Brown. *Story of Nations*. New York: Henry Holt and Company, 1960.

Silver, Daniel Jeremy. *A History of Judaism*. New York: Basic Books, 1974.

_____. *Images of Moses*. New York: Basic Books, 1982.

_____. *The Story of Scripture*. New York. Basic Books, 1990.

Word. *The Journal of The International Linguistic Association*.

Wright, G. Ernest, and Fuller, Reginald H. *The Book of the Acts of God: Contemporary Scholarship Interprets the Bible*. Garden City, NY: Doubleday and Company, Inc., 1960.

Wu Zauji. *Zhonghua Shangxia Wu Qian Nian* (*Five Thousand Years of China, Ancient and Modern*). Beijing: Jinghua Publishing Company, 2002.

APPENDICES

I.

ABBREVIATED POLITICAL CHRONOLOGY OF THE HEBREW PEOPLE, WITH NOTES REGARDING THE ARK OF THE COVENANT

B.C.E (BEFORE COMMON ERA) OR B.C. (BEFORE CHRIST)

c. 1350	God commanded Moses to build the ark of the Covenant to store and carry the stone tablets inscribed with the ten commandments;
c. 933	The Hebrew nation was divided into Kingdoms of Israel and Judah:
	Kingdom of Israel (933-722)
	Kingdom of Judah (933-586)
c. 900	King David brought the ark of the Covenant to the Israeli camp from the hands of the Philistines;
c. 870	King Solomon built the First Temple in Jerusalem to house the ark of the Covenant; during the time of installment rituals, the ark was opened and it was discovered that two of the three sacred articles were missing from the ark;
c. 722	Kingdom of Israel and Jerusalem fell to the Babylonians (or the Assyrians);
c. 700	King Hezekiah constructed tunnel aqueduct through (under) Mount Zion;
c. 586	Babylonian (*i.e.* Chaldean) King Nebuchadnezzar also conquered Kingdom of Judah; soon afterward the entire Hebrew tribes were taken captive and exiled; certain tribes vanished into the Central Asian deserts and mountainous terrains, hence referred to by historians as the 'lost tribes' of Israel, never to be heard again; again;

THE POST EXILIC PERIOD

c. 586–538   *Torah* (the *Pentateuch*, the first five books of the Old Testament) and other OT books were written (compiled) during this period of captivity; King Cyrus of Persia allowed the Hebrew people to return to Jerusalem; the temple was rebuilt and worship rituals restored, but the ark of the Covenant failed to reappear, in spite of the king's command to the Levites to search for the lost sacred chest, the ark of the Covenant and the seat of Yahweh.

II.
ABBREVIATED CHRONOLOGY OF THE POLITICAL POWERS IN THE NEAR AND MIDDLE EAST, FROM ANCIENT TIME TO THE EARLY HELLENISTIC PERIOD

c. 3000–2100	Rise of *Sumerian* city-states farming system collapsed c.1800, marking the end of man's earliest civilization
c. 2450–2193	*Akkadian* Empire (from King Sargon)
c. 2700–1086	*Egyptian* Kingdoms

        Old Kingdom (2686–2160)

        Middle Kingdom (2040–1750)

        New Kingdom (1550–1086)

c. 2500–612	Assyrian Empire (divided into Babylonia and Media)
c. 1800–1600	*Chaldean* (the *Old and Middle Babylonian)* Empires (1792–1595; 1595–1155)
c. 1500–1200	Middle *Assyrian* Empire
c. 1400–1150	New *Hittite* Empire
c. 1400(?)–586	*Hebrew* nation (from Moses)

        (Exodus c.1450?)

        Samuel (c. 1100)

        Saul (r. c. 1050–1010)

        David (r. c. 1010–970)

        Solomon (r. c. 970–930)

        upon Solomon's death, the Hebrew kingdom is divided into Judah (south, two tribes) and Israel (north, ten tribes) (930)

c. 1000–612	Neo-*Assyrian* Empire (from Ashurbanipal to Sargon II and Sennacherib)

        Israel falls to the Assyrians (722)

c. 1000–700	*Aramean* city-states
c. 1000–300	*Phoenecian* city-states
c. 747–539	*Chaldean* (the *Neo*-Babylonian) Empire (from King Nebuchadnezzar)
c. 600–586	The decline and final collapse of the *Hebrew* Nation

        Judah becomes vassal of Nebuchadnezzar II (601)

        Jerusalem falls to the Babylonians (598–7)

        the *diaspora* (Exile) begins (588 to 586)

	Judah falls to the Babylonians (587–6) Nebuchadnezzar II's final destruction of the Temple (586)
c. 660–332	Late *Egyptian* Dynastic Period Egypt falls to the Persians (525)
c. 500–331	*Persian* Empire (from King Cyrus to Darius I and Xerxes I) Cyrus's decree (of religious and ethnic accommodations) that allows the Israelites to return to the land of Judah (536–), to reinstate the rituals of Yahweh worship and to rebuild the (second) Temple (536–519); the revolt of the Jewish populace still remaining within Persia against their Persian overlords, from 359 to 338, B.C.E.
c. 356–323	Alexander the Great (Macedonian Era) defeated Darius III (Persia) in 331 B.C.E.
c. 330–	*The Hellenistic Period* (Greek to *Roman* Empire)
c. 305–51	The Ptolemaic Dynasty of *Egypt* (Ptolemy I, r. 305–282)
c. 280–63	*Syria* (Seleucid Dynasty)

The Hellenistic Period coincided with the period of international expansion and diplomacy of China's Han Dynasty under Emperor Wu (Wu Di), when political and military alliances were established between China and most of the political powers in Central Asia and beyond, including those in the (present) Iran, Persian Gulf, and Eastern Roman region, and as far as northeastern Africa. The 'king's highways,' more famously known later as the "Silk Roads" were established, with Chinese (and Roman) garrisons securing mankind's first communication highway connecting the Far East and the Far West, stretching more than five thousand miles. This is the general period which the present work proposes as the time of the "Second Exodus" of Semitic people, carrying with them the *MiFune-Shiro*, or the *Replica of the Ark of the Covenant*, ultimately arriving on the Japanese archipelago, possibly in at least two major waves of migratory movement, during the approximate period from the third to the second century, B.C.E. The migration of Jewish people from the Middle East and Central Asian regions to the Far East would continue thereafter for many more centuries and throughout the Middle Ages.

INDEX

(The titles of book are in *italics*. Only proper names are capitalized. The items of particular importance are in **bold face**.)

978-0-595-45404-4
0-595-45404-6

Printed in the United Kingdom
by Lightning Source UK Ltd.
127330UK00001B/178/A